WELCOME

RIGHT: Flying Fortresses of the US 384th Bomb Group drop their payloads during a raid on Nazi Germany. Public Domain US Air Force via Wikimedia Commons

BELOW: A Boeing B-17 Flying Fortress soars above the crowd at the Chino Airshow in 2014. Creative Commons Airwolfhound via Wikipedia

BOTTOM: An artist's rendering of a B-17 Flying Fortress adorns a poster promoting the sale of war bonds. Public Domain US National Archives and Records Administration via Wikimedia Commons

The Boeing B-17 Flying Fortress, a four-engine heavy bomber produced in great numbers and deployed in all major theatres of World War Two, has become perhaps the most recognised aircraft of the conflict. Its silhouette and wide wingspan are unmistakable symbols of the war that raged in the skies over Nazi-occupied Europe and the Third Reich itself from 1942 to 1945. The Flying Fortress was also in action in the Pacific, actually engaging Imperial Japanese forces before its epic adventure in Europe.

This captivating volume presents the emergence of the iconic Flying Fortress, its triumphs and its agonies, the stories of the men who served aboard the big bombers and achieved a measure of guts and glory seldom seen in modern warfare. The B-17 remains a symbol of courage and heavy cost. Come and ride along, feel the numbing cold at high altitude and the rush of adrenaline that accompanied encounters with marauding German fighters in the skies above Europe while black puffs of deadly flak scattered hot shards of shrapnel.

The development of the B-17 followed an American perspective on strategic warfare that emerged between the world wars. The concept was that the big bomber, bristling with defensive machine guns, faster than pursuing enemy fighter planes, higher than any interceptor of its day and at altitudes that no antiaircraft

gun could reach, would always find its target. Once overhead, it would devastate that target with an accurate rain of ordnance directed by the top secret Norden bomb sight, and then return to base relatively unscathed.

To that end, senior American military air officers were largely convinced that daylight precision bombing was *the* way. With daylight raids the big bombers flew with the sun in the sky, in ideal weather, and with impunity against enemy fighters and flak. It meant they could bring an adversary to its knees by devastating cities, destroying infrastructure, and demoralising its civilian population. Strategic bombing in itself, they reasoned, might well be a war-winning endeavour.

Influenced heavily by the perspective of visionary Italian air officer Giulio Douhet, whose popular book *The Command of the Air* was published in 1921 and embraced by the fledgling US Army Air Corps quite early, American air officers became enamoured with the idea of the big bomber. By the mid-20s, Douhet's book had been translated into English and widely circulated. It followed that the bomber men of the US military would seek a proper implement for the foreseen strategic bombing campaign, and a series of designs were put forward in the interwar years, each progressing toward the perceived ultimate heavy bomber that implement would deliver.

The saga of the B-17 began in the summer of 1934, when the Air Corps issued specifications for a multi-engine bomber that would replace the Martin B-10 twin-engine monoplane, the first of its type that was actually faster than contemporary pursuit fighters. The B-10 had only entered service in the autumn of 1934, even as the planning for its successor was underway. The new four-engine workhorse was expected to carry a bombload of reasonable weight – perhaps 10,000lb – at an altitude of 10,000ft for a duration of 10 hours with a top speed of at least 200mph. One desirable attribute was an incredible range of 2,000 miles, although this was not made a requirement.

During World War Two, the B-17 developed a reputation for toughness. It became a prime mover in the strategic air war, and it delivered roughly 640,000 of the 1.5 million tons of bombs dropped on Nazi Germany while flying nearly 300,000 sorties. General Carl 'Tooey' Spaatz, commander of US Strategic Air Forces in Europe, commented: "Without the B-17 we might have lost the war." From a practical standpoint, airmen lauded its survivability. One veteran pilot praised: "The plane can be cut and slashed almost to pieces by enemy fire and bring its crew home."

The heroism of the pilots and crewmen of the US Eighth Air Force, the 'Mighty Eighth', and the legend of the B-17 Flying Fortress have been recently burnished with the premiere of the television mini-series *Masters of the Air*. Its gripping realism and unflinching perspective on the air war in Europe are no doubt increasing awareness of those desperate times, and this volume serves well as a companion to the series

In the end, the production run of the B-17 from 1936 to 1945 yielded more than 12,700 aircraft. Of these, more than 4,700 – roughly 37% – were lost in World War Two. Nevertheless, along with the American Consolidated B-24 Liberator and the famed aircraft of the British Royal Air Force, the Avro Lancaster, Handley Page Halifax, Vickers Wellington, and others, the B-17 brought the air war home to Nazi Germany and contributed mightily to the final victory.

Welcome to these pages that chronicle the illustrious story of the Flying Fortress.

CONTENTS

3 Welcome

6 The Bomber Will Always Get Through
US Army strategic bombing doctrine developed in the years between the world wars and was initially based on the concept that heavy bombers could complete unescorted missions over enemy territory.

8 Design and Specifications
The B-17 Flying Fortress was developed in response to the US Army Air Corps requirement for a strategic heavy bomber.

12 Flying Fortresses in the RAF
The British were first to introduce the Flying Fortress to air combat, and the results were less than spectacular.

14 Flying Fortress in the Pacific
B-17s were engaged in World War Two during the December 7, 1941, attack on Pearl Harbor but were later replaced by the Consolidated B-24 Liberator.

18 The Legend of Colin Kelly
Flying a B-17C in the Philippines, Kelly became one of the first American heroes of World War Two.

21 North Africa and the Mediterranean
The Flying Fortress served in North Africa and the Mediterranean in support of the Allied landings of Operation Torch, the invasions of Sicily, Italy, and southern France, and in bombing tactical and strategic targets.

24 The Higher Call
Luftwaffe pilot Franz Stigler spared the lives of nine B-17 crewmen, escorting their damaged bomber to safety. Years later he met the American pilot, Charles Brown.

26 The Mighty Eighth
The Eighth Air Force grew from a fledgling, shoestring operation in World War Two to become one of the most famous air arms in history.

Vapor trails stream from the eight engines of a pair of Boeing B-17 Flying Fortress bombers in this dramatic image captured somewhere over Eastern Europe. Public Domain US Air Force via Wikimedia Commons

30 The Flying Fortress and the First Eighth Air Force Raid
A dozen B-17s conducted the first all-American bombing raid against railroad marshalling yards at Rouen, France, on August 17, 1942.

33 Combined Bomber Offensive
Despite disagreements on the concepts of strategic bombing, the US Army Air Forces and British Royal Air Force conducted a major bombing campaign against Nazi-occupied Europe and the Third Reich.

37 Raid on Schweinfurt and Regensburg
On August 17, 1943, the US Eighth Air Force conducted costly raids on a ball-bearing factory and a Messerschmitt assembly facility in the German cities of Schweinfurt and Regensburg.

40 Second Schweinfurt Raid
The high-priority ball bearing facilities at Schweinfurt, Germany, were targeted for a second Eighth Air Force raid in October 1943, resulting in the heavy losses of 'Black Thursday'.

43 Big Week
Intended to disrupt German aircraft production and gain air superiority over Nazi-occupied Europe, Operation Argument, the resumption of Eighth Air Force daylight bombing in February 1944, was a combined effort with the RAF and the Fifteenth Air Force in Italy.

46 Contemporaries: B-24 Liberator and Avro Lancaster
Some historians point to the fact that the B-17 was obsolescent in World War Two, outclassed by the B-24, its intended replacement, and the British Avro Lancaster.

49 The Luftwaffe Enemy
Nazi fighter pilots fought a dogged defence of the Third Reich against Allied bombers but ultimately were overwhelmed in a war of aerial attrition.

52 The Norden Bombsight
Revolutionary in its potential for bombing accuracy, the US precision daylight bombing strategy was dependent on the top-secret Norden bombsight.

53 General Henry 'Hap' Arnold
General Arnold was a primary advocate of the B-17's development and led American air forces in World War Two.

56 General Frank M. Andrews
An architect of the modern Army Air Forces and the US Air Force that followed, Andrews personally saved the B-17 from obscurity and prepared the US air forces for the strategic bombing campaign in Europe during World War Two.

A beaming Clark Gable in the uniform of the US Army Air Forces and with the rank of captain graces the cover of a Latin American magazine in 1945. Creative Commons A Scena Muda via Wikimedia Commons

59 General Carl 'Tooey' Spaatz
The chief of American strategic air forces in Europe, Spaatz advocated the oil plan that starved the German armed forces of vital fuel.

62 General Ira C. Eaker
Eaker commanded Eighth Air Force Bomber Command and was largely responsible for the establishment of the Eighth Air Force in Britain. He later led all of Eighth Air Force and the Allied Mediterranean air forces.

65 General Curtis E. Lemay
A combat leader and innovator, LeMay refined box formation flying and the lead crew system to American air operations in Europe and then US air forces against Japan.

68 General James H. 'Jimmy' Doolittle
A bomber pilot at heart, Doolittle led the Eighth Air Force in Europe during a battle of attrition against the Nazi Luftwaffe.

71 Anatomy of a Mission
For the crew of a B-17 Flying Fortress the mission was always undertaken with great risk. It was an exercise of long hours and slight monotony punctuated with moments of harrowing air combat.

Boeing B-17 Flying Fortress bombers sit on the ground at Honington Air Depot after arriving in England. Public Domain US Air Force via Wikimedia Commons

74 The B-17 and the Medal of Honor
In the war-torn skies over Europe during World War Two, 17 American airmen earned the Medal of Honor, 11 of them posthumously.

78 The Saga of *Memphis Belle*
The B-17F Memphis Belle flew into legend and lore during World War Two and remains one of the most famous combat aircraft of all time.

80 Memorable Flying Fortress Missions
Many memorable missions were flown by B-17 aircrews, and these are reports of just a few.

83 Reporters Ride Along
Andy Rooney, Walter Cronkite, and other journalists of the Writing 69th flew into battle over Germany aboard B-17s.

86 Operation Aphrodite
An experiment using radio controlled B-17s to demolish high value German targets failed to produce the desired results.

88 Operation Frantic
A programme of shuttle bombing with the cooperation of the Soviet Union and the use of air bases in Ukraine ended with disappointing results.

92 The Death of the Ball Turret Gunner
The poem by Randall Jarrell is descriptive of the experience of a bomber crewman curled into the cramped confines of the ball turret in wartime.

A Boeing B-17 Flying Fortress nicknamed *Aluminum Overcast* comes in for a landing in 2012. Creative Commons Clemens Vasters via Wikimedia Commons

93 Clark Gable and the Flying Fortress
Actor Clark Gable flew at least five combat missions aboard the B-17 and produced a documentary film about the experience with the heavy bomber.

96 The Piggyback Incident
Two B-17s of the 100th Bombardment Group became locked together in a mid-air collision. Some Germans who saw the strangely conjoined bombers thought they were witnessing the debut of a new super weapon.

98 The Bloody 100th
The 100th Bombardment Group earned its nickname in the crucible of the air war, taking tremendous losses from German fighters and flak. Some historians assert that the 100th is the most famous B-17 bombardment group of World War Two.

100 303rd Bombardment Group
The 303rd Bombardment Group completed 364 missions, more than any other B-17 group of the Eighth Air Force and was the parent group of two famous Flying Fortresses, Hell's Angels, and Knockout Dropper.

102 97th Bombardment Group
The 97th Bombardment Group established several 'firsts' in air combat in northwest Europe with the Eighth Air Force and in North Africa and the Mediterranean.

104 91st Bombardment Group
Sustaining higher losses than any other heavy bomber group in World War Two, the 91st conducted 340 missions over Nazi-occupied Europe.

A Boeing B-17 Flying Fortress in olive drab camouflage and early insignia roundel flies in 1942. Public Domain US Air Force via Wikimedia Commons

106 305th Bombardment Group
Among the most active bomb groups of the Eighth Air Force, the 305th was trained by then-Colonel Curtis LeMay, who went on to higher command.

108 Flying Fortress in Film
From Twelve O'clock High to documentaries that emerged to present the experiencesofB-17aircrewsinaction,theFlying Fortress is immortalised in film.

110 Flying Fortress in Captivity
Germany, Japan, the Soviet Union, and neutral nations came to possess examples of the Flying Fortress and sometimes press them into service.

112 The B-17 Mystique
The legend of the B-17 grew from its wartime experience as men who flew aboard it praised the plane that brought them home.

114 The Flying Fortress Today
Nearly 80 years after its last flight of World War Two, the B-17 remains a subject of historical interest, evocative of heroism and hazard, duty, and peril.

A B-17G Flying Fortress of the 348th Bombardment Squadron, 99th Bombardment Group, banks away from a target in Nazi-occupied Europe. Public Domain San Diego Air and Space Museum via Wikimedia Commons

ISBN: 978 1 80282 975 4
Editor: Mike Haskew
Senior editor, specials: Roger Mortimer
Email: roger.mortimer@keypublishing.com
Cover Design: Steve Donovan
Design: SJmagic DESIGN SERVICES, India
Advertising Sales Manager: Sam Clark
Email: sam.clark@keypublishing.com
Tel: 01780 755131
Advertising Production: Becky Antoniades
Email: Rebecca.antoniades@keypublishing.com

SUBSCRIPTION/MAIL ORDER
Key Publishing Ltd, PO Box 300, Stamford, Lincs, PE9 1NA
Tel: 01780 480404
Subscriptions email: subs@keypublishing.com

Mail Order email: orders@keypublishing.com
Website: www.keypublishing.com/shop

PUBLISHING
Group CEO and Publisher: Adrian Cox

Published by
Key Publishing Ltd, PO Box 100, Stamford, Lincs, PE9 1XQ
Tel: 01780 755131 **Website:** www.keypublishing.com

PRINTING
Precision Colour Printing Ltd, Haldane, Halesfield 1, Telford, Shropshire. TF7 4QQ

DISTRIBUTION
Seymour Distribution Ltd, 2 Poultry Avenue, London, EC1A 9PU
Enquiries Line: 02074 294000.

THE BOMBER WILL ALWAYS GET THROUGH

As with most advances in technology, it was no great leap for the military application of the airplane to quickly follow its invention. In 1903, the Wright Brothers flew at Kitty Hawk, and in less than a decade bombs were being dropped from airplanes in wartime.

In 1911-12, Italy was at war with the Ottoman Empire in Libya, and perhaps the first instance of aerial bombing occurred during this period as 2nd Lieutenant Giulio Gavotti of the Italian Aeronautical Battalion dropped ordnance on Turkish soldiers on November 1, 1911, while piloting a German-made Etrich Taube aircraft.

General Giulio Douhet, commander of the Aeronautical Battalion, saw the potential of the strategic bomber to radically change the face of modern conflict, particularly as World War One on the Western Front devolved into a contest of attrition and horrific trench warfare. Rather than ground action that always favoured the defence, the aircraft added a new dimension to waging war, a vertical dimension that was not shackled to the confines of the trenches or invariably slave to local engagements and seizure of territory regardless of the scope of a ground offensive.

The bomber, Douhet averred, would fly over stagnant positions and bomb not only military targets, such as troop concentrations, supply depots, and artillery emplacements, but carry the strategic element to the heartland of the enemy. Strategic bombing would devastate the adversary's infrastructure and destroy its industrial capacity while at the same time demoralising the opposing civilian population to the point that the people would demand a surrender rather than endure further any terrifying aerial assault.

Although aerial bombing did emerge in World War One as the Germans sent their Zeppelins to bomb British cities and the latter retaliated with its own missions against military targets, the phenomenon of strategic bombing began to take shape in the years between the world wars. Douhet, author of the influential book *The Command of the Air*, had written: "A slower, heavily armed plane, able to clear its way with its own armament, can always get the best of a faster pursuit plane…A unit of slower heavily armed planes is in a position to stand up to the fire of enemy pursuit planes and carry out its mission successfully."

The Italian visionary was not alone in his conception of a new and terrible mode of warfare. In Britain, future Marshal of the Royal Air Force Hugh Trenchard was an advocate and later became known as the father of the RAF. In the US, General Billy Mitchell was such a vehement proponent of aerial bombing that he drew a court martial even after demonstrating the vulnerability of naval warships to aerial bombing attack as early as 1921.

Meanwhile, the dark image of what strategic bombing might deliver was captured in the imagination of science fiction author H.G. Wells, who wrote in his book *The War in the Air* as early as 1908, "Quiet people go out in the morning and see air-fleets passing overhead – dripping death – dripping death!"

In the United States, the military establishment rapidly began to consider the prospect of strategic bombing during the inter-war years, and the energy behind the concept gained steady momentum following the relocation of the Air Corps Tactical School (ACTS) from Langley Field, Virginia, to Maxwell Field near Montgomery, Alabama. The officers who served as instructors at ACTS actually constituted an academic think tank that embraced the idea of strategic bombing and reasoned not only that it was plausible, but also that a faster, larger bomber with an adequate death-dealing payload might actually fly higher and at greater speed than enemy fighter planes to bomb industrial and population centres. Furthermore, such air raids would be most effective in daylight, particularly with the development of the accurate Norden bombsight and the introduction of the legendary Boeing B-17 Flying Fortress and Consolidated B-24 Liberator heavy bombers by the mid-to late1930s.

In Britain, Prime Minister Stanley Baldwin warned of the devastation that might be wrought with strategic bombing. He addressed Parliament in 1932 in a speech titled, *A Fear of the Future*. Baldwin seriously intoned: "I think it is well also for the man in the street to realise that there is no power on earth that can protect him from

ABOVE LEFT: Italian air officer Giulio Douhet was an early advocate of strategic bombing. Public Domain www.rusf.ru/fc/img/big/douhet_g.jpg author unknown via Wikimedia Commons

ABOVE RIGHT: As an instructor at ACTS, then-Major Laurence S. Kuter was a key author of AWPD-1. He is pictured years later with the rank of full general. Public Domain US Air Force via Wikimedia Commons

ABOVE: Along with the Consolidated B-24 Liberator, the Boeing B-17 Flying Fortress prosecuted the US component of the strategic bombing campaign in World War Two. This B-17, *Sally B*, was photographed during a 1985 air show.
Public Domain Jan Arkesteijn assumed no machine-readable author provided and released without condition via Wikimedia Commons

being bombed." During his address, Baldwin offered the phrase that became the mantra of the US Army Air Corps senior command. "Whatever people may tell him, the bomber will always get through."

The nexus of air war theory at Maxwell Field produced a confident line of reasoning that military airmen embraced. By 1940, Major General Henry 'Hap' Arnold, commander of the US Army Air Corps and a devotee of Billy Mitchell, declared: "The Air Corps is committed to a strategy of high-altitude precision bombing of military objectives." The American bomber in the war that was sure to come would then concentrate on high-altitude, unescorted missions to destroy high-value targets with devastating accuracy rather than dropping bombs across a wide area – a practice that would certainly reduce such accuracy. The doctrine of daylight precision bombing was taking shape.

In the summer of 1941, the War Plans Division of the US Army was tasked with the formulation of comprehensive blueprints to defeat the potential enemies of the United States should war break out. The so-called Rainbow and ABC series of war plans followed, Rainbow written with colour coded actions depending on the enemy while ABC was developed in anticipation of cooperation with Great Britain and Canada.

Amid these preparations, the Air Corps was permitted to prepare an addendum that outlined the requirements for an effective air campaign, one that some believed might win a future war singlehandedly, ending the need for prolonged ground campaigns. Four officers from ACTS, Lieutenant Colonel Kenneth L. Walker, Lieutenant Colonel Harold L. George, Major Haywood S. Hansel, and Major Laurence S. Kuter, produced the addendum. The quartet had each served as instructors at Maxwell and were confirmed proponents of strategic daylight precision bombing. Their report, Air War Plans Division – Plan 1, or AWPD-1, specified the requirement for more than 13,000 bombers, nearly 8,800 fighters and a final tally of more than 63,000 planes needed. At first, the administration of President Franklin D. Roosevelt was reticent to provide the dollars for such an ambitious programme. However, with the US being draw inexorably into World War Two, soon enough the appropriation of funds amounted to a blank check for the buildup.

In producing AWPD-1 and two subsequent reports, AWPD-4 and AWPD-42, the Maxwell quartet, revered today as among the 'Founding Fathers' of the US Air Force, borrowed statistical information and analysis from the RAF, which was then conducting its own bombing campaign against Nazi Germany. They folded in such data along with details and specifications of German buildings and other targets, some of which had been built after World War One with financing from American banks.

All the while, the fact remained that daylight precision bombing was an untried and unproven concept, although the RAF had attempted a few daylight raids before switching to nocturnal missions after sustaining serious losses in men and planes. The Maxwell cadre acknowledged that air superiority would play a role, but they were confident that the big bombers, well-armed, and flying in mutually supportive formations with interlocking fields of machine-gun fire to deter enemy fighters, would indeed 'get through'.

In tandem with the ability of the bombers to defend themselves, the American ideal of the fighter plane and pilot was one of the hunter, an offensive aircraft with an aggressive operator in the cockpit. Therefore, the notion of the escort fighter, sticking with bomber formations to deter the enemy, was counterintuitive. Only with practical experience and sobering bomber losses during the air offensive of World War Two was the hard lesson of real air superiority learned.

Nevertheless, in the event the Boeing B-17 Flying Fortress and the men who flew it went on to etch an indelible chapter in the history of military aviation.

ABOVE: Cadets assemble in ranks at Maxwell Field, Alabama, in the early 1940s. These aviators were undoubtedly inculcated with the doctrine of daylight precision bombing. Public Domain United States Army Air Forces via Wikimedia Commons

LEFT: Standing at right in the middle row, RAF visionary Hugh Trenchard saw the potential of strategic bombing. Public Domain Air Publication 3003 - A Brief History of the Royal Air Force United Kingdom Government via Wikimedia Commons

LEFT: The officers' quarters at Maxwell Field were home to many men who developed and taught the doctrine of strategic bombing to men of the US Army Air Corps. Public Domain United States Army Air Forces US Government via Wikimedia Commons

DESIGN AND SPECIFICATIONS

The concept of strategic bombing as a decisive instrument in the prosecution of the next major war was pervasive among senior officers of the US Army Air Corps in the 1930s.

Simply put, strategic bombing transcended the tactical application of air power. Rather than attacking relatively small targets closer to the front lines to achieve limited objectives, strategic bombing involved attacks against distant industrial targets and infrastructure located in enemy territory, destroying the capability of an enemy to wage war and the will of its people to support further resistance.

Conceptually, strategic bombing had the potential of a war winning strategy. While it had yet to be proven in actual war, its advocates were confident that sufficient numbers of heavy bombers could bring about the desired result. By the mid-1930s, the essential component that was required – the heavy bomber – had been identified. Since the end of World War One, the burgeoning US Army Air Corps had made use of biplane bombers such as the Keystone B-6, considered sufficient for tactical purposes but lacking in speed (at a maximum of just 115mph), bombload capacity, and defensive capability against enemy fighters.

In November 1934, the Martin B-10, the first all-metal monoplane bomber in US service, was introduced. With a top speed of 213mph, range of 1,240 miles, and bombload of 2,260lb, the B-10 was a leap forward. However, some observers considered it inadequate, far short of an envisioned four-engine aircraft that could fulfil the role of a true 'strategic' bomber.

Even as the B-10 entered service, the Air Corps issued Circular 35-26 in the summer of 1934, seeking an appropriate bomber of the future. The specifications indicated a multi-engine aircraft, and both Martin with its Model 146 and Douglas with its DB-1 interpreted the directive as two engines. Boeing, however, stepped out with a four-engine design. Its Model 299 was immense in comparison to the others and possessed greater range and other attributes that favoured the concept of a true strategic bomber. Other requirements of Circular 35-26 were a payload capacity of 2,000lb over a range of 2,000 miles, a maximum speed of 200 to 250mph, cruising speed of 170 to 220mph, and service ceiling of 20,000 to 25,000ft.

When the Air Corps circular reached Boeing, the company was well acquainted with the military, having produced several biplane fighter models and the all-metal

ABOVE: The shattered Model 299 lies at the crash site in October 1935. The accident nearly killed the future of the B-17 Flying Fortress. Public Domain US Air Force via Wikimedia Commons

LEFT: A line of B-17B Flying Fortress bombers is shown at March Field, California, prior to US entry into World War Two. Public Domain US Air Force via Wikimedia Commons

BELOW: The Boeing Model 299, or XB-17, sits on a runway in January 1935. Public Domain US Air Force via Wikimedia Commons

RIGHT: This B-17E and crew of the 11th Bombardment Group are shown in the Pacific theatre at New Caledonia in January 1943. Public Domain US Air Force via Wikimedia Commons

monoplane airliner 247D that contributed to military applications. The company, however, was in financial straits amid the Great Depression and sales of the 247D were not as brisk as anticipated. Some research in cooperation with the Army Air Corps had been conducted on a heavy bomber as early as 1933. Known as 'Project A', that work had produced the XB-15. If successful, a new prototype dubbed the Model 299 (XB-17) would pivot the company back to prosperity. The Boeing board of directors staked the future of the company on a design team headed by Edward Curtiss Wells and its Model 299, voting to fund $275,000 toward its further development. When cost overruns occurred, more money was allocated.

The Model 299 was powered by four Pratt and Whitney R-1690 Hornet radial engines, and performance was subsequently upgraded to the hefty Wright R-1820-39 Cyclone powerplant. The aircraft measured 68ft in length and just under 103ft wingtip to wingtip. The interior was customised to accommodate a large crew. Just behind the nose, the pilot and co-pilot were seated in the cockpit or flight deck, slightly above the nose positions of the bombardier and navigator. Moving aft, the radio operator's position was past the bomb bay, and to the rear three blisters, two in the sides, or waist, and one ventral, housed machine gun positions.

The Model 299 took to the air for the first time from Boeing Field in Seattle, Washington, on July 28, 1935, during early evaluations against the Martin 146 and Douglas DB-1. Watching from the ground, Richard Williams, a reporter for the *Seattle Times*, noticed the machine-gun positions on the Model 299 and commented that the prototype was a '15-ton flying fortress'. Boeing representatives seized on the name and trademarked it. Then, on August 20, Boeing test pilot Leslie 'Cowboy' Tower flew the Model 299 non-stop 2,100 miles from Seattle to Wright Field near Dayton, Ohio, in nine hours and three minutes with an average cruising speed of 230mph.

Tragedy struck on the morning of October 30, 1935, when the Model 299 crashed and exploded, killing Tower and another pilot, Major Pete Hill. Apparently, the elevator locks had not been disengaged, causing a loss of pitch control as the plane nosed sharply – almost vertically – upward and then plunged to the ground, exploding on impact. An order for 65 Model 299s had been pending at the urging of Brigadier General Frank M. Andrews, commander of General Headquarters Air Force, the combat component of the US Army Air Corps. With the crash, Army Chief of Staff General Malin Craig promptly cancelled the order, and the contract for the new bomber went to Douglas, 133 examples of the B-18 Bolo.

Andrews was still convinced that the Model 299 was the strategic bomber that the Air Corps needed. With specified changes, including the upgrade to the Wright Cyclone engine that burned 100-octane gasoline and significantly improved performance, the Boeing bomber was redesignated the YB-17, allowing Andrews and other officers who were sold on the four-engine design and its numerous technical advantages to purchase 13 of the aircraft for further testing.

With the gathering of war clouds in Europe and the Pacific, several shortcomings in the B-18 were exacerbated. The plane was relatively slow, and its defensive armament was deemed inadequate. The Bolo was subsequently designated for training and transport duty. »

RIGHT: An army sentry stands guard among newly completed B-17F bombers at the airfield adjacent to the Boeing facility in Seattle, Washington. Public Domain Franklin D. Roosevelt Presidential Library National Archives and Records Administration via Wikimedia Commons

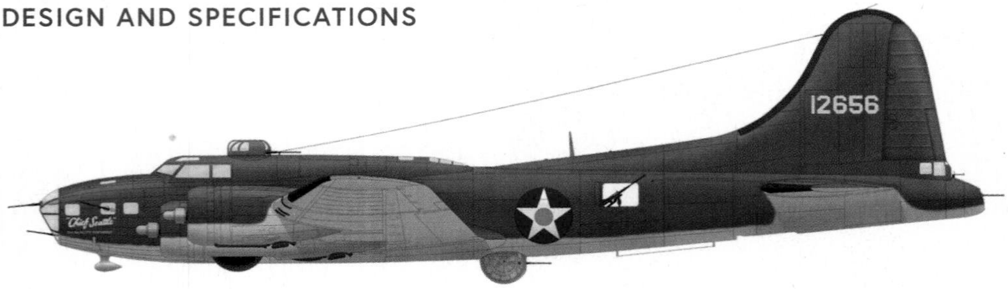

ABOVE: This drawing depicts the B-17E Chief Seattle of the 19th Bombardment Group in the summer of 1942. Note the single .50-calibre machine gun in the waist position, the tail machine gun position, and the enlarged vertical stabiliser with dorsal fin. Creative Commons Martin Čížek via Wikimedia Commons

RIGHT: The B-17G featured the addition of the chin turret mounting twin .50-calibre machine guns and was produced in greater numbers than other Flying Fortress variants. Creative Commons Wilson44691 via Wikimedia Commons

RIGHT: This B-17D was photographed at Wright Field in Dayton, Ohio. Note the bathtub ventral gun position and the shark fin vertical stabiliser. Public Domain US Air Force via Wikimedia Commons

BELOW: Nose art featuring 1940s pinup Betty Grable graces the B-17G *Sentimental Journey* photographed at an El Paso, Texas, air show. Creative Commons Mark Holloway via Wikimedia Commons

Revisions of the YB-17 continued, and a single 14th military airframe, the Y1B-17A, soon flew as the B-17A. By 1938, improvements such as the installation of General Electric turbochargers, enlarged control areas, alterations to the nose section, and a revision of pneumatic brakes to hydraulic operation resulted in an order for 39 B-17B bombers with larger rudders and flaps. The first production model of the heavy bomber, the B-17B also included a .30-calibre machine gun in the Perspex glass nose, its barrel protruding through one of the 10 clear panels.

The outbreak of World War Two marked a renewed sense of urgency within the American military establishment, particularly in its ability to defend the country itself. In 1940, the Air Corps ordered 38 B-17Cs, and 20 of these were delivered to the British Royal Air Force, entering service as the Flying Fortress Mk. I. Rather than three blister machine-gun positions, the B-17C included two waist gunner posts with teardrop shaped Perspex window panels and a gondola or bathtub position in the lower fuselage. Total armament included four .50-calibre Browning machine guns and a single .30-calibre weapon. The B-17C could carry a maximum bombload of 4,800lb with a range of 2,400 miles at a cruising speed of 250mph.

Several deficiencies were discovered during operations of the B-17C, including problems with the onboard oxygen system, poor bombing accuracy, and the freezing of the defensive .50-calibre machine guns at high altitude. Most of the issues were addressed with the B-17D, and the remaining 18 B-17Cs in the Air Corps inventory were upgraded as self-sealing gas tanks were added along with improved armour protection for the crew. Forty B-17Ds were ordered in April 1940, and these bombers appeared quite similar to the B-17C externally with the exception of engine cowling flaps to improve cooling. Armament was improved to twin .50-calibre machine guns in the dorsal and ventral positions along with the single .30-calibre, raising the total number of machine guns to seven. External bomb racks were removed, and a 10th crewman was added for the first time.

Regular Upgrades

Production picked up substantially with the B-17E, and following the initial order in August 1940, a total of 512 were produced. The B-17E was six feet longer than earlier versions and incorporated significant changes, the most obvious of which was the much larger vertical stabiliser and dorsal fin that extended forward. To improve firepower and cover a 'blind spot' in earlier models, a twin .50-calibre machine gun position was installed in the tail, while an electrically operated machine-gun turret was placed on the upper fuselage aft of the flight deck to be operated by the flight engineer. The waist gun positions were modified as rectangular openings with removable windows, and a remotely operated belly turret replaced the gondola configuration.

The B-17E supplanted the B-17D in production by September 1941, and the first delivery was made to the 7th Bombardment Group two months later. Production demands required the establishment of a cooperative relationship between Boeing, the Vega division of Lockheed, and Douglas, referred to comically as B.V.D after a popular brand of underwear. With the 113th B-17E, the remotely controlled ventral turret was removed in favour of the iconic Sperry ball turret, in which the gunner crouched in a confined space. Armament included a .30-calibre machine gun in the nose, which could be relocated to any of six ball-and-socket firing positions, twin .50-calibre machine guns in the dorsal, ventral, and tail positions, and single .50-calibre machine guns in the two waist positions.

The B-17E continued in production through May 1942.

Although the B-17F and its predecessor were virtually indistinguishable externally, more than 400 internal improvements were made to the successor, which first flew on May 30, 1942, and entered combat initially with the US Army Air Forces (USAAF) in a January 27, 1943, raid on the port facilities at Wilhelmshaven, Germany. Improvements included the new ball turret, electrical link to the autopilot, more graphic equipment, better oxygen system, and upgraded Wright R-1820-97 engines generating up to 1,380 horsepower each for short emergency periods. Although there were minor differences in detail, the armament of the B-17F included 11 machine guns, the single .30-calibre in the nose and 10 Browning .50-calibres in waist, dorsal, ball, and tail positions. Later B-17Fs were fitted with additional fuel tanks, called Tokyo Tanks, in the wings.

The B-17F carried a maximum bombload of 9,600lb, cruising speed of 200mph, service ceiling of 37,500ft, and range of 2,880 miles with a 6,000lb bombload. Due to the large number of changes during production of the B-17F, a series of identifying blocks were used to assist ground crews in the field in the performance of routine maintenance. For example, the first block of 50 bombers was identified as B-17F-1-BO, and the second block was distinguished as B-17F-5-BO. Those aircraft built by Boeing in Seattle, Washington, and Dallas, Texas, were designated 'BO,' while Lockheed Vega aircraft built at Burbank, California, were designated 'VE,' and Douglas bombers produced at Long Beach, California, were distinguished with 'DL.' A total of 3,405 B-17Fs were built.

The ultimate combat variant of the Flying Fortress, the B-17G, of which 8,680 were constructed, entered production in July 1943, and its most readily apparent change was the installation of a Bendix turret-mounted .50-calibre machine gun in the chin position. In the B-17G, the waist positions were also permanently enclosed with windows rather than open at times. The B-17G packed 13 machine guns into its airframe, and some observers categorise it, along with the E and F variants, as 'offensive' rather than solely 'defensive' capable.

The B-17G entered service in the autumn of 1943 with a cruising speed of 150mph and maximum speed of 263mph at 25,000ft. Its maximum bombload for short-range missions was 17,600lb, while its range was 1,850 miles with an average bombload of 4,000lb. Some B-17Gs were converted for troop transport, air-sea rescue, training, reconnaissance, target drone, engine testing, and other functions. Through the war years, a relative few B-17s were used by the US Navy as maritime patrol craft, and others, designated the PB-1G, served with the US Coast Guard through the late 1950s.

An interesting variant of the B-17 was the XB-40, conceived as a heavy armed escort. Rather than bombing, the XB-40 was intended to add firepower to formations as a modified B-17F with the Bendix chin turret and a total of 13 machine guns. During testing, it was determined that the heavier and slower XB-40 could not maintain formation with B-17s after they had dropped their bombs. The project was abandoned, but the chin turret was incorporated into the B-17G.

At peak production, the B-17 Flying Fortress was being produced in numbers greater than 200 per month. Of the 12,731 B-17s built between 1936 and 1945, roughly 4,735, or 37%, were lost during World War Two. The Flying Fortress is believed to have dropped 640,000 tons of bombs on Germany and other Nazi-occupied territory during the air war in Europe, about 33% of the total 1.5 million tons delivered. Statistically, some sources report that 58% of those airmen who served aboard the B-17 in combat survived their fiery trial, while about 25% were killed in action, and 17% were shot down and became prisoners of war. Others relate that one in 20 Flying Fortress crewmen were lost.

LEFT: This modified B-17G of the US Air Force's 5th Rescue Squadron was photographed in 1950. Public Domain US Air Force via Wikimedia Commons

LEFT: A B-17G sits in a hangar while undergoing restoration at the Mighty Eighth Air Force Museum in Pooler, Georgia. Creative Commons Bubba73 via Wikimedia Commons

BELOW: Seen here liveried as 448846 *Lucky Lady* and photographed in 1988, this B-17G Flying Fortress was airworthy for a time as a warbird and then later grounded. GNU Free Documentation License Mike Freer Touchdown Aviation cdn-www.airliners.net/aviation-s/s/6/6/9/2144966.jpg via Wikimedia Commons

FLYING FORTRESSES IN THE RAF

For the October 18, 1941, edition of the *Saturday Evening Post*, reporter W.L White penned an article titled *The Dying and the Buying.* He highlighted the deployment of the Boeing B-17 Flying Fortress heavy bomber with Britain's Royal Air Force, at that time engaged in a strategic bombing effort against Nazi Germany.

White noted that the RAF command establishment had for some months waged its air war with light and medium bombers, some of them outmoded. He mourned the brave airmen who had lost their lives in the widening war and then pointed to an expected boost to the air campaign.

"A good many of them died for their country, it turns out, only because in 1940 rigid-minded superiors were convinced that they already had the best planes in the world, and when better bombers were built, the British would build them…They know better now, because the American Flying Fortress has at last gone into action. The British bomber pilots who do the actual dying have taken them up, have seen that they can carry on long raids five times the bomb load of the standard British bomber, carry it higher, faster, farther and with infinitely less risk to the crew. Today only a few dozen are in England. They could have had 500 or more, and with these they might have made, this summer, substantial changes in the map of Germany, and maybe in the whole outlook of the war."

White's perspective was one of the contemporary press. His assessment is accurate on one count. The combat debut of the B-17 Flying Fortress occurred with the RAF in the summer of 1941. But then, even as the *Saturday Evening Post* went to press just weeks after that debut the story of its first days in hostile skies was actually quite different from that implied by White and consumed by the American public.

By the summer of 1941, RAF bombing raids against Nazi-occupied Europe and targets inside Germany itself were occurring regularly. Handicapped by air losses and the sheer number of bombers available to carry on its offensive, the British sought the rapid development of their own bombers, particularly the heavy four-engine Avro Lancaster and Handley Page Halifax. They knew of the big Boeing bomber that had incorporated some innovative improvements in air design, particularly the machine guns intended for the plane to protect itself during daylight raids, and other follow-on innovations. However, they kept the B-17 at arm's length even after it was made available through Lend Lease by the US government.

In the spring of 1941, the British did accept an American offer of 20 B-17C bombers, the variant then in production. Only 38 of this type were completed, and that score of Flying Fortresses allotted to Britain arrived at West Raynham and were assigned to No. 90 Squadron RAF. The British designated the new bomber the Fortress Mk I, and crews were trained at far-off McCord Field near Tacoma, Washington, from January to April 1941. The British would take advantage of a few American bombers, nowhere near the 500 considered by White, while they would provide the Americans with data on the bomber's combat performance, information the US Army Air Corps was eager to obtain.

By the time the 20 B-17Cs reached No. 90 Squadron, the unit had relocated to RAF Polebrook in Northamptonshire, and perhaps as a harbinger of things to come, the first Flying Fortress to approach the field there ground looped on landing, skidded off the runway, and was so badly damaged that it

ABOVE: Crewmen of No. 90 Squadron RAF don electrically heated flight suits prior to boarding their Fortress Mk I heavy bomber and embarking on a mission over Nazi-occupied Europe. Public Domain collections of the Imperial War Museums via Wikimedia Commons

LEFT: A Fortress Mk I of No. 90 Squadron RAF is shown in flight during an air raid on Berlin. Public Domain United Kingdom Government via Wikimedia Commons

BELOW: This B-17C of No. 90 Squadron RAF was photographed on June 20, 1941, just weeks before the Flying Fortress was introduced in the British bombing campaign. Public Domain United Kingdom Government via Wikimedia Commons

RIGHT: Photographed in August 1944, this Fortress Mk III was deployed in radar jamming activities by No. 214 Squadron RAF at Prestwick. Public Domain collections of the Imperial War Museums via Wikimedia Commons

RIGHT: A Fortress Mk II of No. 220 Squadron RAF is shown in flight over the Hebrides islands in 1943. Public Domain collections of the Imperial War Museums via Wikimedia Commons

was written off for spare parts. Soon the remaining Flying Fortresses were readied for action. Their first combat mission was undertaken on July 8, 1941, and the results were underwhelming to say the least.

Three Fortress Mk Is took off at 3pm that summer day to attack the German Kriegsmarine base at Wilhelmshaven situated along the Jade Bight and the North Sea. Designated aircraft C, G, and H, their task was to drop bombs from high altitude while testing the aircraft's performance in numbing cold, its bombing accuracy, and its defensive capability should any Nazi fighters be encountered.

The mission assessment was less than glowing. "Aircraft G and C attacked the primary target between 1650 and 1700 hours from 28,000 and 30,000ft respectively," it read. "Aircraft G dropped 4 X 1,100-pound demolition bombs and aircraft C had 2 X 1,100-pound bombs hang up and only two were released." Aircraft H developed engine trouble and began to bleed oil profusely at 28,000ft. It was forced to divert from the primary target and drop its bombs on the island of Nordeney in the North Sea. The bombs were loosed at 4:45pm and were observed to explode about 500 yards distant from the German-occupied town; photographs failed to document any real damage, and the plane was forced to drop to 15,000ft to allow the oil to thaw from its horizontal stabilisers.

Compounding the poor results of the mission were the fact that camera failure precluded the documentation and assessment of damage inflicted by those bombers that reached Wilhelmshaven. At the same time, machine guns froze solid at the high altitude and were rendered useless. At 18,000ft the Plexiglas astrodome froze up in aircraft G. Normally used for navigation, the report nevertheless indicated that it caused problems with 'fire control'. This bomber also had a brush with a pair of Luftwaffe Me-109 fighters, but no fire was exchanged.

A second mission was launched on July 23, as three B-17s flew against Berlin. The high altitude bombing run was thwarted by bad weather and thick cloud cover. One of the bombers was so riddled with flak that it was scrapped, the first Fortress lost to enemy combat. A third mission was undertaken against targets near Oslo in occupied Norway. All three Fortresses participating were lost to German fighter attacks.

By the end of September, two weeks before White's article appeared in the popular American magazine, the RAF had actually flown 26 raids against enemy targets involving 51 sorties. The results were dismal. Half the individual missions had been aborted due to some sort of mechanical issue. As of September 12, only 19 bombers had dropped their payloads on primary targets, while two had hit secondary targets and only two 1,100lb bombs could be confirmed as having accurate drops. Eight of the original 20 Flying Fortresses had been lost, and in less than two months the RAF pulled the B-17 from strategic bombing operations.

Despite the disappointment, the US officers who received discouraging reports pointed out that the British had flown the B-17s in small numbers rather than the larger box formations they had envisioned for mutual defensive support against German fighters. They added that bombing from such high altitude and with seriously overloaded aircraft was an exercise in futility. Nevertheless, the British saw the experience as validating their contention that daylight bombing could not be conducted in the face of existing German defences, further backing their subsequent switch to nocturnal operations.

The Flying Fortress continued to serve with the RAF for the remainder of World War Two, the lion's share used by Coastal Command. Additionally, No.220 Squadron deployed the remaining B-17s of No. 90 Squadron in the Far East before receiving the Fortress II for anti-submarine patrol duties. Radar jamming activities were conducted by No. 214 and No. 223 Squadrons of No. 100 Group.

By war's end, the RAF had received its 20 Fortress Is (B-17C), 19 Fortress IIs (B-17F), and 11 Fortress IIIs (B-17G). Despite the negative experience with the British, American air officers were not dissuaded. With the urgency of rearmament sponsored by the administration of President Franklin, the B-17 found new life and became an icon of the strategic bombing campaign.

BELOW: Ground crewmen load 250lb depth charges aboard a Fortress Mk II at RAF Benbecula in the Hebrides, Scotland, 1943. Public Domain collections of the Imperial War Museums via Wikimedia Commons

FLYING FORTRESS IN THE PACIFIC

ABOVE: Japanese Aichi D3A 'Val' dive bombers are seen from a B-17E Flying Fortress arriving over Oahu on December 7, 1941. Public Domain Staff Sergeant Lee Embry US Air Force via Wikimedia Commons

It was supposed to be a routine flight. A dozen B-17 Flying Fortress heavy bombers were just about to complete the 14-hour leg of their journey from Hamilton Field, California, to Hawaii, en route to Clark Field in the Philippines.

The date was December 7, 1941, and the sudden Japanese attack on Pearl Harbor and other American military installations on the island of Oahu thrust the Flying Fortresses into action during the first day of US involvement in World War Two. Major Truman 'Ted' Landon of the 38th Reconnaissance Squadron, 19th Bombardment Group, was leading six of the big bombers, four early model B-17Cs and two more up to date B-17Es, as they approached Hickam Field.

The first of the B-17s to reach Hawaiian airspace quickly came under attack by Japanese Mitsubishi A6M Zero fighters, escorting the torpedo-, dive- and level bombers that were sowing destruction across Oahu. Lieutenant Robert Richards, pilot of the B-17C nicknamed *Skipper*, spotted something unusual, a smaller aircraft closing fast and appearing to line up a firing pass at his bomber. Seconds later, he heard the thud of bullets impacting the plane. One of the crewmen yelled forward, "There are damned holes in the wings!"

RIGHT: A B-17C of the 38th Reconnaissance Squadron lies burned and destroyed at Hickam Field after the Japanese attack on Pearl Harbor and other facilities on the island of Oahu. Public Domain US Air Force Historical Research Agency via Wikimedia Commons

Richards headed for cloud cover, dodging the attack momentarily. But when *Skipper* came out of the clouds briefly, Japanese Zeros pounced again. The B-17s were not armed for their long 'peacetime' relocation and had no way to fight back. Richards decided to head for nearby Bellows Field and set *Skipper* down safely but shot up to the extent that the B-17 would never fly again.

The harrowing morning of the infamous Japanese raid brought the B-17 into combat, but not as American war planners had envisioned. There was no doubt that the US and Japanese governments had reached a diplomatic impasse and that war clouds were looming. In preparation, General Henry 'Hap' Arnold, commander of the US Army Air Forces, had authorised the movement of B-17s to the Philippines in the event of an outbreak of hostilities. Those caught up in the attack on Pearl Harbor were just the latest of the bombers headed to their new Far East station at Clark Field near Manila.

In the months leading up to the outbreak of the Pacific War, B-17 heavy bomber strength in the region was steadily augmented. The first reinforcement flight departed Hamilton Field for Hawaii on May 13, 1941, as 21 Flying Fortresses later designated for assignment to the 5th and 19th Bombardment Groups made the first transit of a large formation of bombers across such a great stretch of open sea in history, reaching their destination within five minutes of their estimated time of arrival. The US War Department envisioned a peak bomber strength in the Pacific to reach 165 B-17s and Consolidated B-24 Liberators by the spring of 1942, their numbers split evenly between the two heavy types.

Another 26 B-17s were sent to the Philippines on November 26, and by the end of 1941, a total of 29 B-17Ds and six B-17Cs of the 19th Bombardment Group had taken up station there, while plans were being made to relocate the 35 new B-17Es of the 7th Bombardment Group from their base at Salt Lake City, Utah, to Clark.

LEFT: A B-17 Flying Fortress of the 14th Bombardment Squadron is serviced at Clark Field in the Philippines prior to the outbreak of hostilities on December 8, 1941. Public Domain US Army Air Corps via Wikimedia Commons

Twelve B-17Ds of the 5th Bombardment Group were located at Hickam Field on Oahu when the Japanese struck. Their bombers and strafing Zero fighters destroyed five of these on the ground and damaged the others.

When war broke out, two of the five bombardment groups that would deploy the B-17 in the Pacific, the 5th and 11th, constituted the nucleus of the Seventh Air Force in Hawaii, later to be transferred to the Thirteenth Air Force in the Central Pacific. Those bombers in theatre on December 7, 1941, suffered heavy losses at the hands of the Japanese. Enemy aircraft attacked the airfields in Hawaii and the Philippines on December 8 (across the International Date Line). A total of 18 B-17s were destroyed on the ground at Clark Field on opening day, leaving only 17 serviceable bombers.

Contrary to popular belief, the US Army Air Forces in the Philippines were not caught off-guard, unprepared, and like sitting ducks. General Douglas MacArthur, commander in the islands, and his chief of the Far East Air Force (FEAF), General Lewis Brereton, expected a Japanese attack. In actuality, Brereton had dispersed his bomber and fighter strength to other bases in the Philippines on the eve of the Japanese attacks. Two of the 19th's bombardment squadrons had been ordered to the airfield at the Del Monte plantation on the »

LEFT: The B-17E *Suzy-Q* of the 93rd Bombardment Squadron, 19th Bombardment Group, is shown on February 7, 1942. *Suzy-Q* took part in numerous early Pacific engagements. Public Domain US Army Air Forces via Wikimedia Commons

LEFT: The B-17E *Chief Seattle* of the 435th Bombardment Squadron was lost over Buna, New Guinea, on August 14, 1942. Public Domain US Air Force via Wikimedia Commons

island of Mindanao, and these were a safe distance, roughly 500 miles, from Manila and Clark Field on December 8.

When word was received that Pearl Harbor had been attacked, the squadrons at Clark Field were ordered to conduct reconnaissance missions. That afternoon, an air raid against Japanese installations on the island of Formosa was being organised, and these bombers were recalled to Clark. While they were on the ground being armed and fuelled, the Japanese appeared overhead, roughly 200 aircraft strong, and destroyed all but three of these American planes. Rather than a case of unpreparedness, the devastating result was a prime example of plain bad luck for the American air forces in the Philippines.

Still, the two bomber squadrons at Mindanao remained intact and conducted operations against the Japanese in the earliest days of the war. As American air power in the Pacific grew, these would become the foundation of the US Fifth Air Force. Between December 17-20, a total of 14 B-17s, the only serviceable bombers of FEAF to escape the Philippines, relocated to Batchelor Field near Darwin Australia. In the meantime, the exploits of Captain Colin Kelly had occurred in the Philippines, as he sacrificed his life piloting a B-17 and received a posthumous Distinguished Service Cross. The B-17s of the 19th Bombardment Group relocated to the island of Java in the Dutch East Indies, and a trickle of 7th Bombardment Group bombers reached Java as well, but never more than 20 B-17s were available for action at any given time. FEAF headquarters was transferred to Australia in February. Renamed Fifth Air Force, its Brisbane command was given to General George Kenney in late July 1942.

The 5th and 11th Bombardment Groups, flying B-17s and B-24s, were deployed to the New Hebrides in the summer of 1942 and participated in the Solomons campaign and the later Allied offensive launched to liberate the Philippines.

LEFT: A B-17E Flying Fortress of the 72nd Bombardment Squadron, 5th Bombardment Group sits on a runway at Midway Atoll in 1942. Public Domain US Air Force Historical Research Agency via Wikimedia Commons

LEFT: This B-17D of the 19th Bombardment Group is being loaded with bombs at Del Monte Field on the Philippine island of Mindanao in preparation for a strike against the Japanese early in 1942. Public Domain US Army Air Corps via Wikimedia Commons

LEFT: A Japanese transport manoeuvres violently to avoid American bombs during the Battle of the Bismarck Sea, March 3, 1943. Public Domain collections of the Australian War Memorial via Wikimedia Commons

The B-17s of the 7th and 19th Bombardment Groups moved to Australia, conducting raids against enemy forces in the Solomon Islands and the burgeoning base at Rabaul on the island of New Britain. The 19th then relocated to a base at Townsville, Australia, and conducted small-scale air raids, some with only three Flying Fortresses involved,

LEFT: Personnel of the 19th Bombardment Group stand at attention at Mareeba Airfield, Australia, in late 1942, prior to departure for the United States after months of action. Public Domain US Air Force Historical Research Agency via Wikimedia Commons

RIGHT: B-17E Flying Fortresses of the 431st Bombardment Squadron await maintenance at an air depot on the island of New Caledonia. Public Domain US Air Force via Wikimedia Commons

against Rabaul. These were shuttle missions in which the aircraft took off from Townsville, staged through Port Moresby at the southeastern tip of New Guinea, and after spending a night there continuing their mission across the peaks of the Owen Stanley Mountains and the Bismarck Sea to hit their intended target.

The 7th Bombardment Group was transferred to India and Tenth Air Force in the spring of 1942, and within weeks the 43rd Bombardment Group arrived at Darwin. Both the 19th and 43rd groups provided air support during the campaign in Papua, New Guinea, and while the 43rd remained in the southwest Pacific, trading its B-17s for B-24s in 1943, the 19th Group returned to the US in 1942. By the time of General Kenney's arrival in theatre, the Fifth Air Force included five bombardment groups, and only the 43rd was flying the B-17.

The B-17's anticipated primary mission as a high altitude bomber suggests that its performance in an anti-shipping role might be less than stellar. However, in late May 1942, the 5th and 11th Bombardment Groups, Seventh Air Forces, transferred 16 Flying Fortresses from Hawaii to Midway atoll, 1,150 miles northwest of Oahu, to defend against an expected Japanese invasion. During the first week of June, nine of these B-17s opened the Battle of Midway with a raid against the Japanese invasion force, roughly 570 miles from the atoll. Although the returning crews claimed several hits, postwar analysis suggests that only a single near-miss occurred.

Nevertheless, the Midway-based B-17s flew 55 sorties in 16 missions during the battle. They disrupted enemy operations even though no real damage was reported. At the same time, Japanese fighters flying combat air patrol were often unable to reach the high altitudes from which the Flying Fortresses attacked. When the Japanese fighter pilots were able to close with the B-17s, they often decided against engaging the heavily-armed bombers, bristling with machine guns.

On August 7, 1942, the day of the American landings on Guadalcanal in the Solomons, 15 bombers of the Fifth Air Force flew in support. Other raids against Japanese shipping took place regularly. General Kenney issued the order that sent the 19th Bombardment Group, in continual action since December 8, 1941, back to the US shortly after he took command of Fifth Air Force.

Some historians assert that Japanese naval officers showed little concern for the B-17 since its bombing accuracy against moving targets such as ships at sea was quite questionable. However, the Flying Fortress did achieve a measure of success during the Battle of the Bismarck Sea, March 2-4, 1943. American aircraft decimated a Japanese troop convoy out of Rabaul destined for Lae, New Guinea, with reinforcements and supplies for its troops fighting on the island. The Japanese lost eight transport ships and four destroyers sunk, other vessels damaged, and nearly 3,000 dead.

The B-17s of the 43rd Bombardment Group, Fifth Air Force carried out multiple attacks, dropping to altitudes below 9,000ft at times to deliver their ordnance. They were credited with sinking a Japanese destroyer and a transport which was carrying 1,200 combat soldiers of the Imperial Army intended to reinforce the garrison at Lae, while damaging several other troop ships. One B-17 was lost during the Battle of the Bismarck Sea, and Japanese fighter planes were seen machine-gunning surviving crewmen in their parachutes.

After the Battle of the Bismarck Sea, the command decision was made that no further replacement B-17s would be sent to the Pacific theatre. The last Flying Fortresses, those of the 43rd Bombardment Group, were withdrawn by the end of 1943. Demand for the B-17 in the European theatre was steadily increasing due to heavy Eighth Air Force losses, while the longer range and heavier payload of the B-24 were more suitable for missions against distant targets across vast stretches of open water.

By the end of World War Two, it was estimated that the Flying Fortress had flown only 2% of its total sorties during the conflict while operating in the Pacific theatre.

RIGHT: General George Kenney took command of Fifth Air Force in the summer of 1942. Public Domain US Air Force via Wikimedia Commons

FAR RIGHT: A diver explores the wreckage of a submerged B-17 Flying Fortress bomber lost in action during the Pacific War. Creative Commons Pacific Aviation Museum via Wikimedia Commons

THE LEGEND OF COLIN KELLY

RIGHT: This romanticised painting of Captain Colin Kelly was painted by artist Deane Keller of Yale University. Public Domain Deane Keller US Air Force via Wikimedia Commons

During the dark days after the Japanese attack on Pearl Harbor plunged the United States into World War Two, the American people were in tremendous need of a hero. Twenty-six-year-old Captain Colin Kelly of the US Army Air Corps and the B-17C Flying Fortress provided the much-needed morale boost, although Kelly lost his life in the process.

The story of Kelly's courage, death in combat, and stirring example grew in the weeks and months that followed his fateful mission against the invading Japanese in the skies above the Philippines on December 10, 1941, just three days after the US had been attacked without warning. The American press carried accounts of the event and lauded the patriotism of young men like Colin Kelly. And rightly so. American military planners had once written off the Philippines, concluding that the islands were not defensible in the event of war with Japan. Nevertheless, US and Filipino forces under the command of General Douglas MacArthur were posted there when war came.

Commensurate with the attack on Pearl Harbor, Japanese bombers and fighters hit targets in the Philippines, destroying much of General MacArthur's air power as the planes sat on the ground at Clark Field, near the Philippine capital of Manila. However, a few American bombers of the 14th Bombardment Squadron, 19th Bombardment Group, had been spared. Some were actually operating from other airfields in the Philippines and managed to put up a fight against the marauding Japanese.

Kelly was among those pilots who still had a plane to fly, and on the fateful morning of December 10, he was one of six who took to the air in their B-17s under the command of Major Emmett O'Donnell. According to records, the bombers flew from San Marcelino Airfield on the island of Luzon to Clark Field, arriving overhead in a driving rainstorm. The authorities at Clark were expecting another Japanese air raid and allowed only three of the B-17s to land. The others returned to San Marcelino and then moved to the island of Mindanao the next day, probably landing at the airfield near the Del Monte pineapple plantation.

O'Donnell flew on that morning and mounted an attack against Japanese warships near the town of Vigan off the western coast of Luzon but did not score any hits on an enemy cruiser and destroyer that he reportedly made five passes against. Meanwhile, the three bombers that landed at Clark Field were hurriedly serviced. In their haste to get the B-17s into the air, the ground crewmen managed to load one plane, flown by Lieutenant George Schaetzel, with eight 600lb bombs. Lieutenant G.R. Montgomery's bomber had only a single bomb aboard. Kelly's B-17 was armed with three bombs, and its fuel tanks were not completely filled.

BELOW: The probable focus of Colin Kelly's bombing run on December 10, 1941, was the Japanese light cruiser *Natori*. Public Domain Mikasa Memorial Museum unknown author via Wikimedia Commons

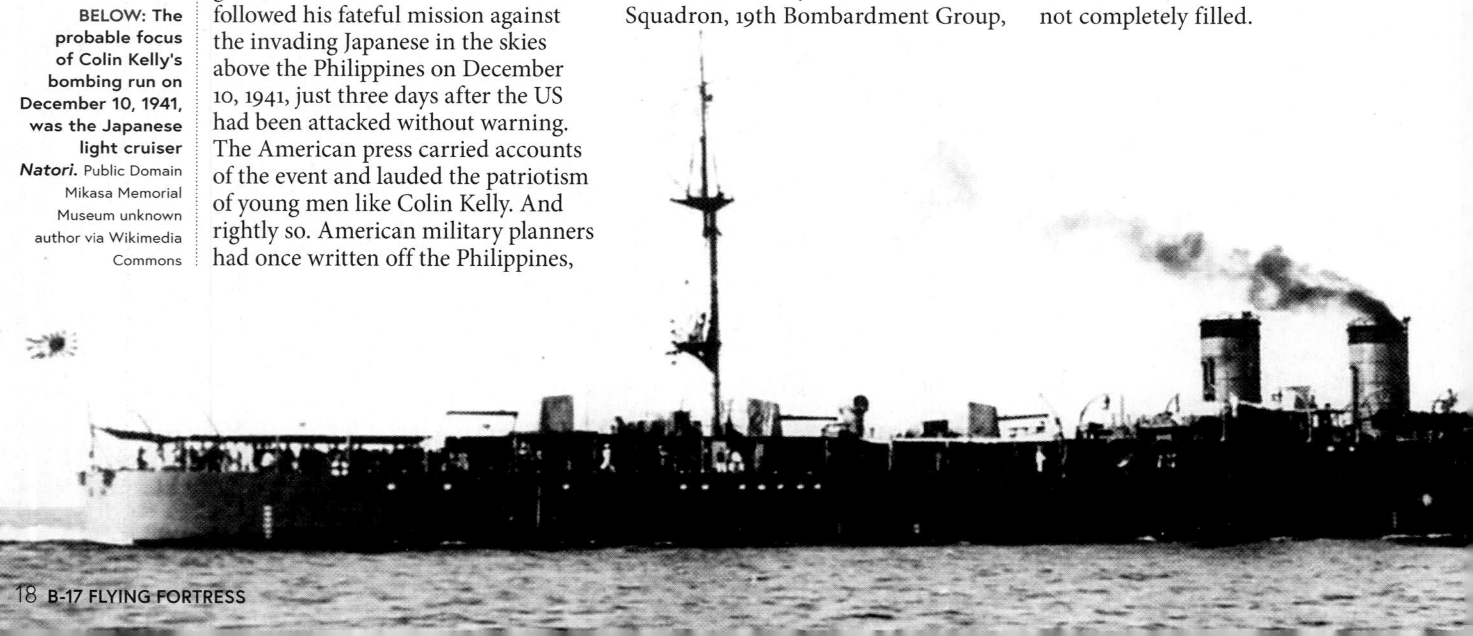

After take-off, Montgomery headed for Vigan and dropped his single bomb. After returning to Clark, his B-17 was loaded with 20 100lb bombs for a run at Japanese transport craft off the northern coast of Luzon. After-action reports indicate that the attack left one enemy vessel smoking. The bomber was later caught in a violent storm, causing Montgomery to ditch in open water. Although the B-17 was lost, the crew was rescued.

Kelly and Schaetzel flew north in search of a Japanese aircraft carrier that had been reported off the coast near Aparri. The pilots located the enemy task force, including troop transports and escorting warships. Schaetzel attacked, dropping his bombs before he was set upon by at least four Mitsubishi A6M Zero fighters of the Tainan Air Group, based on the island of Formosa, that were flying cover above the landing area. His B-17 was riddled with bullets but managed to limp to San Marcelino, where it touched down safely. Miraculously, there were no injuries to the crew.

Meanwhile, Kelly and his crew were not so fortunate. From an altitude of 20,000ft, the pilot made two passes while bombardier Sergeant Meyer Levin hunched over his bombsight to acquire a target. Coming around a third time, Levin released the three bombs, which plummeted earthward and evidently bracketed a Japanese warship that has been since identified as either the light cruiser *Natori* or less likely the heavy cruiser *Ashigara*. Most reports assert that the target was indeed the *Natori*, which sustained some damage from the near misses, as did the adjacent destroyer *Harukaze*. However, in the heat of the moment the Americans mistakenly identified their target as a Japanese battleship, the *Haruna*, or so they thought. Subsequently, the story would circulate that Kelly and company had actually bombed and sunk the enemy battleship.

After their bombs were dropped, Kelly turned for Clark Field, and the drama of the lone B-17 and its crew played out in the skies above the Philippines. Zeros, with veteran fighter pilots at the controls, slashed at the vulnerable Flying Fortress. With guns blazing in its first pass, one of the Tainan Air Group fighters killed Technical Sergeant William J. Delehanty and wounded Private First Class Robert E. Altman. Fire erupted when the fuel tank in the left wing was shot up, and the big bomber was shaken with the impact of more hits that severed the elevator cables when the Japanese fighters made another pass.

Kelly ordered the crew to bail out and maintained as much control of the burning bomber as he was able. Levin and navigator 2nd Lieutenant Joe M. Bean managed to exit the stricken plane through the escape hatch in the nose. Co-pilot Lieutenant Donald Robins worked to open the upper escape hatch and was thrown clear when bomber exploded in mid-air, reportedly the first American-manned Flying Fortress lost to enemy action in World War Two. With the safety of his crew in mind, Kelly had willingly tried to remain aloft, sacrificing himself. His body was found near the wreckage, still clad in an unopened parachute harness, while that of Delehanty was recovered about 50 yards away from the crash site just east of Clark Field. The surviving crewmen parachuted to safety and were taken prisoner.

The famed Japanese ace Saburo Sakai was among the enemy pilots who attacked Kelly's B-17 that day. He claimed to have shot down the bomber, but that was never confirmed. Credit was later shared by several other Tainan Air Group »

LEFT: Sergeant Meyer Levin served as bombardier aboard the B-17C piloted by Captain Colin Kelly. Public Domain Baltimore Sun Archive World Wide Photos via Wikimedia Commons

LEFT: Bombers of the US Fifth Air Forces are shown at Clark Field, Philippines, in 1945. Colin Kelly's final flight began at Clark Field. Public Domain San Diego Air and Space Museum via Wikimedia Commons

BELOW: **Colin Kelly flew a B-17C on December 10, 1941. Twenty of these were also sent to the British RAF, and this example is emblazoned with the RAF roundel.** Public Domain US Air Force via Wikimedia Commons

LEFT: **Japanese fighter pilots of the Tainan Air Group that downed Colin Kelly's B-17 pose for a photo.** Public Domain Hajime Yoshida Uruguay Round Agreements Act via Wikimedia Commons

pilots, and Sakai, who ended the war with 64 aerial victories, was not among them.

On February 19, 1942, Colonel Eugene L. Eubank, commanding headquarters of 5th Bomber Command at Malang, Java, reported on Kelly's mission. "The battleship was seen about four miles offshore and moving slowly parallel to the coastline," his summary read in part. "A quartering approach to the longitudinal axis of the ship was being flown. The three bombs were released in train as rapidly as the bombardier could get them away. The first bomb struck about 50 yards short, the next alongside, and the third squarely amidship…A great cloud of smoke arose from the point of impact. The forward length of the ship was about 10 degrees off center to portside. The battleship began weaving from side to side and headed toward shore. Large trails of oil followed in its wake…."

The story of Kelly's heroism resonated across the United States. He was the all-American boy. Born in Madison, Florida, on July 11, 1915, he was a 1937 graduate of the United States Military Academy at West Point, New York. He was a boxer, football player, cross country, and track athlete who married his sweetheart in the academy chapel just weeks after graduation. In January 1939, he earned his pilot's wings at Randolph Field, Texas.

Kelly cut the figure of a dashing and patriotic hero, and a legend was created – partly fact and partly fiction. His valour was lionised in newspapers and even in the popular song *There's A Star Spangled Banner Waving Somewhere*, which placed him alongside other larger-than-life personas in the pantheon of American heroes. The story also circulated that Kelly was posthumously awarded the Medal of Honor, the nation's highest recognition for heroism in the face of an enemy. However, he actually received the Distinguished Service Cross. An excerpt from the citation reads, "…With his airplane a focal point of fire from the strong hostile naval forces, Captain Kelly exhibited a high degree of valor and skill in placing three direct hits upon an enemy battleship, resulting in its destruction." The reference to the young airman's valour is certainly accurate, even though the details had become shrouded in the inevitable 'fog of war'.

General MacArthur was subsequently moved to comment: "It is my profound sorrow that Colin Kelly is not here. I do not know the dignity of Captain Kelly's birth, but I do know the glory of his death. He died unquestioning, uncomplaining, with a faith in his heart and victory his end. God has taken him unto Himself, a gallant soldier who did his duty."

With Colin Kelly's sacrifice, America had its first war hero of the great conflict. When he died, Kelly left his wife and young son to mourn his patriotic passing. A wave of national pride swept the country, lifting the spirit of its people for the long fight that lay ahead. A Liberty ship was named in his memory.

In 1941, President Franklin D. Roosevelt wrote a letter addressed to 'the President of the United States in 1956' requesting that the little boy, Colin 'Corky' Kelly III, receive an appointment to West Point when he came of age. The younger Kelly did actually graduate from the military academy with the class of 1963.

Kelly's remains were temporarily interred in the Philippines and repatriated to the US after the war. He now rests in Oak Ridge Cemetery in his hometown.

LEFT: **Mitsubishi A6M Zero fighters of the Tainan Air Group are shown in flight over the Solomon Islands.** Public Domain Imperial Japanese Navy Uruguay Round Agreements Act via Wikimedia Commons

FAR LEFT: **Japanese fighter ace Saburo Sakai was among those who attacked Colin Kelly's B-17C on December 10, 1941.** Public Domain unknown author flyanddrive.com Uruguay Round Agreements Act via Wikimedia Commons

LEFT: **A bust of Colin Kelly at Clark Field honours the heroic pilot who lost his life in the Philippines.** Creative Commons E911a via Wikimedia Commons

NORTH AFRICA AND THE MEDITERRANEAN

RIGHT: A B-17 Flying Fortress in service with the Royal Air Force is shown at Shallufa, Egypt, in 1941. Public Domain collections of the Imperial War Museums via Wikimedia Commons

The first Flying Fortresses deployed to North Africa and the Mediterranean theatre of World War Two were loaned to the British. Reassigned following the less than spectacular Royal Air Force daylight bombing experience with the B-17 in western Europe, these Fortresses of No. 90 Squadron RAF were dispatched to Egypt to bolster Vickers Wellington bombers already in action against the Axis.

Operated as a detachment of No. 220 Squadron RAF Coastal Command from December 1941, the B-17Cs carried out some daylight raids on targets in Libya while the Wellingtons flew missions at night. Only four B-17s participated in the RAF bombing, and they also flew night missions against enemy shipping in the Mediterranean Sea as well as concentrations of supplies and the city of Benghazi. At least one of the aircraft was lost, and the remaining B-17s were withdrawn by mid-January 1942 and returned to the US Army Air Forces (USAAF).

During Operation Torch, Allied troops landed at Oran and Algiers in Algeria and Casablanca, Morocco, on the western coast of Africa on November 8, 1942. Within days, as airfields became operational, the 97th and 301st Bombardment Groups were detached from the Eighth Air Force in England and sent to North Africa and the Twelfth Air Force. The move slowed the buildup of the Eighth Air Force and the momentum of the American strategic bombing effort in northwest Europe, but it was deemed necessary to provide heavy bombing support for the troops on the ground in North Africa.

In time, the Consolidated B-24 Liberator became the predominant American heavy bomber in the Mediterranean theatre, but the B-17 was always present in some numbers. In February 1943, the 2nd and 99th Bombardment Groups reached bases in North Africa. Following the invasion of the Italian mainland in September 1943, two more B-17 bombardment groups, the 463rd and 483rd, were assigned to the US Fifteenth Air Force, activated on November 1, 1943, at Tunis, Tunisia, and later moving to the European continent with bomber groups based in the vicinity of Foggia in southern Italy. At peak strength, the six B-17 groups in the Mediterranean reached 669 heavy bombers. Although the Eighth Air Force has gained more prominence in the decades since the end of World War Two, the Fifteenth Air Force made a major contribution to victory in Europe during the last 18 months of the conflict.

During the early days of Mediterranean operations, both the Ninth and Twelfth Air Forces operated the B-17 and B-24 in North Africa. Consolidation took place in late 1943 as the Twelfth Air Force was reassigned to a tactical role in theatre and the Ninth relinquished its heavy bombers prior to transferring to England to form a tactical air force that would operate in northwest Europe. The heavy bombers in the Mediterranean were placed under the command of the 5th Bombardment Wing, and the Fifteenth Air Force was commanded by General Nathan F. Twining.

During the following months, the Fifteenth Air Force conducted »

BELOW: This B-17, nicknamed *Starduster* and now on display at the March Field Museum in Riverside, California, was assigned as transportation for General Ira C. Eaker and later served with the Fifteenth Air Force in the Mediterranean. Creative Commons Eric Salard via Wikimedia Commons

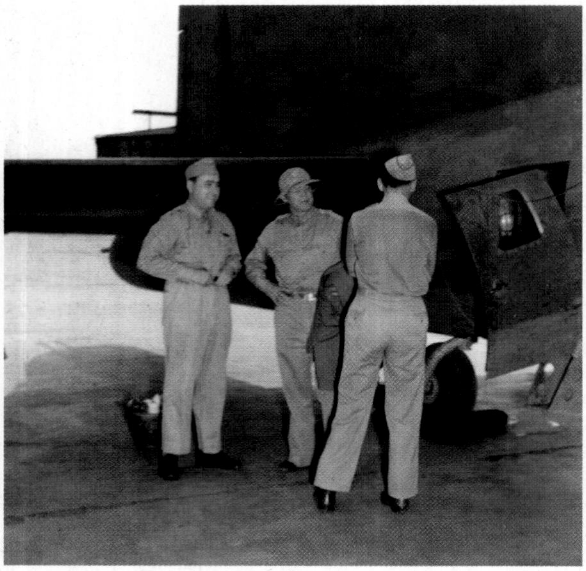

ABOVE: Officers chat near the open door of a B-17 at an airfield in North Africa in 1943. Creative Commons John Atherton via Wikimedia Commons

both strategic raids against targets in southern and eastern Europe that were out of range of bombers based in England, as well as striking tactical military targets throughout the Allied advance into Sicily and Italy. They bombed oil refineries at Ploesti, Romania, supported the Red Army advance on the Eastern Front, conducted shuttle bombing raids during Operation Frantic, and participated in the controversial bombing of the abbey of Monte Cassino on February 15, 1944.

With only two groups of B-17s, three medium bomber groups, and a few light bombers, the initial operations of the Twelfth Air Force had been limited in scope. Bombing commenced in mid-November 1942 with raids on targets in Tunisia, and 78 missions were flown, delivering more than 1,300 tons of bombs. B-17s of the 97th and 301st Bombardment groups struck shipping in the harbours of Bizerte and Ferryville. Although bad weather hampered operations, a series of notable raids occurred on January 9, 12, and 18, when as many as 25 B-17s, complemented by five Martin B-26 Marauder medium bombers, hit Castel Benito airfield south of the Libyan capital of Tripoli. At least 20 enemy aircraft were destroyed on the ground, while 20 enemy fighters were claimed as shot down in air battles. In exchange, one Flying Fortress and one escorting Lockheed P-38 Lightning fighter were lost.

One of the most experienced bomber groups among the Americans, the 97th had reached England in the spring of 1942 and conducted the first USAAF raid against Nazi-occupied Europe, hitting railroad marshalling yards near the city of Rouen, France, on August 17, 1942. It was the only American bomber group to take part in the ill-fated Dieppe Raid two days later, flying a diversionary raid against a German airfield at Abbeville. In the first raid against Axis forces in North Africa, the 97th sent six B-17s against Sidi Ahmed airfield near Benghazi, Libya, on November 16.

After the victory in North Africa, the 97th participated in raids against enemy transportation, supply lines, and fortifications, in support of Operation Husky, the Allied invasion of Sicily in July 1943. One of the targets was the enemy-occupied Mediterranean island of Pantelleria, which was later occupied by Allied troops. The port of Messina was a frequent target. After transferring to bases in Italy after the September 1944 Allied landings at Salerno, the 97th Bombardment Group continued strategic bombing and earned two Distinguished Unit Citations, the first for valour during a raid against ball bearing and aircraft assembly facilities at Steyr, Austria, during Big Week on February 24, 1944, and the second for the August 18, 1944, raid on the oil production facilities at Ploesti.

Later, tactical missions were flown in support of the Allied Fifth and Eighth armies as they pushed northward up the boot of Italy and during Operation Anvil-Dragoon, the Allied invasion of southern France.

The 301st Bombardment Group flew missions against Axis targets in North Africa as well and received the first of two Distinguished Unit Citations for a raid on an enemy shipping convoy off the coast of Bizerte on April 6, 1943. Its second Distinguished Unit Citation was earned during a mission against the Messerschmitt Me-109 assembly plant at Regensburg, Germany, on February 25, 1944, the last day of Big Week operations. The group was also involved in missions supporting Operation Husky and later flew against targets across Italy, southern France, eastern Europe, and the Balkans.

The 2nd Bombardment Group received its first Distinguished Unit Citation for the same raid on Steyr, Austria, as the 97th. The bombers were set upon by large numbers of Luftwaffe fighters that day, and the pilots of the 2nd were lauded for maintaining their formations and carrying out their assigned bomb runs. Sharing in the arduous bombing of Regensburg the next day, the group earned its second Distinguished Unit Citation.

RIGHT: A Consolidated B-24 Liberator heavy bomber, cohort of the B-17 in the Mediterranean, takes off from an airfield in Libya in 1943. Public Domain US Air Force via Wikimedia Commons

RIGHT: This B-17 Flying Fortress nicknamed *Rangy Lil* is shown in flight above the Tunisian desert. Public Domain US Air Force via Wikimedia Commons

RIGHT: General Nathan F. Twining commanded the US Fifteenth Air Force in the Mediterranean from the autumn of 1943. Public Domain US Air Force via Wikimedia Commons

FAR RIGHT: Trailing smoke, a damaged B-17 of the 99th Bombardment Group makes an emergency landing at Tortorella airfield, Italy, in 1944. Public Domain US Army Air Forces via Wikimedia Commons

BELOW: A B-17 of the 301st Bombardment Group drops its bombs on a railyard at Terni, Italy, on August 11, 1943. Public Domain US Army Air Forces via Wikimedia Commons

BOTTOM: A B-17 Flying Fortress of the 301st Bombardment Group sits at a dusty airfield in North Africa. Public Domain US Army Air Forces via Wikimedia Commons

Meanwhile, its B-17s were active in raids across the Mediterranean theatre, hitting tactical objectives to bolster the sluggish advance of the Allied forces in Italy. They also bombed industrial targets across eastern Europe and in Greece.

The 99th Bombardment Group earned praise for a productive strike on the enemy airfield at Gerbini, Sicily, on July 5, 1943, fending off attacks from more than 100 Axis fighters and sowing great destruction. The group earned its first Distinguished Unit Citation that day and followed up with a second on April 23, 1944, when it was the lead group during a raid on aircraft assembly plants at Weiner Neustadt, Austria. Remarkably, no B-17s were lost during the Weiner Neustadt raid, but 31 Flying Fortresses returned to base in Italy with varying degrees of damage from flak and fighter attacks.

The 463rd Bombardment Group received two Distinguished Unit Citations during combat in the Mediterranean, first for a May 18, 1944, raid on Ploesti, and second for a hazardous mission to bomb armoured vehicle factories in the vicinity of the Nazi capital of Berlin on March 24, 1945. The unit achieved notable tactical successes in destroying bridges that hampered the German response to the Allied liberation of Rome in June 1944, and again in the invasion of southern France that August.

Along with the 463rd, the 483rd Bombardment Group's pilots and aircrew displayed tremendous courage during the March 1945 raid on Berlin and earned a Distinguished Unit Citation, its second. The first for the 483rd was awarded for an attack against a Luftwaffe airfield at Memmingen in southern Germany, which was completed on July 18, 1944, without fighter escort. When World War Two in Europe ended, the 483rd participated in the massive airlift of American personnel from Italy to North Africa during their return to the US.

From its activation in November 1943 through to the end of the war, the Fifteenth Air Force dropped 303,842 tons of bombs on territory in 12 countries. A total of 148,955 air missions were flown, and the six B-17 groups accounted for their fair share.

One of the most unusual missions flown by B-17s in the Mediterranean theatre was Operation Reunion, the rescue of former prisoners of war from Romania following that country's exit from the Axis in August 1944. Colonel John A. Gunn, a B-24 pilot of the 454th Bombardment Group, had been shot down and taken prisoner during a raid on Ploesti. After the Romanians switched sides and joined the Allies, he met with sympathetic Romanian leaders who agreed to fly him to Italy. He made the hazardous trek as a passenger in the cramped space of a German-built Me-109 piloted by a Romanian Air Force officer.

Gunn brought the prospect of a rescue operation to the attention of the Fifteenth Air Force command, and up to 40 B-17s of the 5th Bombardment Wing were converted into transport planes, some of them rigged to carry wounded men on stretchers. The B-17s completed the Operation Reunion airlift between August 31 and September 3, 1944. On the first day, 38 Flying Fortresses departed their bases around Foggia and reached air installations outside the Romanian capital of Bucharest, where they picked up 740 former POWs and flew them to freedom. On the second day another 310 were rescued. By the end of Operation Reunion, 1,166 men had been rescued, 1,135 of them downed American airmen.

THE HIGHER CALL

ABOVE: Me-109 fighters of JG 27 fly over the North African desert. Franz Stigler was a veteran of air combat in North Africa. Public Domain US Air Force via Wikimedia Commons

RIGHT: The emblem of the 379th Bombardment Group depicts a four-engine B-17 bomber. Public Domain US Air Force via Wikimedia Commons

It was the first mission for the crew of the B-17 Flying Fortress nicknamed *Ye Olde Pub*, 527th Bombardment Squadron, 379th Bombardment Group, based at RAF Kimbolton, and the pilot and captain of the 10 men aboard was 2nd Lieutenant Charles Lester 'Charlie' Brown, just 21 years old. It was an all-out effort as nearly every bomb group of Eighth Air Force Bomber Command was participating, roughly 475 B-17 and B-24 Liberator bombers.

The target for the day, the Focke Wulf Fw-190 fighter assembly plant in the German city of Bremen, was daunting indeed. When it was revealed during the mission briefing early that morning, every man knew of the hazards. Bremen was heavily defended by clusters of anti-aircraft guns, and the Luftwaffe would no doubt raise swarms of fighters to contest the approaching bombers. On the morning of December 20, 1943, the crews went through their obligatory pre-flight rituals, and *Ye Olde Pub*, initially flying in the highly vulnerable position on the outer edge of its formation known as Purple Heart Corner, lifted into the sky laden with its high-explosive cargo. No. 4 engine was soon experiencing problems, but not enough to cause the crew to turn back.

The simple fact that Bremen was the target weighed heavily on the crews of the B-17s as they droned across the North Sea, and the limited range of their fighter escort was known to everyone. The briefing officer had warned that as many as 500 German Me-109 and Fw-190 fighters could be expected to attack the bomber formations with their characteristic ferocity. This day presented the usual risky business, but by the end of the mission this bomb run to Bremen would prove extraordinary.

Three B-17s were forced to abort the mission due to mechanical problems, and *Ye Olde Pub* moved up in formation. Flak, heavy and accurate, rocked the bombers, and Brown's aircraft took a direct hit, shattering its Plexiglas nose. More hits disabled the no. 2 engine and damaged no. 4 engine, already malfunctioning, and requiring it to be throttled back. Despite the fact that his B-17 was slowing, Brown stuck to the flight plan. Once *Ye Olde Pub* reached the target, the bombardier, 2nd Lieutenant Robert M. 'Andy' Andrews, took over and delivered the cargo from 27,300ft.

As the American bombers began turning for home, the German fighters descended on them in waves. At least a dozen of them made for *Ye Olde Pub*'s formation, guns blazing steadily. Brown's B-17 shuddered with the impact of machine-gun bullets and cannon shells. No. 3 engine sustained damage, but the plane stayed in the air at less than half normal power. Seriously damaged, the big bomber had much of its rudder and port side elevator shot away. Its hydraulic and electrical systems were damaged, and its internal oxygen system was malfunctioning. Guns had frozen due to the loss of heat at high altitude, and several crewmen were wounded. One man, tail gunner Sergeant Hugh S. 'Ecky' Eckenrode, was dead – decapitated by a direct hit from a 20mm cannon shell.

Ye Olde Pub was in dire straits, falling out of formation. Stragglers were usually easy pickings for Luftwaffe fighter pilots, who raced in to finish them off.

While Brown and the rest of the crew, shocked by the violent

RIGHT: Second Lieutenant Charlie Brown, pilot of *Ye Olde Pub*, is shown in a 1945 portrait. Public Domain Valor Studies via Wikimedia Commons

FAR RIGHT: Luftwaffe ace Franz Stigler spared the lives of American airmen aboard the B-17 *Ye Olde Pub* on December 20, 1943. Public Domain allthatsinteresting.com/franz-stigler-charlie-brown via Wikimedia Commons

death of their comrade, struggled toward home, a German fighter pilot, Oberleutnant Ludwig Franz Stigler of JG-27, an ace with 22 victories in North Africa and in the West, had landed at the airfield at Jever, Germany, for refuelling and rearming. Jever was not his home field, but Stigler knew it from earlier days as a Luftwaffe flight instructor. An eager ground crewman asked if he had scored, and Stigler replied that he had shot up a B-17 but was forced to break contact before he could confirm that it had gone down.

LEFT: The crew of B-17 Flying Fortress *Ye Olde Pub* stand before their bomber prior to the Bremen mission of December 20, 1943. Public Domain US Army Air Forces via Wikimedia Commons

Stigler was told that a .50-calibre bullet had lodged in the radiator of his Me-109's engine. Dismissing the suggestion that the plane should be wheeled away for repair, Stigler informed the astonished ground crewmen that he was going back into the air. German fighter pilots received bonus points for shooting down four-engine bombers, and with those added Stigler's score stood at 27. Another victory would ensure that he topped 30 victories and would qualify for the award of the coveted Knight's Cross of the Iron Cross.

Within minutes of taking off, Stigler spotted the grievously wounded *Ye Olde Pub* limping through the air. He approached warily and saw the condition of the B-17 and its crew clinging to the forlorn hope that they might survive the ordeal. Brown saw Stigler too. He concluded that his life and those of his remaining crew would end within minutes.

Surprisingly, as he closed Stigler remembered a warning from Oberst Gustav Rödel, his JG-27 commander in North Africa: "If I ever see or hear of you shooting at a man in a parachute, I will shoot you myself," he had said. Stigler later remarked, "To me, it was just like they were in a parachute. I saw them and I couldn't shoot them down."

Coming alongside, Stigler signalled to Brown that he should land at a Luftwaffe airfield and turn his wounded crew over to the Germans. He also tried to communicate that neutral Sweden was an alternative to land. Brown, confused that the enemy pilot had not already shot down his bomber, could not understand the gestures and kept flying toward England. Stigler took up position just off the B-17's port wing, hoping to prevent German flak gunners from opening fire. Brown ordered his available gunners to watch the German closely but not to fire on the Me-109.

Once *Ye Olde Pub* reached the North Sea, Stigler was assured that his stricken foe would be out of danger from German attack. He saluted and headed back to base. Brown landed the shattered B-17 at RAF Seething, where the crew received treatment. Miraculously, nine men survived. Brown told of the incident during debriefing but was admonished to keep the story to himself, lest Allied pilots gain a favourable impression of their aerial enemy. The German fighter pilot said nothing, aware that court martial probably awaited anyone who allowed a bomber to escape.

Decades went by. Brown completed his combat tour, worked for the US State Department, and retired from the US Air Force with the rank of lieutenant colonel. Stigler emigrated to Canada in 1953 and became a business executive. While attending a reunion event at Maxwell Air Force Base, Alabama, in 1986, Brown told the story of the Bremen mission and decided at long last that he should try to find the gallant German pilot who had spared nine American lives. There was little information available, but a letter to a pilot's association resulted in a response from Stigler.

During a telephone conversation, the two men corroborated each other's memories of the Bremen mission. They became friends, exchanging letters, phone calls, and photographs. Then, on June 21, 1990, they met face to face. In his bestselling book *A Higher Call*, author Adam Makos wrote: "Franz saw Charlie and ran to him. The two former enemies hugged and cried."

The men remained close until Stigler's death at 92 on March 22, 2008. Brown passed away on November 24, 2008, at age 86. Stigler had lost a brother in the crash of a bomber in 1940, but in presenting a book about his 'Squadron of Experts' to Charlie, he wrote: "…I had the chance to save a B-17 from her destruction, a plane so badly damaged it was a wonder that she was still flying. The pilot, Charlie Brown, is for me, as precious as my brother was…."

Even in the deadly skies above Europe in World War Two, chivalry was not dead. Generations of children, grandchildren, and more have been born to those American crewmen spared by Franz Stigler.

BELOW: Franz Stigel flew an Me-109 fighter similar to this example, also of JG 27. Creative Commons Bundesarchiv Bild via Wikimedia Commons

THE MIGHTY EIGHTH

The Eighth Air Force has been lauded, lionised, and criticised in the decades following the end of World War Two. Its history of heroism and sacrifice has inspired the content of books and films, stirred continuing debate as to its role in the air war in Europe, and engendered a mystique of nostalgia, romance, and respect for its veterans along with continued mourning and remembrance for the lost.

The story of the Eighth Air Force from its beginnings through the end of World War Two is remarkable indeed. It grew from 1942 to 1945 from a cadre of only seven Army Air Forces officers without quarters, offices, telephones, desks, chairs or even paperclips, into a formidable machine of war. At its peak, the Eighth Air Force was the largest of the US Army Air Forces engaged in World War Two in terms of personnel, aircraft, and other resources deployed.

General Ira C. Eaker, the advance man for the burgeoning US air presence in the European theatre, commander of VIII Bomber Command and later the Eighth Air Force, arrived in England about February 23, 1942, with six other officers, travelling from the US to England via neutral Portugal. The small group established its headquarters and went to work amid the constraints on manpower and planes as US industry switched to a war footing which meant that both production of military machines and recruiting increased. The Americans came to Daws Hill and then to High Wycombe in Buckinghamshire, where wartime headquarters were established at Wycombe Abbey, a former girls preparatory school.

One of the young officers with Eaker was Captain Frederick W. Castle. Promoted to major and then to colonel by January 1, 1943, Castle was given the job of A-4, Air Chief of Supply. He did, however, yearn for a combat command, and on June 19, 1943, he took charge of the 4th Bombardment Group, tasked with improving morale and overall efficiency within the unit. By April 1944, he was in command of the entire 4th Combat Bomb Wing, and in November he was promoted to brigadier general. Castle personally flew numerous bombing missions and was killed in action during a raid on December 24, 1944. The general had taken temporary control of a stricken B-17 while the pilot got into his parachute. Seconds later, the Flying Fortress exploded in mid-air. Castle received a posthumous Medal of Honor.

By mid-1944, the Eighth Air Force had grown to more than 200,000 personnel and an air strength that could put 2,000 heavy, four-engine bombers and 1,000 fighters aloft

ABOVE: Flying Fortresses of the Eighth Air Force fly in formation on April 13, 1945, during a raid on Neumünster, Germany. Public Domain US Air Force via Wikimedia Commons

LEFT: The Mighty Eighth was the most famous of the numbered US air forces deployed during World War Two. Public Domain US Air Force via Wikimedia Commons

LEFT: The effects of Allied bombing on the Nazi capital of Berlin are revealed following a 1945 raid. Public Domain United States Air Force Historical Research Agency via Cees Steijger (1991) via Wikimedia Commons

LEFT: **A B-17 of the 96th Bombardment Group, 339th Bombardment Squadron, is shown at its base in England.** Public Domain National Archives via the US Air Force Historical Research Agency via Wikimedia Commons

LEFT: **The B-17 *Nine-O-Nine* of the 91st Bombardment Group, 323rd Bombardment Squadron, displays specific identification markings.** Public Domain National Archives via US Air Force via Wikimedia Commons

in a single raid, with orders and directives being relayed through an efficient chain of command. An estimated 350,000 personnel served with the Eighth during the course of World War Two, and slightly more than two years from inception, the 'Mighty Eighth' had earned its lasting nickname through blood and toil.

In the execution of the Allied Combined Bomber Offensive, the Eighth executed the American strategy of daylight precision bombing and paid an enormous price for its contribution to air supremacy and ultimately victory over Nazi Germany. From May 1942 through the end of the war, the Eighth conducted 440,000 bomber sorties, dropping 697,000 tons of bombs, while more than 5,100 of its aircraft were lost, nearly 1,000 of these to accidents, and 11,200 enemy planes were claimed as shot down by its bombers and fighters.

Along the way, the Boeing B-17 Flying Fortress became a legend, its crews taking many of the casualties absorbed by the Eighth Air Force. Nearly half the US Army Air Forces' casualties in World War Two were among the men of the Mighty Eighth, 47,483 of 115,332, and 26,000 of these were killed in action or died of wounds. Seventeen men received the Medal of Honor, 11 of them posthumously. Further, Eighth Air Force personnel received 220 Distinguished Service Crosses and 442,000 Air Medals.

The Eighth became the first strategic US air force designated as such during World War Two, and on February 22, 1944, a restructuring of the air forces in theatre led to the renaming of the Eighth as the Strategic Air Forces in Europe, under General Carl 'Tooey' Spaatz, and elevating VIII Bomber Command to the Eighth Air Force designation. In the same timeframe, General Eaker was reassigned to command US air forces in the Mediterranean and General James H. 'Jimmy' Doolittle took command of Eighth Air Force. At the conclusion of the war in Europe in 1945, the Eighth Air Force began relocating to the island of Okinawa in the Pacific; however, Imperial Japan surrendered before offensive operations were undertaken.

The Eighth Air Force was authorised on January 19, 1942, at Langley Field, Virginia, and activated on January 28, 1942, as it relocated to Savannah Army Airfield, Georgia. The Eighth Air Force encompassed three component units: VIII Bomber Command, VIII Fighter Command, and VIII Ground Air Services Command. From its slight beginnings in Britain, its first combat element, the ground support and air units of the 97th Bombardment Group, reached their bases at RAF Polebrook and RAF Grafton Underwood in early June 1942. Less than a month later, the VIII Bomber Command's first offensive air mission of World War Two took place as six Douglas A-20 Havoc light bombers joined a like number of »

LEFT: **Shown as a West Point Cadet, General Frederick Castle was an early officer with the Eighth Air Force and received a posthumous Medal of Honor.** Public Domain US Army via Wikimedia Commons

ABOVE: Painted in olive drab camouflage, this B-17 of the 379th Bombardment Group, Eighth Air Force sits at its airfield in England. Public Domain collections of the Imperial War Museums via Wikimedia Commons

ABOVE RIGHT: The Consolidated B-24 Liberator was the Eighth Air Force strategic bombing partner of the B-17 Flying Fortress. Public Domain US Air Force via Wikimedia Commons

RAF Bostons (the British nickname for the Havoc) in attacks on four Nazi airfields in the Netherlands.

The missions of Eighth Air Force included the strategic bombing of Nazi-occupied Europe and the Third Reich itself as assigned through the Casablanca directive and the specifications of Operation Pointblank. Targets included military and industrial infrastructure, transportation centres, U-boat bases on the coasts of the Atlantic and in Germany, as well as oil production, aircraft assembly, and component manufacturing facilities. During the course of World War Two, the B-17s and Consolidated B-24 Liberator bombers of the Eighth carried out the orders that were issued concurrently with the initiation of the Combined Bomber Offensive.

The first Eighth Air Force raid on Nazi-occupied Europe occurred on August 17, 1942, as 18 Flying Fortresses participated in the bombing of rail marshalling yards near the city of Rouen, France. Steadily, despite the diversion of assets to the Mediterranean theatre in late 1942 and beyond, the strength of the Eighth grew. At the same time, daylight precision raids penetrating into German-controlled airspace resulted in an unsustainable casualty rate, some groups experiencing losses as high as 88%, in both planes and personnel. Among its costliest raids were those conducted against the Messerschmitt aircraft assembly plants at Regensburg, Germany, and the ball bearing manufacturing nexus at Schweinfurt. Daylight raids were suspended for five months after October 14, 1943, remembered as 'Black Thursday@ for the loss of 60 B-17s at Schweinfurt.

The Eighth Air Force renewed its bombing campaign against Nazi Germany in February 1944, with the offensive dubbed Big Week. For five straight days, US and RAF heavy bombers hit various targets. At Big Week's inception, 1,000 B-17s and B-24s hit multiple aircraft assembly plants. The B-17s concentrated on Leipzig, Bernburg-Strenzfeld, and Oschersleben. Eleven B-17s were lost on February 24 during another raid on Schweinfurt. Augsburg and Regensburg were targeted on February 25, and Eighth Air Force losses totalled 31 big bombers.

On March 6, 1944, the Eighth carried out its first major raid on the Nazi capital of Berlin as 700 B-17s and B-24s struck. Two more raids followed as 600 bombers heavily damaged the ball bearing production facility at Erkner, a suburb of the capital, on March 8. A third raid saw B-17s drop their bombs via radar through heavy cloud cover above Berlin. During the first week of March, Eighth Air Force bombers dropped 4,800 tons of bombs on the city.

Through the following spring, Eighth Air Force operations supported preparations for the D-Day landings of June 6, 1944. B-17s and B-24s struck rail lines, bridges, and other transportation infrastructure to impede any German reinforcement response to the upcoming landings. On May 1, more than 1,300 bombers of all Eighth Air Force types conducted raids, and this was followed up by a 1,000 bomber effort to disable coastal fortifications and rail lines along the enemy-held coast of France.

Daylight missions were costly to the Eighth Air Force and its heavy bombers, which initially were required to fly missions deep into German airspace without fighter escort all the way to and from targets due to the short range of available fighter types. The situation changed in late 1943 with the introduction of the long-range P-51 Mustang fighter. By early 1944, Mustangs flew escort for the big bombers regularly. General Doolittle altered the fighters' tactical directive, allowing them to range forward of bomber formations to seek air combat with Luftwaffe fighters and ultimately win control of the air through a battle of attrition.

At first, the bomber crews were nonplussed by the tactic, believing their escorts had been diverted from their primary task of protecting bomber formations. In the end, however, the offensive fighter tactic – using the bombers as bait to lure the Luftwaffe into the air – actually offered increased protection for the B-17s. With air supremacy won, General Dwight Eisenhower, supreme Allied commander in Europe, said prior to D-Day: "If you see fighter aircraft over you, they will be ours."

A concerted effort to damage or destroy Nazi oil production was undertaken by Eighth Air Force bombers in mid-May 1944. Through early 1945, oil facilities in Germany, Romania, Czechoslovakia, and across the shrinking territory of the Third Reich were carried out. During the waning days of the war, Eighth Air Force bombers encountered

BELOW: This photo of the B-17 Flying Fortress *Sally B* was taken in 1985. Public Domain Rotterdam Airport Airshow via Wikimedia Commons

LEFT: This contemporary aerial photograph depicts RAF High Wycombe, headquarters of the Eighth Air Force and RAF Bomber Command in Britain during World War Two. Creative Commons Tony Crowe via Wikimedia Commons

LEFT: This modern photo depicts a B-17 painted in World War Two markings as it comes in for a landing. GNU Free Documentation License Mike Freer Touchdown Aviation via Wikimedia Commons

the first operational jet fighters in history, particularly the Luftwaffe's Messerschmitt Me-262. The Me-262 was a deadly aircraft in the hands of an experienced pilot, but the jets were available in too few numbers and too late in the war to alter the outcome of the conflict.

The Eighth Air Force launched its last bombing raids of the war on April 25, 1945, when B-17s attacked the Skoda armaments factories in Czechoslovakia while B-24s struck rail yards and installations in eastern Germany at Bad Reichenall and Freilassig. Through the course of World War Two in Europe, the B-17 became a workhorse of the Allied strategic bombing campaign, sharing the American heavy bombing load with the B-24. However, during the years that followed, the Flying Fortress's fame and status seem to have eclipsed that of its big Consolidated partner.

The Flying Fortress has since seen its combat record evaluated and re-evaluated, its capabilities and shortcomings analysed, and its story burnished with the memoirs and recollections of the diminishing number of men who knew it during the war years.

As the number of Eighth Air Force planes grew into the thousands, identification of various units and individual planes became increasingly difficult, particularly when many bomber formations were in the air at the same time. The VIII Bomber Command had quadrupled in size by December 1942, and at the end of the year, the Eighth and other US air forces deployed in the European and Pacific theatres adopted a simple identification system first employed by fighter groups and then by 16 squadrons of B-17s.

Within months, however, the increasing number of aircraft had nearly exhausted the available two-letter identifications. By June 1943, a more sophisticated identification system was introduced utilising a painted geometric figure on the bomber's vertical stabiliser, initially 80 inches wide and painted white, to denote a specific bomber wing. A triangle, for example, indicated the 1st Bombardment Wing (later designated as the 1st Air Division). The 4th Bombardment Wing, flying the B-17, was recognised with a square.

It followed that bombardment groups were designated by a letter painted atop the geometric symbol. After some aircraft were painted with yellow letters, the colour was changed to blue for better visibility. Beginning in February 1944, most bombers were delivered without olive paint and in their natural aluminium. For these planes, the geometric symbol was painted in black and the superimposed number in white. The bombers were also emblazoned with these identifying marks on the upper surface of the right wing.

Individual bombers were identified with combinations of numbers on the vertical stabiliser, such as the B-17 *Kentucky Colonel* of the 384th Bombardment Group. Its aircraft number was 42-107121, and the number was painted on the lower edge of its triangle wing/division insignia and just below its bombardment group letter 'P'. The national insignia, or cocarde, was painted on both sides of the fuselage. By mid-1943, Eighth Air Force planes were further identified with a squadron code consisting of two letters. These were 48 inches tall and painted in assigned colours on the port side of the fuselage just forward of the cocarde and on the starboard fuselage between the waist window and the cocarde.

A single letter was added to identify a specific plane within its squadron, group, and wing/division. This letter was also 48 inches tall and painted aft of the cocarde and forward of the waist window on the B-17's port side and just forward of the squadron code on the starboard side. The single letter was used in radio communications with lead aircraft, other planes within its squadron, or ground control personnel, as each bomber identified itself with the single letter and the last three digits of its serial or identification number as shown on the vertical stabiliser.

Letters and combinations were reused when aircraft were transferred from one unit to another, or lost aircraft were replaced.

LEFT: A B-17 of the Eighth Air Force kicks up a cloud of dust as it starts its four engines at an airfield in England. Public Domain US Air Force via Wikimedia Commons

THE FLYING FORTRESS AND THE FIRST EIGHTH AIR FORCE RAID

General Ira C. Eaker, head of Eighth Air Force Bomber Command in England, penned an optimistic letter to General Henry 'Hap' Arnold, commander of US Army Air Forces (USAAF) on August 5, 1942. It read in part: "The tempo is stepping up as we approach the zero hour...Our combat crews have the heart and stamina, the keenness, the will to fight, and the enthusiasm...We not only have the best collection of officers ever assembled in one place, but they are all working like one congenial, happy family."

Eaker's communication was in response to Arnold's growing displeasure with the pace of the Eighth Air Force actually getting its heavy bombers, particularly the B-17 Flying Fortress, into action against Nazi Germany. It did little to soothe Arnold's ire, and on August 14, the top commander, his patience wearing thin, whisked off a terse cable to General Carl 'Tooey' Spaatz, chief of the Eighth Air Force and Eaker's direct superior, demanding to know why the brand new Flying Fortresses sitting at air bases in Britain had not yet dropped a bomb in anger.

The primary task of the Eighth Air Force was to put American bombers in the skies over Nazi-occupied Europe as soon as possible. However, training airmen, producing big bombers in sufficient numbers, and flying them across the expanse of the Atlantic Ocean, and then coordinating their deployment took time. Never mind the fact that as Arnold fumed, Eaker and his entourage of six had only arrived in England to establish the Eighth Air Force in February 1942, just weeks after the US entry into World War Two following the December 7, 1941, Japanese attack on Pearl Harbor. Forget the fact that the Americans had come with nothing so much as a paperclip in hand to set up the headquarters, therefore relying on what they could borrow from the British.

The time had come, and results were demanded. President Franklin

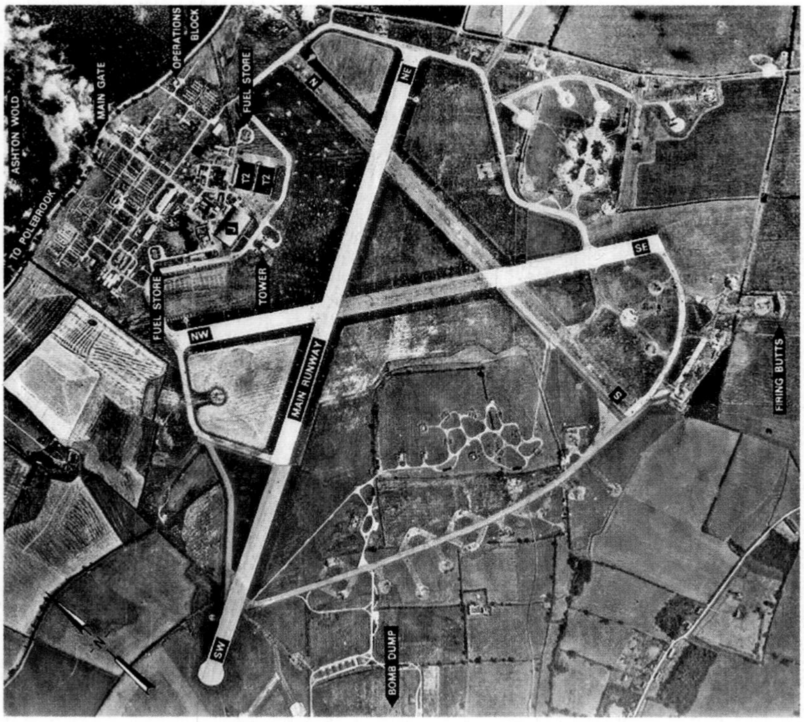

ABOVE: The B-17 Flying Fortress raided the marshalling yards at Rouen in the first all-American heavy bomber mission of the Eighth Air Force on August 17, 1942. Public Domain US Air Force via Wikimedia Commons

LEFT: RAF Polebrook was the home base for the B-17s that raided Rouen on August 17, 1942. Public Domain United Kingdom Government via Wikimedia Commons

RIGHT: Flying Fortresses of the 97th Bomb Group are shown in flight while the group was assigned to the Fifteenth Air Force in Italy. Public Domain US Air Force via Wikimedia Commons

RIGHT: Colonel Frank A. Armstrong piloted *Yankee Doodle*, the lead Flying Fortress of the 414th Bombardment Squadron, 97th Bomb Group on the raid against marshalling yards at Rouen. Public Domain US Air Force via Wikimedia Commons

BELOW: This B-17 Flying Fortress, serial no. 41-2578, was dubbed *Yankee Doodle* and led the August 1942 raid on Rouen. The plane became the longest serving B-17 in the Eighth Air Force. Public Domain US Air Force via Wikimedia Commons

D. Roosevelt was anxious to see American bombers get into the fight, demonstrating that the US was an active partner in the war, while cooperation with Royal Air Force Bomber Command was essential. Although it mattered little by mid-August, Spaatz and Eaker had actually been working hard to get their bombers into the fight. They had identified earlier dates for the first raid by USAAF heavy bombers against the enemy, but predictably bad weather had forced the postponement of the historic mission on two prior occasions.

Finally, in mid-August, Eaker was ready to try once more. The 97th Bomb Group was alerted for the third time on the morning of the 16th. If the weather cooperated, American bombs would be plummeting earthward within a few hours. Although the number of aircraft would be minimal and the target somewhat less than ambitious, there was no doubt that much was at stake. An anxious press wanted to tell the story of American bombers in action, while the Eighth Air Force needed to raise its profile positively as well.

Early on the morning of August 17, General Eaker arrived at his headquarters, a former girls' preparatory school, at High Wycombe, in Buckinghamshire. By 11am, he had assembled a group of officers for an operations conference, informing them that the first USAAF heavy bomber raid of World War Two was scheduled for that afternoon. Indeed, compared to the size and scope of later missions, this initial effort was less than impressive. But it was full of expectations.

A dozen B-17Es were scheduled to attack the railroad marshalling yards at Sotteville on the left bank of the River Seine near the ancient French city of Rouen, where Joan of Arc had been burned at the stake in the 15th century. Only 35 miles inland from the English Channel, the target was 65 miles northwest of Paris. Fighter escort was be supplied by four squadrons of RAF Supermarine Spitfire IXs, while the remaining six B-17s of the 97th Bomb Group would fly a decoy mission along the French coastline, hopefully drawing away at least some of the expected Luftwaffe fighter opposition from the main effort.

After the morning conference broke up, Eaker flew to RAF Polebrook in Northamptonshire, the first B-17 base in England and home to the 97th Bomb Group, where hasty preparations for the day's effort were well underway. He exchanged his uniform for flight gear and steeled himself for the coming test. Both Eaker and Spaatz had been authorised to fly combat missions, although not at the same time. A former fighter pilot, Eaker had been given the first opportunity.

Eaker met briefly with Colonel Frank A. Armstrong, Jr., commander of the 97th, and then rode out to the planes with other airmen, who hoisted themselves into their respective bombers. Eaker took his place in the radio operator's compartment aboard Armstrong's B-17, nicknamed *Yankee Doodle*, belonging to the 414th Bombardment Squadron, and settled in. The co-pilot aboard *Yankee Doodle* that day was Major Paul W. Tibbets, later to fly the Boeing B-29 Superfortress bomber *Enola Gay*, which dropped the first atomic bomb on the Japanese city of Hiroshima in 1945.

Shortly after 3pm, the dozen B-17s began taxiing toward the runways, and one after another they climbed upward into fair skies. By 3:39, all were aloft and headed toward the marshalling yards. Within minutes, they had climbed to their cruising altitude of 22,500ft. The Spitfires joined up on the bomber formations as the English Channel came into view, and crossing over the continent the gunners aboard each bomber kept their eyes open for German fighters, their .50-calibre machine guns at the ready. As the four engines of *Yankee Doodle* droned on, Eaker took a turn manning the topside machine-gun turret.

The minutes dragged by slowly, but as the navigators stayed on course and the bombers approached their target, bombardiers crouched and peered through their Norden bombsights. No Luftwaffe »

ABOVE: Freight unloaded from ships on the River Seine at Rouen awaits rail transportation in 1944. Public Domain US Army via Wikimedia Commons

RIGHT: Then Major Paul Tibbets was the co-pilot aboard *Yankee Doodle* during the Rouen raid. He later piloted the B-29 Superfortress *Enola Gay* that dropped the atomic bomb on Hiroshima. Public Domain US Air Force via Wikimedia Commons

interference had been encountered so far. Only a few scattered blossoms of German flak had been seen, and the weather was clear, ideal for the visual sighting necessary. The bomb bay doors opened, and General Eaker, after clambering into the bomb compartment to experience the conditions and feeling the numbing cold of an air temperature nearing 350 below zero Fahrenheit, then watched from a side window as the modest *Yankee Doodle* payload of only five 600lb bombs was released.

Only 18½ tons of bombs were dropped that historic day, and some damage was inflicted on the marshalling yard, a roundhouse, siding tracks, rail cars, storage buildings, and a repair shop. It was virtually a pin prick compared to the massive number of planes and tonnage of bombs to be carried in future Eighth Air Force and RAF Bomber Command raids on military and industrial targets and cities across Nazi-occupied Europe and deep in the heart of the Third Reich. Regardless, the raid of August 17, 1942, was a trial by fire for those who participated – a combat baptism for the Flying Fortress flown by American aircrew in Europe, and a harbinger of things to come.

Shortly after the bombers turned for home, five squadrons of Spitfire Vs met them for the return flight. No B-17s were shot down during the raid, even after three Luftwaffe Focke-Wulf Fw-190 fighters swept in to take look at the big bombers. The German pilots were apparently dissuaded from pressing home their attacks when the machine gunners aboard the Flying Fortresses opened up on them. They turned away quickly.

A pair of B-17s had incurred some damage from enemy flak, and one of these was noticeably trailing smoke from a stricken engine while lagging behind the others in formation. All aircraft landed safely, the first touching down at RAF Polebrook at 7pm; the entire mission had concluded in just about four hours. A flock of pigeons had smashed into the Plexiglas nose of a B-17 in the diversionary group as it headed back to the satellite airfield at Grafton Underwood in Northamptonshire. Two crewmen had suffered minor cuts.

When the raid was over, Spaatz congratulated Eaker on its success. Both men were overjoyed. Their inexperienced bomber crews had accomplished the mission without loss, and the outcome seemed to bolster the American perspective that daylight precision bombing could produce the desired results. Over time, both officers would see their expectations dimmed amid heavy losses. But on this day, they were well satisfied. Eaker was even-tempered in his assessment. "The raid went according to plan, and we are satisfied with the day's work." He paused and then cautioned, "…but one swallow doesn't make a summer."

The reporters quickly dashed off stories relaying the news that the Eighth Air Force heavy bombers were in the war at last. RAF observers, engaged in their own air campaign against the enemy for months, concluded that the raid on the Sotteville marshalling yard was definitely not a 'really big show'. It was, though, a resolute beginning.

In a display of Allied camaraderie, the day after the raid, Air Chief Marshal Sir Arthur Harris, a personal friend of Eaker and head of RAF Bomber Command, dashed off an appreciative telegram. It read: "Congratulations from all ranks of Bomber Command on the highly successful completion of the first all-American raid by the big fellows on German-occupied territory in Europe. Yankee Doodle certainly went to town and can stick yet another well-deserved feather in his cap."

RIGHT: General Ira C. Eaker, commander of Eighth Air Force Bomber Command, rode along on the historic raid against rail marshalling yards at Rouen in 1942. Public Domain US Air Force via Wikimedia Commons

FAR RIGHT: The cathedral of Rouen smoulders after being damaged in an Allied bombing raid in 1944. Creative Commons Bundesarchiv Bild via Wikimedia Commons

COMBINED BOMBER OFFENSIVE

ABOVE: The RAF's legendary Avro Lancaster made its World War Two debut with the Combined Bomber Offensive. Public Domain United Kingdom Government via Wikimedia Commons

RIGHT: Pictured at right with Army Chief of Staff General George C. Marshall, General Henry 'Hap' Arnold led the USAAF strategic daylight precision bombing advocacy. Public Domain Franklin D. Roosevelt Presidential Library via Wikimedia Commons

RIGHT: Churchill, Roosevelt, and the Combined Chiefs of Staff met at Casablanca in 1943. The two leaders posed with their senior advisors as the Casablanca Directive was issued. Public Domain National Museum of the US Navy via Wikimedia Common

By the time the US Eighth Air Force had established itself and had been equipped with sufficient bombers and aircrew to conduct its first independent raid against Nazi-occupied Europe in August 1942, the British Royal Air Force had been conducting raids against targets on the continent since 1939. When the Americans arrived, it might have been logical for some RAF senior officers to assume that the US bombers would work together with the British in a sustained campaign of night area bombing.

However, armed with the Boeing B-17 Flying Fortress bomber and later the Consolidated B-24 Liberator, the Americans brought with them a firm conviction in the effectiveness of daylight precision bombing. They based their confidence on two pillars. First was the theory that the heavily armed Flying Fortress and Liberator could take care of themselves against attacking Luftwaffe fighters and did not require the defence of long-range fighter escorts. Therefore, the development of such a fighter lagged behind. Secondly, the Norden bombsight, a complicated airborne computer of sorts, was so accurate, they asserted, that it could put a bomb into a proverbial 'pickle barrel' from extremely high altitude.

For their part, the RAF had already tried daylight precision bombing and sustained serious losses that led to a strategic shift to night area bombing. The British had also put the B-17 to its first combat test in the European theatre, and the results had been disheartening to say the least.

Nevertheless, the Americans were determined to execute their daylight bombing strategy. Even as Air Chief Marshal Arthur 'Bomber' Harris took control of RAF Bomber Command in February 1942 to execute a War Cabinet directive on area bombing and see to the deployment of the formidable Avro Lancaster, the Americans continued to muster what strength they could in England. Despite demands on resources in the Mediterranean theatre and in the Pacific, B-17s and crews allotted to General Ira C. Eaker's Eighth Bomber Command grew in numbers. »

While the British maintained their nocturnal raids, for the balance of 1942, Eighth Air Force missions were limited in scope. The B-17s hit U-boat pens along the Atlantic coast of France, rail lines and marshalling yards, and factories in France and the Low Countries. Escort fighters included the British Supermarine Spitfire and the American Republic P-47 Thunderbolt and Lockheed P-38 Lightning. The long-range North American P-51 Mustang also made its combat debut late in the year.

By the end of 1942, American bombers had delivered more than 1,700 tons of bombs against targets in France, Belgium, and the Netherlands, but the effort was dwarfed by that of the RAF. Losses mounted, and the British were ever sceptical. While the American senior commanders, including Eaker, Eighth Air Force commanding officer General Carl 'Tooey' Spaatz, and General Henry 'Hap' Arnold, head of the US Army Air Forces (USAAF), were staunch in their advocacy for the continuing daylight offensive, the cost in men and planes was climbing. British Prime Minister Winston Churchill and RAF leaders began a steady attempt to convince President Franklin D. Roosevelt to order a switch to night area bombing in concert with the ongoing RAF campaign.

The first Eighth Bomber Command raid against a target inside Germany did not take place until January 27, 1943, when 64 bombers hit the port facilities at the city of Wilhelmshaven. The historic raid came three days after the Allied leaders had concluded their conference at Casablanca, Morocco, where Churchill and Roosevelt met along with the Combined Chiefs of Staff. In addition to other urgent matters, Churchill intended to close the deal with Roosevelt during their face-to-face discussions and bring the American's bombing effort in line with the RAF. Some historians say that Churchill had already succeeded, and that Roosevelt was ready to issue such orders.

General Arnold, however, became aware of the coming coup and sent Eaker to visit Churchill in an effort to persuade the Prime Minister to stand down. The American general and the British premier met for lunch, and Eaker was well prepared for his mission. A fine writer, he penned a concise single page of lucid argument regarding daylight precision bombing. Churchill appreciated the brevity and the prose, particularly a phrase that Eaker turned which read: "If the RAF continues night bombing and we bomb by day, we shall bomb them around the clock and the devil shall get no rest."

Eaker prevailed, and Churchill explained afterward that the American officer had "…pleaded his cause with skill and tenacity. Considering how much had been staked on this venture by the United States and all they felt about it, I decided to back Eaker and his theme, and I turned around completely and withdrew all my opposition to the daylight bombing by the Fortresses… They went ahead and soon began to pay dividends. All the same, I still think that if at the beginning they had put their money on night bombing, we should have reached our climax much sooner."

Consequently, among other business, the Combined Chiefs of Staff issued the Casablanca Directive on January 21, 1943. At the time, the notion that Allied

LEFT: An Eighth Air Force B-17 Flying Fortress completes a bomb run against the Focke Wulf assembly plant at Marienburg, Germany, in October 1943. Public Domain National Archives and Records Administration via Wikimedia Commons

LEFT: Air Chief Marshal Sir Arthur 'Bomber' Harris led RAF Bomber Command during the Combined Bomber Offensive. Public Domain Royal Air Force official photographer via Wikimedia Commons

LEFT: U-boat pens such as these at Trondheim, Norway, were early targets of the Allied Combined Bombing Offensive. Public Domain collections of the Imperial War Museums

air power alone might be sufficient to bring Nazi Germany to its knees was still plausible, and the directive to 'appropriate British and US Air Force commanders' specified: "Your Primary object will be the progressive destruction and dislocation of the German military, industrial, and economic system, and the undermining of the morale of the German people to a point where their capacity for armed resistance is fatally weakened."

The Casablanca Directive further specified targets in order of importance – German submarine construction; German aircraft production; transportation; oil refineries and storage facilities; and enemy industrial and war related infrastructure. These priorities were modified from time to time, particularly as the Allied preparations for D-Day, June 6, 1944, the invasion of Normandy, matured. In response to the directive, Operation Pointblank was implemented to execute the programme. Early American raids in the spring of 1943 had hit industrial targets in the cities of Bremen and Recklinghausen among others. The Allied Combined Bomber Offensive officially began on June 10, 1943.

The details of the Casablanca Directive were left to the military planners, and Pointblank was introduced on June 14, 1943. One significant Pointblank modification included a major additional objective for the Americans – the facilities that produced German fighter aircraft and the components that were critical to their manufacture. It was understood that these facilities were key to the support of sustained Luftwaffe air defence, and the D-Day landings could not move forward unless the Germans were defeated in the skies above the invasion beaches in northwest France. Air superiority was prerequisite to launching of the major ground offensive.

LEFT: RAF bombs burst on a railroad marshalling yard in northern France during a rare daylight raid in 1941. Public Domain Air Ministry Photograph via Wikimedia Commons

LEFT: B-17 Flying Fortress bombers drop their payloads through cloud cover over Bremen, Germany, on November 13, 1943. Public Domain US Air Force via Wikimedia Commons

While the British conducted their night raids, the Eighth Air Force embarked on a series of costly daylight raids of its own. The first coordinated raids by the British and Americans took place in July 1943 and were aimed at the second-largest city in Germany - the port of Hamburg. The Americans followed RAF nocturnal raids and bombed by day; however, the smoke from raging fire obscured targets and made the Americans reticent to follow the RAF in the future.

Particularly sobering were the results of a two-pronged attack against the Messerschmitt aircraft factory at Regensburg and the complex of ball bearing facilities at Schweinfurt on August 17, 1943, and a second raid against Schweinfurt on October 14 of that year, which will forever be remembered as 'Black Thursday'. Sixty B-17s were shot down in each of the raids, while heavy casualties among crews and the write-offs of bombers so damaged that they could not return to action yielded »

LEFT: B-17 Flying Fortresses are lined up at an airfield in the United States prior to their deployment in 1943. Public Domain United States Army Air Forces via Wikimedia Commons

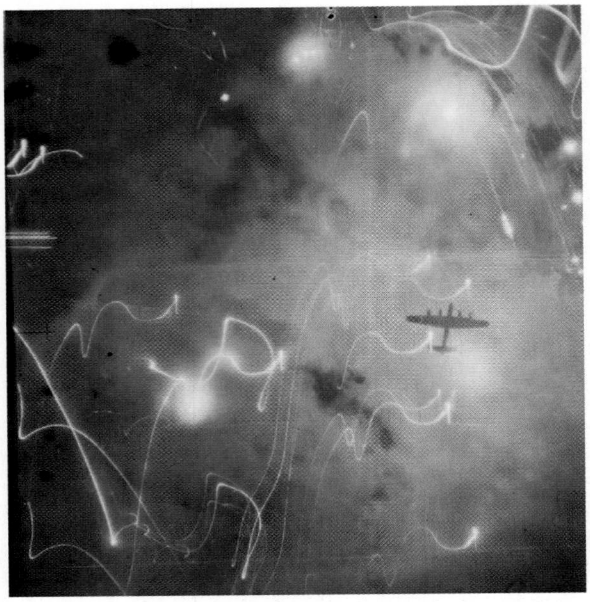

ABOVE: RAF Lancaster heavy bombers attack Hamburg, Germany, by night in 1943. Public Domain collections of the Imperial War Museums

an unsustainable loss rate. American daylight raids were suspended for five months until the long-range Mustang could be deployed in numbers to provide escort against German fighters on missions deep inside the Fatherland.

When the American daylight raids were resumed in early 1944, another modification in standing orders led to a directive that emphasised the destruction of the Luftwaffe in the air and on the ground. General Jimmy Doolittle assumed command of the Eighth Air Force in January and implemented a new, aggressive order. While the Mustangs were capable of escorting the B-17s and B-24s all the way to targets deep inside Germany, they were also authorised to range ahead of the formations and seek out air combat with German fighters, while further strafing enemy airfields and targets of opportunity. Along with the P-47s, P-38s, and allocated British fighter strength, the Mustang fighter pilots went about their task with grim determination and prosecuted a war of attrition. Though the bomber crews at first were dismayed with the new orders, fearing that their fighter escort would be less effective, the offensive tactic proved to be beneficial for the bomber formations as well.

By February 1944, the top priority of Operation Overlord prompted more modification of the Pointblank orders. Operation Argument, known popularly as Big Week, included a series of Eighth Air Force bomber raids against targets in Germany, signalling the commitment to the attrition of Luftwaffe fighter strength and continuing prosecution of the daylight precision bombing effort. Throughout the implementation of the USAAF strategy, the Americans sought greater participation from RAF fighter units. However, the American fighters bore the brunt of the daylight Pointblank fighter initiative. A third raid on Schweinfurt during Big Week was conducted on February 24, and during the maximum effort the loss rate among the big bombers for the duration was reduced to less than seven percent as 247 Flying Fortresses were lost during 3,500 Big Week missions flown.

Meanwhile, as the RAF continued to bomb German cities and industrial targets at night, the American daylight bombing compelled the Luftwaffe to draw much of its fighter strength away from the front lines to defend the Third Reich itself, facilitating the air superiority that was required for D-Day to proceed. In fact, by June 6, 1944, the Luftwaffe could muster only a few dozen aircraft along the coast of the English Channel, and these are believed to have flown fewer than 300 sorties on the day. Conversely, overwhelming Allied air strength flexed its muscle with nearly 14,000 sorties on D-Day alone.

As the air superiority aspect of Operation Pointblank succeeded, strategic bombing faced another challenge in the eradication of launch sites for the V-1 buzz bomb and V-2 rocket, a pulse-jet aircraft and the world's first operational ballistic missile respectively. These were Hitler's 'vengeance' weapons, and their random attacks led to many civilian casualties in British cities. Therefore, the destruction of the launch sites became a priority. This bombing initiative was concluded as many of the sites were overrun by Allied ground troops by early 1945.

The reduction of German oil production was always a priority for the Allied air forces, and in the spring of 1944, Eighth Air Force bombers conducted their initial raids on synthetic oil production facilities inside Germany. Earlier raids had taken place against oil fields and refineries at Ploesti, Romania, and other locations with B-24 bombers of the Fifteenth Air Force making an epic attack against the target on August 1, 1943. Following the May 1944 raid against the synthetic plants, Reich Minister of Armaments Albert Speer told Hitler: "…The enemy has struck us at one of our weakest points. If they persist at it this time, we will soon no longer have any fuel production worth mentioning."

Allied bombing did in fact reduce German oil production in June 1944 from a previous 734,000 tons per month to 511,000 tons. At the same time, aviation fuel production decreased to a dangerously low 53,000 tons while diesel dropped from an April level of 88,900 tons to 66,000 tons in June as well. In July, German refined oil output dropped to 438,000 tons. By early September, oil production in the Third Reich was less than 43% of its April output at 345,000 tons.

Without doubt, such rapid declines impacted the availability of fuel for ground and air operations while essentially bringing to a halt the expenditure of the vital oil resource for any training or non-military purposes. By the time of Nazi Germany's surrender in May 1945, its oil production infrastructure had completely collapsed.

Historians have continued to debate the cost versus return of the Allied Combined Bomber Offensive during World War Two. However, there is no dispute in the claim that heavy bombers brought the war home to the Reich and contributed substantially to the ultimate victory.

RIGHT: A pair of B-17 Flying Fortresses is shown in flight in 1942, the year the Eighth Air Force began its buildup in Britain. Public Domain US Army Air Forces via Wikimedia Commons

RIGHT: The Boeing B-17 Flying Fortress was a mainstay of the Combined Bomber Offensive from 1943-1945. GNU Free Documentation Licence Kogo via Wikimedia Commons

RAID ON SCHWEINFURT AND REGENSBURG

FAR LEFT: B-17 Flying Fortresses of the 1st Bombardment Wing fly over Schweinfurt, Germany, August 17, 1943. Public Domain US Air Force via Wikimedia Commons

LEFT: Clouds of smoke rise from the ball bearing factory at Schweinfurt, Germany, as US bombs explode. Public Domain US Air Force Wikimedia Commons

In response to the Pointblank Directive of June 14, 1943, the US Eighth Air Force and RAF Bomber Command stepped up their raids on German aircraft production facilities and the factories that produced the components that went into the Luftwaffe's fighters. The intent was to compel the German air defenders to protect such vital infrastructure and pull away from the proposed frontlines of the invasion of Western Europe scheduled for the spring of 1944, while also eroding the combat effectiveness of the Luftwaffe through attrition.

In theory, a concerted bombing effort against aircraft production facilities would require the German fighters to pull back into the airspace of the Third Reich itself, leaving the Allied forces with air superiority over the English Channel and the coast of France, particularly Normandy, where the D-Day landings were to take place. While RAF Bomber Command continued its campaign of nocturnal area bombing of industrial targets, the Eighth Air Force sent large-scale daylight bomber formations, including B-17 Flying Fortresses and B-24 Liberators, to attack selected high-value targets.

Among these were a major Messerschmitt Me-109 fighter assembly plant at Regensburg, Germany, where an estimated 300 aircraft were produced per month, and the Schweinfurter Kugellagerwerke ball bearing factory located in the city of Schweinfurt. The American daylight raids had increased steadily in size and scope through early 1943, and commensurate with the offensive, losses in big bombers had escalated at an alarming rate. Luftwaffe senior officers recognised the growing threat to their infrastructure and transferred no fewer than 600 fighters to advantageous locations to intercept the great streams of American bombers. Conversely, US senior air commanders were well aware of the importance of Operation Pointblank and remained keen on validating their doctrine of precision daylight bombing.

In lock step with the Pointblank directive, US air planners organised a two-pronged air assault scheduled for August 17, 1943. At total of 376 Flying Fortresses from the 1st and 4th Bombardment Wings were assigned to the task. The former would hit the ball bearing plant at Schweinfurt with 230 bombers, while the latter would attack the Messerschmitt factory at Regensburg simultaneously with 146 B-17s. Flak, as always, was a concern, and the air staffs worked to develop flight plans that minimised exposure to German fighters. They expected the Regensburg group to take on the brunt of fighter opposition en route to its target, hopefully allowing the Schweinfurt raid to proceed close behind with lesser interference. When the Regensburg bombers had completed their runs, they would proceed to bases in North Africa to refuel rather than running the gauntlet of enemy defences a second time on their return to England. Consequently, the Schweinfurt bombers were expected to have their toughest exposure to the Luftwaffe on their return flight to England.

General Ira C. Eaker, commander of Eighth Air Force, was somewhat reticent in approving the dual missions to Schweinfurt and Regensburg. Losses in recent raids had been »

BELOW: Republic P-47 Thunderbolt fighters like this one provided limited escort for bombers headed to Regensburg and Schweinfurt. Creative Commons Tim Felce via Wikimedia Commons

heavy, and such an investment of men and planes would strain available resources in light of the pace of replacements due to demands in other theatres. Compounding Eaker's concerns was the simple fact that the fighters assigned to escort the missions, 18 full squadrons of American Republic P-47 Thunderbolts and 16 of RAF Supermarine Spitfires, lacked the range to go all the way to the targets with the bombers. Their depleted fuel tanks would cause them to break off and turn for home well before the heaviest concentrations of Luftwaffe fighters would press their attacks.

On the morning of August 17, the pilots and aircrews taking part in the day's missions were roused from their sleep at 2am at bases across East Anglia and elsewhere. After breakfast, they headed for the morning briefing, aware that something was up. However, many of them were taken aback when the ambitious missions were disclosed. One officer of the 100th Bomb Group remembered the atmosphere in the briefing room when the target of Regensburg was revealed.

"...Everybody had been chatting away and horsing about a little as usual," he recalled, "but when they pulled the curtain back and revealed that route with the line going so deep into Germany...there was dead silence for a moment...We all knew there were going to be a few of us not coming back." The Bloody 100th lost nine B-17s that day. A sergeant remembered the response during the 384th Bomb Group briefing. "A moan went up," he said. "Some men stood, cursed, and expressed their bitter dissatisfaction – too deep, so many miles without fighter protection. It was sheer fear that gripped us."

At approximately 6:20am, the first bombers headed for Regensburg began taking off, their departure delayed more than 90 minutes by heavy cloud cover. As they clawed their way into the leaden grey sky, the expectations for a coordinated dual raid evaporated quickly. The bombers assigned to Schweinfurt did not begin taking off until 11:20am, and by that time the Regensburg raiders were already deep inside the airspace of the Third Reich.

The flight path of the 4th Wing bombers took them over the Nazi-occupied Netherlands and Belgium, while German trackers watched their progress almost from the moment of take-off. Two dozen P-47 escorts engaged about 60 Me-109s and Fw-190s from I/JG 26 and III/JG 26 respectively. Flak bursts blossomed, the impact of shrapnel with a bomber's fuselage creating a noise reminiscent of gravel being thrown against a metal roof.

Captain Frank Murphy, a navigator aboard a 100th Bomb Group B-17, vividly remembered the initial morning air encounter. "... Approximately 1025 hours, two Fw-190s appeared at 1 o'clock level and whizzed through the formation ahead of us in frontal attack," he wrote in his war memoir *Luck of the Draw*, "nicking two B-17s of the 95th Group in the wings and breaking away beneath us in half-rolls. Smoke immediately trailed from both B-17s, but they held their stations. As the fighters passed us at a high rate of closure, the guns of the group went into action. The pungent smell of burnt powder filled our cockpit, and the B-17 trembled to the recoil of nose and ball-turret guns. I saw pieces fly off the wing of one of the fighters before they passed from view."

Prior to entering German airspace, six B-17s were shot down. The P-47s turned toward home above the town of Eupen, Belgium, and for a while there was a lull in the air battle.

German trackers had, in fact, been surprised to see American bombers venturing so deep into the Fatherland, and they worked feverishly to move a substantial number of fighters into

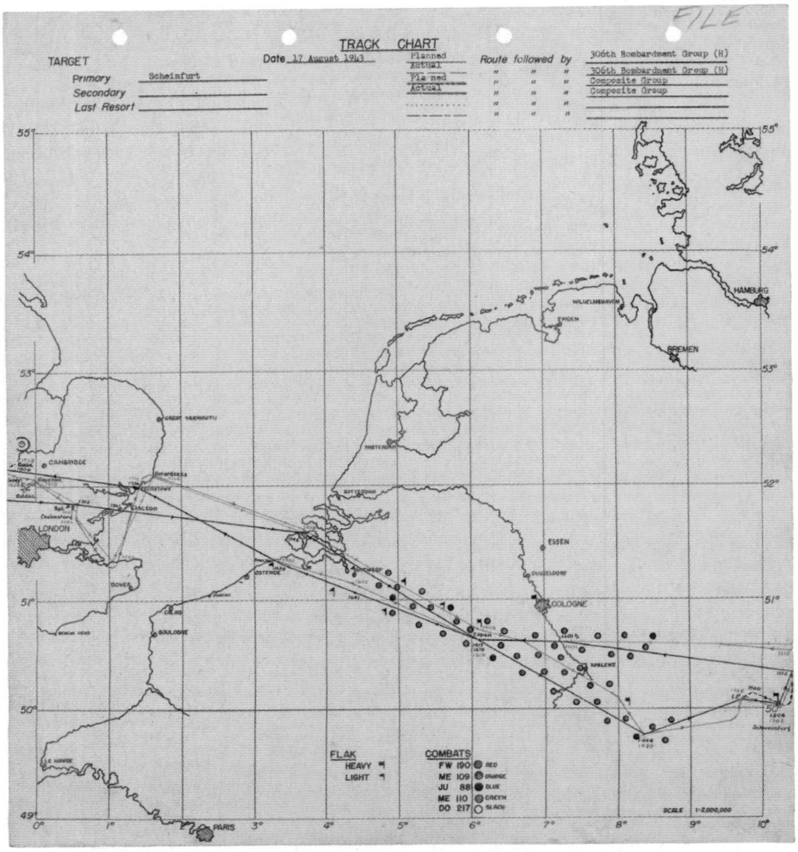

LEFT: This track chart depicts the flight paths of the US bombers during the Regensburg and Schweinfurt raids. Public Domain US Army via Wikimedia Commons

LEFT: General Ira C. Eaker, commander of Eighth Air Force, reluctantly approved the dual bombing missions against Schweinfurt and Regensburg in August 1943. Public Domain US Air Force via Wikimedia Commons

BELOW: The wreckage of a B-17 Flying Fortress lies in a field after the big bomber was shot down during an air raid. Creative Commons Bundesarchiv Bild via Wikimedia Commons

RIGHT: P-47 Thunderbolt fighters fly in formation. Note the additional fuel drop tanks attached to their fuselages. Public Domain US Air Force via Wikimedia Commons

position to intercept. The respite was brief, and the second Luftwaffe fighter onslaught brought down nine more Flying Fortresses. Once over the target, the remaining bombers trained above Regensburg for 20 minutes, dropping their bombs from 20,000ft. After turning toward their North African haven, the formations of the 4th Bombardment Wing had noticeably thinned. Twenty-four of their number had been shot down, and 240 airmen were killed, missing, or in enemy hands.

The Schweinfurt bombers lagged more than three hours behind the Regensburg B-17s. Over two hours had been required for the four bombardment groups of the 1st Bombardment Wing to get airborne and form up for the long flight. Heading over the North Sea, they climbed to an altitude of 21,000ft, and as they approached the continent, Luftwaffe fighters had been rearmed, refuelled, and readied to meet the next big raid. Instead of attacking the B-17s of the 4th Bombardment Wing on their flightpath to North Africa, the German controllers sent swarms of Me-109s and Fw-190s against the inbound Schweinfurt bombers. An estimated 250 to 300 fighters rose to meet the Flying Fortresses, and when the P-47s turned back toward England, 48 minutes of unescorted flying time remained before the bombers made Schweinfurt.

Just as the Thunderbolts withdrew, a crewman aboard one B-17 watched in horror as he saw "an overwhelming number of fighters steadily climbing." He later remembered the chill of the spectacle and commented that it was "the largest number of enemy fighters that I ever saw in my tour." During the half hour of flying time from Eupen to the River Rhine, the German onslaught was relentless. Messerschmitts and Focke Wulfs slashed through the formations, machine guns chattering and cannon thumping. The fighters had a field day, and 21 Flying Fortresses went down in smoke and flame.

The loss was substantial, with great gaps blasted through the bomber formations, but the remaining B-17s flew on toward Schweinfurt. The target factory buildings were dispersed across a rather wide area, and the first American bombs fell at approximately 3pm. As they made their turns for the homeward leg of the hazardous mission, the B-17 aircrews noticed a pause in the fighter attacks. However, as they flew above the German city of Meiningen in southern Thuringia, a torrent of Luftwaffe planes descended on them and another 11 B-17s were shredded by enemy fire, some of them exploding in mid-air while others careened out of formation or began a long earthward death spiral. Parachutes billowed while pieces of damaged and downed planes, American and German, spun wildly.

As the bombers approached Eupen once again, P-47s with drop tanks for extra fuel to extend their range came into view. The American fighters pitched into the marauding enemy, and swirling dogfights ensued. The Germans were surprised to see American fighters so far from the coastline, but another B-17 fell in flames before the Luftwaffe assault abated. The Luftwaffe pilots had flown 500 sorties and accounted for the majority of bombers shot down. The Schweinfurt raid cost the Eighth Air Force another 36 Flying Fortresses and their precious crews.

The butcher's bill for the combined Schweinfurt and Regensburg raids amounted to 60 heavy bombers, and 565 airmen were casualties. In exchange, the Luftwaffe lost 25 fighters. Compounding the American toll, another 20% of the attacking bombers were so severely damaged that they were written off as total losses even though they had managed to make it home, some literally 'on a wing and a prayer'. In total, a staggering 40% of the combined bomber strength hurled at Schweinfurt and Regensburg had been shot down or blasted into scrap.

Post-raid bomb assessment rendered a verdict of average accuracy, something of a bitter pill considering the great losses. Ball bearing output at Schweinfurt was cut 38% immediately, but the shortfall was covered with surplus product while damage was repaired. Fighter production at Regensburg was halted but recovered within weeks.

The cost of the August 17 raids in men and machines had startled the Eighth Air Force command. However, its commitment to precision daylight bombing did not waver. Schweinfurt and Regensburg remained high on the target list for Operation Pointblank, and the American heavy bombers were fated to return another day.

BELOW LEFT: B-17s of the 95th Bombardment Group fly in formation with P-47 Thunderbolt fighters nearby. Public Domain US Air Force via Wikimedia Commons

BELOW RIGHT: A German Messerschmitt Me-109 fighter begins to blaze under the guns of an American fighter in the sky over Nazi-occupied Europe. Public Domain US Air Force via Wikimedia Commons

SECOND SCHWEINFURT RAID

The Pointblank Directive of March 1943 had clearly indicated the high priority target value of the German ball bearing industry. In fact, ball bearing production actually ranked second on the list of enemy industrial enterprises designated for heavy bombing.

In August, the twin raids on the ball bearing facility at Schweinfurt, Germany, and the Messerschmitt Me-109 fighter assembly plant at Regensburg curtailed aircraft output temporarily and cut ball bearing production nearly 40% for time. However, this modest interruption had come at the price of 60 B-17 Flying Fortress bombers destroyed with the loss of approximately 600 airmen killed, wounded, and captured.

Nevertheless, firmly committed to the doctrine of daylight precision bombing, the senior commanders of the US Eighth Air Force planned a second raid against the ball bearing facilities in Schweinfurt, where the critical components of many German weapons systems – the aircraft construction industry alone used 2.4 million per month – were fabricated in massive quantities.

Amid a growing chorus of criticism from strategic bombing partners in the RAF, who considered the B-17 highly vulnerable with a tail gunner position that was too cramped, a belly gunner position that all but useless, and overall deficient defensive fire capability, the Americans believed staunchly in the big bombers and daylight precision bombing. In March, the US Army Air Forces Committee on Operations Analysis had declared: "...It is better to cause a high degree of destruction in a few essential industries...than to cause a small degree in many." Perhaps there was some truth in the theoretical statement, but in practice the Eighth Air Force was being sorely tested.

The results of the August raid had been disappointing, and in short order a follow-up mission had been cancelled as depleted bomber groups absorbed replacement airmen and planes. Planning continued, however, for a second mission to Schweinfurt, and the date of October 14, 1943, was chosen.

Apparent lessons were gleaned from the experience of the August raid, and the groundwork for the second Schweinfurt mission was laid accordingly. Fighter escort was beefed up for both the inbound and return legs of the mission; however, the limited range of the available Republic P-47 Thunderbolt fighters meant that the 'Little Friends' could stay with the bombers only for the first 200 miles of their long approach flight to the target and then only pick the returning bombers up as they neared the coastline of continental Europe

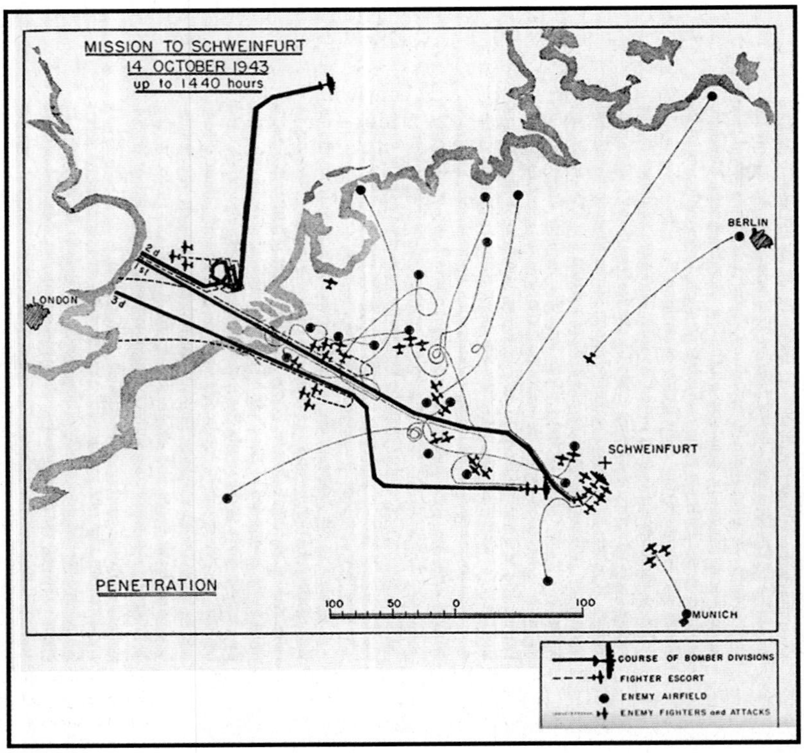

ABOVE: A B-17 bomber heads for home as a pall of smoke shrouds the city of Schweinfurt on October 14, 1943. Public Domain US Army via Wikimedia Commons

LEFT: This map depicts the inbound flight path of the second raid on Schweinfurt in October 1943. Public Domain US Army via Wikimedia Commons

BELOW: Flying Fortresses of the 384th Bombardment Group drop their payloads on a target in Europe. Public Domain US Air Force via Wikimedia Commons

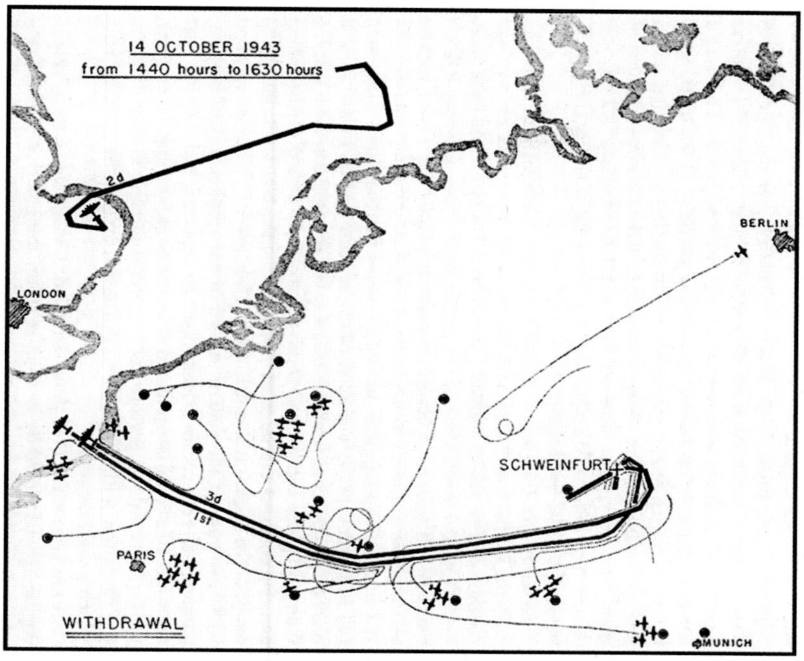

LEFT: German fighters harassed the US bombers during the return flight from Schweinfurt. Public Domain US Army via Wikimedia Commons

ABOVE: A B-17 Flying Fortress of the 545th Bomb Squadron wings its way above the English countryside. Public Domain US Air Force via Wikimedia Commons

during their return flights. In addition, the October mission would be directed toward Schweinfurt alone rather than dividing the strength of the available bombers between two major targets as had been done in August.

An imposing force of 291 Flying Fortresses from the 1st an 3rd Air Divisions were ordered to carry out the raid, and B-17s from 16 bomber groups took part. Just as they had bemoaned the hazards of the earlier Schweinfurt mission, the bomber crewmen were well aware that another long trek deep into Germany would lead to significant losses when they entered morning briefings on October 14 and spotted the red yarn string stretching ominously again toward Schweinfurt.

In addition to running the gauntlet of Luftwaffe fighters, now perfecting the technique of the head-on attack against the American bombers, the ever-improving accuracy of German flak guns would pose a tremendous hazard. The aircrews had good reason to be concerned, and the second Schweinfurt mission proved even costlier than the first. Sixty B-17s were shot down by German fighters and flak, accounting for more than 600 men killed, wounded, or taken prisoner. Well over 100 more bombers sustained some degree of damage, and 17 were so riddled with enemy bullets and cannon shells that they were completely written off as scrap. The second Schweinfurt raid was the last unescorted Eighth Air Force unescorted deep penetration bombing raid into Germany during World War Two. Its staggering losses amounted to 26% of the aircraft involved, and as 2,900 American air personnel had been engaged the human casualty rate was an intolerable 22%. October 14, 1943, is forever remembered in the history of the US Air Force as 'Black Thursday'.

On that fateful morning, plans were completed, weather reports were reviewed, and bomber crews moved out to their explosive-laden planes based across East Anglia. The skies were sullen and grey when the first B-17s began taking off at approximately 10:15am. Despite considerable dense and slowly dissipating fog, the mission was a go. However, there was some immediate confusion as the aircraft began to form up. One group joined with planes of another division when it was unable to find its own. Thirty-three bombers were soon forced to abort their missions due to mechanical issues.

There were 60 B-24 Liberators assigned to fly the mission, but these became scattered early, eight of them unable to form up at all and returning to base, while only 21 went on to fly a diversionary mission against the German city of Emden due to the bad weather. The diversionary raid attracted little attention from German fighters as directors tracked the incoming streams headed for Schweinfurt and kept the majority of their strength focused on the main American effort.

After earlier air battles with the American bombers, the German fighter pilots had not only refined their tactics but also had seen their Messerschmitt Me-109, Focke Wulf Fw-190, and other fighter aircraft types upgunned in some cases from 20mm cannon to 30mm while others were at times equipped with the werfer-granate 21 rocket launcher, a relative of the 210mm nebelwerfer 42 infantry rocket system. The rockets allowed fighters so equipped to stay out of range of the .50-calibre machine guns aboard the American bombers and lob these shattering weapons capable of bringing down a bomber with one direct hit into the formations.

After the escorting Thunderbolt fighters turned toward home, their fuel tanks depleted, the Schweinfurt bombers fought a running battle with the Luftwaffe, whose pilots knew well the limited range of the P-47s. Within moments the first German fighters, specks that grew larger during swift closing runs, were spotted by American crewmen, and radios crackled with warnings. The last of the Thunderbolts in the vicinity took on the Me-109s of JG 3 and shot down seven of the attackers for the loss of one P-47 before withdrawing. »

LEFT: A building at a ball bearing factory in Schweinfurt lies in ruins after the second raid on the German city. Public Domain US Army via Wikimedia Commons

While the bombers flew over the Netherlands, two more fighter groups, JG 1, and JG 26, joined in. The 305th Bombardment Group was devastated. Thirteen of its 16 Flying Fortresses were shot down in the span of just a few minutes.

Colonel Budd J. Peaslee commanded the mission and flew as co-pilot aboard a B-17 of the 92nd Bombardment Group. He vividly remembered the earliest onslaught. "The opening play is a line plunge through centre," he said in a 1960 interview with author Martin Caidin. "The fighters whip through our formation for our closing speed exceeds 500 miles per hour. Another group of flashes replaces the first, and this is repeated five times, as six formations of Me-109s charge us…I can see fighters on my side…their paths marked in the bright sunlight by fine lines of light coloured smoke as they fire short bursts. It is a coordinated attack…Their timing is perfect, their technique masterly."

One airman remembered: "We took rocket hits that resulted in damage to the left wing, severe enough to salvo the bomb load in order to keep up with the formation." That particular B-17 absorbed more damage from antiaircraft fire, and the crew eventually was forced to bale out.

A tail gunner with the 388th Bombardment Group recalled: "The intercom was a constant chatter as the crew called out Luftwaffe fighter locations…I knelt in silence. I had nothing to say . . . .No one had to tell me there were bandits at six o'clock and there was no need for me to report their presence. The Luftwaffe was all around us. . . We were being mauled."

Roughly 300 Luftwaffe fighters took to the air that fateful day, many of them exhausting fuel and ammunition, then landing for replenishment and rejoining the fray. The fighters concentrated on B-17s approaching the target, allowing a brief respite for those who completed their bombing runs, but then once again setting upon the masses of Flying Fortresses that had made the great turn for their bases in England. During the return flight, Luftwaffe pilots from JG 11 counted claims for 18 bombers.

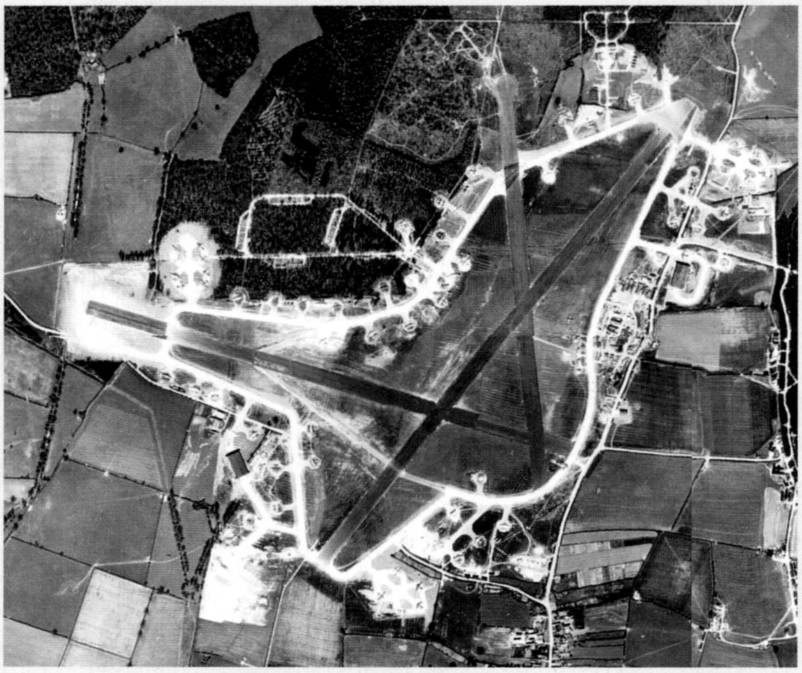

LEFT: RAF Grafton was home to American Flying Fortresses that participated in the second raid on Schweinfurt. Public Domain US Army Air Forces via Wikimedia Commons

The losses in bombers were mounting well before Schweinfurt was in sight and a single bomb was loosed. A full 37 Flying Fortresses were either shot down or damaged so severely that they fell out of formation without dropping bombs, and only 228 of the original complement of B-17s reached the ball bearing complex. By the time the 40th Bombardment Wing's bombers droned above Schweinfurt, seven of its 49 Flying Fortresses had been shot down. In addition to the marauding fighters, intense flak claimed a number of planes.

In the wake of the shattering Black Thursday raid, morale among the Eighth Air Force bomber crews reached a new low. Clearly, the Luftwaffe had established air superiority over the Third Reich. Eighth Air Force planners were taken aback, and the decision was made to suspend the daylight bombing campaign until long-range escort fighters could be deployed in numbers great enough to defend the bomber formations on deep penetration raids.

In early 1944, General James 'Jimmy' Doolittle took command of Eighth Air Force. At roughly the same time, the North American P-51 Mustang fighter, its range capable of shepherding the bombers deep into Germany, made its debut in the escort role. The debate surrounding the resumption of daylight precision bombing continued both during and after the five-month suspension of the heavy raids.

However, with the introduction of the P-51 the air game changed. Coupled with a revision of fighter tactics under Doolittle allowing American fighter pilots to assume a 'hunter-killer' role, the Luftwaffe was inevitably depleted in experienced pilots and planes while air superiority was wrested from them.

Even so, the bitter memory of Black Thursday was never to be forgotten.

BELOW: German controllers tracked the incoming and return routes of the B-17s during the second Schweinfurt raid and coordinated Luftwaffe fighter deployments. Creative Common Bundesarchiv Bild via Wikimedia Commons

BOTTOM: A B-17 bomber sits on the ground at RAF Grafton during the buildup of American heavy bombers in England. Public Domain US Army Air Forces via Wikimedia Commons

BIG WEEK

ABOVE: An RAF Handley Page Halifax heavy bomber drops its payload on an oil refinery in Germany during a 1944 raid. Public Domain United Kingdom Government via Wikimedia Commons

RIGHT: A B-24 Liberator of the 44th Bombardment Group trails smoke after taking hits from flak over a city in Germany. Public Domain US Air Force via Wikimedia Commons

BELOW: Many B-17s such as this one were lost during the Big Week bombing period, crashing due to battle damage. Public Domain US Air Force via Wikimedia Commons

The disastrous losses sustained in the summer and autumn of 1943 laid bare the fallacy of the heavy bomber's ability to complete unescorted raids into German territory without fighter escort, destroy targets, and return to bases in England with an acceptable casualty rate among men and planes. B-17 Flying Fortresses and B-24 Liberators of the US Army Air Forces (USAAF) had fallen under the guns of Luftwaffe fighters and to concentrated antiaircraft fire at an alarming rate.

The official USAAF history of the period put it succinctly. "The fact was that the Eighth Air Force had, for the time being, lost air superiority over Germany." For the balance of 1943, after the disastrous 'Black Thursday' raid of October 14 against the ball bearing facilities at Schweinfurt, the Eighth Air Force flew 27 more missions over Nazi-occupied Europe, only missions within the range of escorting fighters. None of the raids were against targets in Germany. The heavy bomber offensive against the Third Reich itself was suspended.

However, by February 1944 the Mighty Eighth would set about regaining the edge in air superiority. Even earlier, General Ira C. Eaker, commander of the Eighth Air Force, had dubbed a new tactical approach as 'bait and kill'. The big bombers would serve as the bait, and as they flew toward their targets, centres of industry, transportation, and military value, Luftwaffe fighters would be obliged to confront them. When the Germans rose up, the American fighter escorts would engage them in repeated battles of attrition that would whittle away the combat efficiency of German defensive air power.

Eaker's offensive effort, though, was stalled by bad weather, and when he was replaced as commander of the Eighth Air Force by General Jimmy Doolittle in January 1944, a new dimension was added to the American tactic. The escorting fighters would be allowed to range ahead of the bomber formations rather than staying close to them, hunting the Luftwaffe even more aggressively. Although bad weather postponed Doolittle's first raid, by February 20, Operation Argument was underway. For six straight days, Eighth Air Force bombers cooperated with those of the RAF and the Fifteenth Air Force based in Italy in a major aerial assault that became known popularly as Big Week.

The Big Week roll out was in response not only to the Operation Pointblank directive of June 1943, but also to the pointed admonition General Henry 'Hap' Arnold, commander of the US Army Air Forces, delivered to both the outgoing Eaker and incoming Doolittle on December 27, 1943. It read tersely, "...my personal message to you—this is a MUST—is to destroy the enemy Air Force wherever you find them, in the air, on the ground, and in the factories."

Operation Argument signalled the resumption of the American »

RIGHT: B-17 Flying Fortresses fly in formation and drop their bombs on an industrial target inside Germany. Public Domain US Air Force via Wikimedia Commons

BELOW RIGHT: Scores of Luftwaffe fighters such as this Messerschmitt Me-109 shown being readied for combat, were shot down during Big Week. Creative Commons Bundesarchiv Bild via Wikimedia Commons

BELOW LEFT: The Augsburg city hall was destroyed by American bombing during Big Week, February 20-25, 1944. Creative Commons Fred Romero via Wikimedia Commons

strategic daylight bombing campaign against the Third Reich, and its purposes were to cripple German fighter production with major blows against factories and assembly plants while forcing the Luftwaffe fighters into the air where they would be overwhelmed by Allied fighter strength. Synthetic oil production was another target, while the air superiority aspect was also necessary for the coming D-Day invasion of northwest Europe to have a reasonable chance of success. When the maximum effort of Big Week was over on February 25, 1944, the Eighth and Fifteenth Air Forces had flown 3,800 missions and dropped 10,000 tons of bomb, more than the Eighth Air Force had delivered in its entire first year of operations. Overall, Allied bomber and fighter sorties topped 6,000.

More than 2,500 airmen were killed, wounded, or captured, while 357 Allied bombers and 28 fighters were lost during the desperate six days, but the Luftwaffe lost a whopping 262 fighters destroyed with more than 150 damaged. At least 250 German airmen, 100 of whom were irreplaceable experienced pilots, were killed or wounded. Although German fighter production was damaged - estimates said that it was set back approximately two months - deliveries of new aircraft did rebound and actually increase. Nevertheless, Big Week was the beginning of the end for the Luftwaffe as its pilots were pushed to the breaking point and replacements with relatively little training made the sheer number of planes available a moot point when only ill-trained pilots – or no pilots at all – were available to fly them in combat.

Thick cloud cover obscured the sun on the morning of February 20, 1944, and a light covering of snow lay on the ground, but General Carl 'Tooey' Spaatz, commander of US Strategic Air Forces in Europe, had received a weather report that stated conditions were tolerable for the inception of Operation Argument. At bases across the Midlands and East Anglia, the four engines of the big American bombers, more than 1,000 B-17s and B-24s, coughed to life, as did Fifteenth Air Force bombers in Italy. The bombers then formed up and headed for a dozen targets inside Germany that were related to the aircraft production industry. Their escort of 660 Allied fighters took to the air in formations that were 25 miles wide with some clusters ranging as far as 50 miles ahead of the bombers to seek out German fighters in the air or on the ground.

During the raids of February 20, American losses were relatively light, 21 bombers and four fighters. The Luftwaffe pilots who rose to do battle were shocked to see American escort fighters so deep into German airspace. They were also shaken as the US fighter pilots were decidedly more aggressive and the erstwhile hunters often became the hunted. On the second day of Big Week, General Doolittle ordered 767 heavy bombers into the air to attack aircraft factories in Brunswick, Germany, along with numerous airfields that served the German fighter groups. Only three bombers were lost on February 21.

Despite a forecast of more cloudy weather in the skies over England on February 22, Doolittle remained resolute and sent 250 heavy bombers against the city of Halberstadt, a regional centre of aircraft production for the Junkers company. A second target that day was the Messerschmitt aircraft assembly works at Regensburg, where B-17s had suffered grievous losses the previous August. An hour after the bombers from England turned for home, 84 Liberators of the Fifteenth Air Force followed up from their bases around Foggia, Italy. Later bomb assessment suggested that the Regensburg facility had been decimated. But the butcher's bill was a stark reminder of the hazards of daylight bombing with 35 Flying Fortresses and 13 Liberators shot down. Forty-one Eighth Air Force planes were lost that

day, and six more had sustained such damage that they were rendered useless.

The following day, the Flying Fortresses of the Eighth Air Force returned to another target that held bitter memories from the previous year, the ball bearing facilities at Schweinfurt. On February 24, a contingent of 231 B-17s hit that familiar location along with industrial sites in the cities of Rostock and Eisenach. On the same day, 236 B-24s struck the assembly plant at Gotha, which produced the twin-engine Messerschmitt Me-110 fighter. The losses were again heavy, and aircrews were still a precious commodity, with 11 Flying Fortresses and 37 Liberators lost to enemy fighters and flak. Meanwhile, Fifteenth Air Force bombers attacked the Daimler Puch factory at Steyr, Austria, targeting ball bearing production, and struck the oil refineries surrounding the city of Fiume in Croatia.

That night, a strong raid of 734 RAF Avro Lancaster and Handley Page Halifax heavy bombers returned to Schweinfurt, adding to the destruction there. Through the course of Big Week, the RAF flew more than 2,300 nocturnal missions and dropped about 9,200 tons of bombs, losing 157 bombers to Luftwaffe night fighter and anti-aircraft fire.

On the last day of Big Week, Eighth Air Force bombers hit Regensburg and Schweinfurt yet again, while also damaging the Messerschmitt assembly plant at Augsburg, Germany. They also bombed the ball bearing production facilities in the city of Stuttgart. Overall losses totalled 31 big bombers.

Indicative of the arduous missions mounted during Big Week was the ordeal of Lieutenant Edward G. Reppa's aircrew of the 457th Bombardment Group. Just as his Flying Fortress crossed the French coastline en route to Augsburg on February 25, an engine was knocked out by flak. After completing the bomb run against the factory where the Messerschmitt Me-210 fighter was assembled, Reppa's Flying Fortress lost a second engine. The aircraft could not make the flight all the way back to base at RAF Glatton, and Reppa managed as best he could as the plane came down near another airfield in England. With no brakes, the B-17 careened into a tree and then came to rest in a deep ditch. Incredibly, there were no casualties. Every member of the crew walked away from the crash site, but the bomber was a total loss.

At least one other bomber of the 457th managed to get home on two engines, while another, piloted by Lieutenant Clarence Schumann, lost three engines before losing its fourth during a down-wind approach to its airfield, compelling the pilot to make a skilful dead stick landing. Big Week had been a baptism of fire for the 457th Bombardment Group.

As Big Week ended, it was apparent that American fighter pilots had taken a severe toll on the Luftwaffe despite the fact that some of the new P-51 Mustangs experienced problems with their .50-calibre machine guns jamming. The 56th Fighter Group, flying the Republic P-47 Thunderbolt, had accounted for 72 enemy fighters by itself. Approximately 33% of the available single-engine fighter planes of the Luftwaffe were lost in combat, while the pilot loss rate had reach a prohibitive 20%.

Big Week had slowed the pace of German aircraft production temporarily, but by spring of 1944, output had risen to roughly 1,500 planes per month as some factories were moved into caves or underground spaces and substantial machinery had survived the repeated air raids even though buildings had been extensively damaged around them. Still, the days of Luftwaffe dominance in the air over Nazi Germany were numbered after Big Week

LEFT: The devastation of Allied bombing is reflected in this image of the city of Stuttgart, Germany, a target of Big Week. Public Domain collections of the Imperial War Museums via Wikimedia Commons

FAR LEFT: RAF bombs rain down on a German city during a sustained attack by night. Public Domain collections of the Imperial War Museums via Wikimedia Commons

LEFT: General Jimmy Doolittle, shown here with the rank of brigadier, unleashed the Eighth Air Force fighters during Big Week. Public Domain National Museum of the US Navy via Wikimedia Commons

CONTEMPORARIES: B-24 LIBERATOR AND AVRO LANCASTER

LEFT: This B-24D Liberator, nicknamed *Betsy*, flew with the 90th Bombardment Group in the South Pacific. Public Domain US Air Force via Wikimedia Commons

Five years after the B-17 Flying Fortress heavy bomber prototype took its first flight in July 1935, the US Army Air Forces (USAAF) command establishment realised that another heavy bomber design, one more up to date in many respects, would be required for the future.

With the leadership of General Henry 'Hap' Arnold, chief of the (USAAF), the development of the Consolidated B-24 Liberator was undertaken in early 1939 with the expectation that the new bomber could exceed 300mph at top speed and reach a service ceiling of 35,000ft with a range of 3,000 miles. When Consolidated Aircraft Corporation was approached in January 1939 with the opportunity to produce more B-17s for the expected conflict that was brewing with the Axis, founder Reuben Fleet and design engineer I.M. 'Mac' Laddon offered to develop the better bomber that had been talked about for some time.

Taking on the task with alacrity, Consolidated produced a contemporary design that made a considerable leap forward, even though at times that leap raised questions. The new bomber was powered by four Pratt & Whitney Twin Wasp radial engines, while its tricycle landing gear, innovative for a big bomber, would allow for faster take-off and landings. A distinctive tail assembly featured a twin design borrowed from the Consolidated Model 31 flying boat. But the most unusual aspect of the new plane, selected by the US Army as the Model 32 on February 21, 1939, with a single prototype designated the XB-24 ordered a month later, was the slender wing fixed above its twin bomb bays. High-set and producing lower drag, the wing designed and patented by engineer David R. Davis and known simply as the 'Davis Wing', increased the bomber's range, speed, and bombload capacity.

The US Army placed an order for seven YB-24 bombers for testing after the aircraft's first flight on December 29, 1939. The French government placed an order for 139 of the planes, and after the fall of France to the Nazis in 1940, that order was transferred to the British as construction was distributed among four companies, North American at Dallas, Texas, Douglas at Tulsa, Oklahoma, Ford at its legendary Willow Run facility in Michigan, and Consolidated at San Diego, California, and Fort Worth, Texas.

Initially, the US Army Air Forces used the B-24 as a transport and ferry plane, while the first deliveries to

LEFT: A formation of Consolidated B-24 Liberator bombers of the 446th Bombardment Group flies from its base at RAF Bungay. Public Domain US Air Force via Wikimedia Commons

BELOW: A restored B-24J Liberator nicknamed *The Dragon And His Tail* sits at Roberts Field, Oregon, in 2004. Creative Commons Tequask via Wikimedia Commons

Britain were employed by the British Overseas Airways Corporation and Royal Air Force Ferry Command. Subsequent aircraft were delivered to RAF Coastal Command in Scotland and refitted for anti-submarine patrols against marauding German U-boats. The Liberator proved a formidable weapon in the war against the U-boats and throughout the Battle of the Atlantic, its long range helping to plug the gap in the mid-Atlantic where previously convoys were beyond air cover. The Liberator carried 2,500 gallons of fuel and reached 1,100 miles out to sea.

The Liberator was also, as many historians point out, intended as a successor to the B-17 as the primary four-engine heavy bomber of the USAAF. The big bomber had a wingspan of 110ft, length of 67ft, and cruising speed of 290mph. Each of these was indicative of a performance that exceeded that of the B-17, but most interestingly its bombload of 8,000lb or more was routinely considerably heavier than that of the Flying Fortress. The B-24 incorporated state-of-the-art technology for its time. While the B-17 was all electric and the B-24 required electrical workings too, some critical mechanics of the B-24 were operated hydraulically and offered better reliability.

Although it was complex, the B-24 assembly process and time were refined during the course of World War Two. By March 1944, the Ford plant at Willow Run was producing a finished B-24H every 100 minutes, including 1,225,000 parts and 313,237 rivets. The efficiency generated a substantial surplus of the bombers as they were coming off the assembly line faster than the USAAF could place them in service. The cost of the B-24, with its advantages, was not substantially more than the B-17 at $215,000 per plane while the B-17 cost per unit averaged $187,000. At Willow Run, an astounding 19,203 Liberators were eventually built along an assembly line that stretched half a mile. More than 18,000 B-24s were produced between 1940 and 1945, more than any other aircraft of the conflict, and it served with the armed forces of 15 nations. Early versions were equipped with five defensive machine guns, but later variants sported as many as 11 .50-calibre machine guns, and the B-24H introduced twin machine guns mounted in a chin turret.

The B-24 was deployed to all theatres of World War Two, and its introduction to the Pacific preceded the Japanese attack on Pearl Harbor. The Liberator operated alongside the B-17 for a time, but the last Flying Fortresses were withdrawn from service in the Pacific at the end of 1943, and from that time every new heavy bomber group in theatre flew the Liberator, its strength in the Pacific peaking at 992 bombers in service by May 1944. In the Mediterranean, B-24s flew the first USAAF heavy bomber mission in the European theatre from bases in North Africa against Axis oil fields and production facilities at Ploesti, Romania, on June 12, 1942. The August 1, 1943, raid against Ploesti during Operation Tidal Wave brought the B-24 perhaps its greatest wartime recognition, although the attack was costly.

B-24s were modified for use as tankers, carrying vital fuel across the 'Hump' of the Himalayas from India to China. They also participated in bombing raids against the Japanese home islands, and a modified version designated the PB4Y-2 Privateer served as a long-range maritime patrol plane with the US Navy. Prime Minister Winston Churchill was provided with a B-24 nicknamed Commando for many of his long flights to wartime summit meetings and elsewhere.

The B-24 came into wide use by late 1943, growing to more than one-third of the Eighth Air Force strength in England and exceeding the number of B-17s serving in the Mediterranean. More than 550 B-24s were flying in Europe by the end of the year. As World War Two progressed, both the Eighth and Fifteenth Air Forces were operating more than 2,000 Liberators by the spring of 1944 and nearly 2,700 that August. Around the world, an incredible 6,000 were serving in September 1944, and more than 45 US bomber groups were flying B-24s at the end of the war.

The Lancaster

The Royal Air Force had been bombing targets in Nazi-occupied Europe since the early months of the war, but the leaders of Bomber Command realised that the existing twin-engine types employed were inadequate for longer-distance, »

ABOVE: A 448th Bombardment Group B-24 flies high above its base at RAF Seething in Norfolk, England. Public Domain US Air Force via Wikimedia Commons

LEFT: Smoke billows from oil refineries at Ploesti, Romania, as B-24 Liberators deliver their payloads on May 31, 1944. Public Domain Library of Congress via Wikimedia Commons

BELOW: An Avro Lancaster painted in markings of No. 460 Squadron RAF flies above Lincolnshire in 2018. Open Government License Cpl Phil Major ABIPP

ABOVE LEFT: An RAF Lancaster heavy bomber is shown over the city of Hamburg, Germany, in 1943. Lancasters devastated the city during Operation Gomorrah. Public Domain United Kingdom Government via Wikimedia Commons

ABOVE RIGHT: A formation of No. 44 Squadron RAF Lancasters shown in flight in 1942. Public Domain Collections of the Imperial War Museums via Wikimedia Commons

BELOW: A Lancaster loaded with a 22,000lb Grand Slam bomb sits at an airfield in Lincolnshire, 1944. Public Domain Collections of the Imperial War Museums via Wikimedia Commons

heavy raids even into Germany itself during the prosecution of the RAF nocturnal area bombing campaign. In response, three four-engine heavy bomber types were accepted into service by 1942, the Short Stirling and Handley Page Halifax entered service in 1940. The Stirling flew more than 10,000 sorties but suffered a severe loss rate to Nazi night fighters and flak, while a total of 6,176 Halifax bombers were built and the type saw extensive deployment during World War Two.

The third heavy bomber introduced became the workhorse of the strategic bombing campaign against the Third Reich and took its place among the great aircraft of the conflict in the process. The Avro Lancaster was designed by engineer Roy Chadwick as a larger adaptation of the disappointing twin-engine Manchester bomber. Chadwick's innovations included the introduction of the Rolls-Royce Merlin engine rather than the underpowered Vulture that had equipped the Manchester. He repositioned the wing in the Lancaster prototype to accommodate the Merlins, which produced 1,280hp each, a cruising speed of 200mph, and a range of 2,530 miles with a service ceiling of 21,400ft.

The Lancaster carried a standard bomb load of 14,000lb, more than its American contemporaries. It was easily identified by its distinctive profile and tail structure with three fins. For protection against enemy aircraft, it was equipped with two Browning .303 machine guns in an upper turret, two more mounted in a nose turret, and four others in a rear turret. Early models also carried two .303 machine guns in a ventral turret, operated through a periscope from inside the bomber.

The prototype Lancaster, BT308, flew first on January 9, 1941, and some modifications followed, one of which was the removal from the second prototype, DG595, of the middle tail fin that was found to be unnecessary. The initial variant, the Mk I, entered service in February 1942, and remained in production throughout World War Two. Avro built 7,377 examples of the Lancaster, affectionately known as the 'Lanc', during the conflict at its Chadderton factory in Oldham, Lancashire, and the first aircraft equipped No. 44 Squadron based at RAF Waddington. The bomber was also produced in Canada. One of the Lancaster's virtues was its simple construction, which allowed its active numbers to increase rapidly.

The Lancaster was deployed in both the European and Pacific theatres. Among its well-known variants were the Mk I (Special) capable of carrying the massive Tall Boy and Grand Slam bombs, the B.II, powered by Bristol Hercules radial engines during a shortage of Merlin availability, the B.III, which flew with Merlins built by the American Packard company, the Mk III (Provisioning) modified to carry the Upkeep weapon used during the famed 'Dambuster' raid by No. 617 Squadron, and adaptations for air-sea rescue.

No. 44 Squadron made the first offensive use of the Lancaster in a minelaying operation in March 1942, and a week later Lancasters bombed for the first time, hitting armaments factories in Essen, Germany. Within weeks of its combat debut, 73 Lancasters participated in Operation Millennium, the first 1,000-bomber raid of the war, against the city of Cologne, Germany. Lancasters also inflicted such heavy damage on the Nazi super battleship *Tirpitz*, anchored in a Norwegian fjord, that the warship was unfit for further service.

By the end of World War Two in Europe, the Lancaster had flown approximately 156,000 missions and dropped 608,612 tons of bombs. Although 35 Lancs completed 100 missions or more, they averaged 21 missions before being shot down or damaged so seriously as to be written off. By war's end, some 3,250 Lancasters had been lost to enemy action. During its career that stretched into the 1960s, the Avro Lancaster served with the forces of numerous countries.

THE LUFTWAFFE ENEMY

Before he was killed in action on October 8, 1943, Luftwaffe ace Lieutenant Colonel Hans Philipp amassed 206 aerial victories, flying both on the Eastern and Western fronts. He knew the risks and the challenges of aerial combat well, and among the most daunting missions he flew were those opposing the box formations of B-17 Flying Fortress bombers in the skies above the Third Reich.

Philipp was wary of the big bombers and the interlocking fields of fire from their multiple .50-calibre machine guns. In fact, on his last day alive Philipp's Messerschmitt Me-109 fighter was reportedly damaged by a bomber's rear gunner. He had already shot down a B-17, but the damage sustained and the swirl of combat with the bombers and Republic P-47 Thunderbolt escort fighters of the 56th Fighter Group brought his spectacular career to an end. Post-war research has revealed that he may have been the victim of American ace Robert S. Johnson.

Philipp's respect for the B-17 was born of experience. In a letter written to fellow Luftwaffe ace Johannes Trautloft just four days before his death, Philipp commented: "Against 20 Russians trying to shoot you down, or even 20 Spitfires, it can be exciting, even fun. But to curve in towards 40 Fortresses and all your past sins flash before your eyes. And when you yourself have reached this state of mind, it becomes that much more difficult to have to drive every pilot of the Geschwader (Jagdgeschwader or fighter wing), right down to the youngest and lowliest NCO, to do the same."

Philipp and his fellow Luftwaffe pilots were dedicated hunters of the air, many of the "experten" with dozens of victories against Allied aircraft. But the Luftwaffe's resources, particularly precious veteran pilots, were limited, and as World War Two in Europe dragged on, the toll in killed, wounded, and captured, doomed the defenders of the skies »

ABOVE: Engulfed in flames, a stricken B-17 goes down during a raid over Nazi Germany. Public Domain US Army Air Force via Wikimedia Commons

LEFT: German fighter ace Egon Mayer was largely responsible for the head-on attack tactic against B-17s. Public Domain State Treasury of Poland via Wikimedia Commons

LEFT: This B-17 was apparently heavily damaged by a head-on Nazi fighter attack over the city of Cologne, Germany. Public Domain US Air Force via Wikimedia Commons

over the Reich to defeat. The fact that a single Jagdgeschwader, JG 26, lost 158 fighter pilots in 1943, double the loss rate of 1942 and equivalent to an attrition rate of 100%, is indicative of the condition.

Nevertheless, the Luftwaffe was a formidable opponent in the air, while German flak guns were capable of putting up a veritable curtain of lethal anti-aircraft fire. Both made duty aboard Allied bombers indeed hazardous, at times harrowing, during the Allied bomber offensive. The Germans earned grudging respect, and one bomber crewman lamented: "No matter the target they were defending, they were balls to the wall. They were brave. They didn't hesitate."

Early in World War Two, the Luftwaffe had demonstrated its ability to gain tactical air superiority, taking control of the airspace as ground forces overran vast territory, East and West. However, the vaunted air arm of Reichsmarschall Hermann Göring failed to assert strategic control of the air over the English Channel and lost the Battle of Britain in 1940. When the Allies seized the air initiative, the Luftwaffe was compelled to transition from an offensive to a defensive posture. A defence in depth was created to battle the increasing number of American bombers which attacked by day in tandem with the Royal Air Force nocturnal area bombers that regularly visited targets across Germany.

For the Luftwaffe pilots, the requirement to develop air tactics that were effective against the heavily armed B-17s and B-24 Liberators that executed the American programme of daylight precision bombing became readily apparent. One pilot quickly concluded that taking on a bomber formation was like "trying to make love to a porcupine that was on fire." Another said that the red tracers from their .50-calibre machine guns were continually "swarming like wasps" around his fighter.

In a 1994 interview, Luftwaffe ace Johannes Steinhoff, who recorded 176 air victories including at least three against B-17s, confirmed the dangers of attacking bomber formations. When asked which of the Allied aircraft was most difficult to take on, he responded immediately: "The B-17 Flying Fortress without a doubt. They flew in defensive boxes, a heavy defensive formation, and with all of their heavy .50-calibre machine guns they were dangerous to approach. We finally adopted the head-on attack pioneered by Egon Mayer and Georg Peter Eder, but only a few experts could do this successfully, and it took nerves of steel. Then you also had the long-range fighter escorts, which made life difficult, until we flew the Me-262 jets armed with four 30mm cannon and 24 R4M rockets. Then we could blast huge holes in even the tightest formation from outside the range of their defensive fire, inflict damage, then come around and finish off the cripples with cannon fire."

Instinctively, the Luftwaffe pilots initially pursued the classic attack from behind the B-17s, but the supporting fire of the combat box formation and the presence of the rear gunner heightened the risk of such attacks. One fighter pilot remembered the resistance encountered in an attack from the rear of a bomber formation. "I open fire at short range," he recalled. "My cannon shells land beautifully in the centre of the fuselage. The rear gunner persistently returns my fire. I calmly close, guns blazing. Holes appear in my right wing as I am hit. That sod of a rear gunner! He will not leave me alone – must have a lot of guts."

As the air war continued, some Luftwaffe fighters were equipped with heavier 30mm cannon to replace their 20mm weapons, while the German

LEFT: The Messerschmitt Me-109 fighter was a nemesis of American bomber formations during the air campaign of World War Two. Public Domain Jacobst via Wikimedia Commons

LEFT: Luftwaffe ace Johannes Steinhoff is shown in 1966. He was severely burned in a crash during World War Two and had a healthy respect for the B-17. Creative Commons Bundesarchiv Bild via Wikimedia Commons

LEFT: The Luftwaffe used training models to educate fighter pilots on the perils of attacking a Flying Fortress. Public Domain Bundesarchiv Bild via Wikimedia Commons

fighters, primarily the Messerschmitt Me-109 and Focke-Wulf F2-190, were also armed with machine guns. However, assessments of the 20mm cannon performance revealed that at least 20 hits were required to bring down a Flying Fortress. Considering the volume of fire emanating from a German fighter's guns, such results required an extended time on the target and usually multiple passes.

Through the examination of B-17s shot down over German territory and the evaluation of their defences, Mayer, and Eder, who recorded 102 and 78 victories respectively - 24 of Mayer's and 36 of Eder's against four-engine bombers - discovered an area of vulnerability with the B-17. Earlier models had a single machine gun in the nose, and it might do little damage if an attack were pressed home swiftly. The rapid closing speed of the attacking fighter would minimise the time exposed to the bomber's defensive fire, while the pilot and co-pilot positions would be the focus of the attack. Any significant hits would likely disable the control of the bomber, causing it to fall out of formation.

The head-on attack made its deadly debut on November 23, 1942, during a bombing raid on the French port of St. Nazaire. Through experience, it was determined that the attack had to be made directly head-on, wavering only slightly caused difficulty in target acquisition and increased the risk of a mid-air collision.

In his book *Luftwaffe Fighter Aces*, author Mike Spick described the tactics adopted by one fighter group. "...III/JG 2 met the bombers well forward and followed them for a short while to determine their exact course and altitude. They then pulled off to one side and accelerated past, out of range to a position about two miles ahead. Once there, the fighters turned through 180 degrees, lined up and ran in to attack. The closing speed of about 700 feet per second meant that the firing pass was very brief: less than two seconds elapsed between reaching maximum effective firing range and having to break to avoid a collision."

LEFT: An example of the Focke Wulf Fw-190, a frontline fighter of the Luftwaffe during World War Two, is shown in flight at the 2014 Chino, California, air show. Creative Commons Airwolfhound via Wikimedia Commons

LEFT: The introduction of the long-range North American P-51 Mustang fighter contributed to the demise of the Luftwaffe while protecting US bomber formations over Germany. Creative Commons Airwolfhound via Wikimedia Commons

The fighter pilot was instructed to remember the phrase 'gently does it'. Pulling too hard on the stick resulting in a loss of airspeed and greater vulnerability to return fire. Clearing the targeted bomber closely and remaining in level flight through the interlocking cones of defensive fire were essential in surviving the attack. Few bombers were actually shot down during the first pass, while a number of them would often lose power due to damage, falling out of formation and away from the relative safety of the combat box formation. From there, the straggler was easy pickings for the German fighters.

Through the course of World War Two, the growing numbers of Allied heavy bombers and the introduction of the long-range North American P-51 Mustang fighter tipped the balance of the air war in favour of the Allies. In addition, drop tanks were added to virtually all Allied fighter aircraft to extend their range substantially. Coupled with the refocus of Allied fighter tactics to one of offensive search and destroy rather than close-support escort duty tethered to bomber formations, such changes resulted in catastrophic losses for the defenders of the Reich. As the pressure mounted, it became more difficult for German fighter pilots to attack incoming bomber formations until their fuel and ammunition was exhausted, land, and replenish, and then take-off to harry the formations on their homeward trek.

Despite their courage and relentless pursuit of the B-17 and other bomber formations, the casualty rate among German fighter pilots soared. In the first four months of 1944 alone, a full 1,000 were killed or wounded. Such losses were unsustainable despite the introduction of the Messerschmitt Me-262 Swallow, the world's first operational jet fighter, the rocket-propelled Me-163 Komet fighter, and an array of innovative weapons.

The Allied air forces, however, paid a heavy price during the months-long aerial onslaught, and the names of cities such as Bremen, Stuttgart, Schweinfurt, Regensburg, and Berlin took on a terrible, dark connotation in counting the cost. The price was paid in blood and the wreckage of thousands of aircraft. In truth, the Luftwaffe fighters and anti-aircraft did bring the American daylight bomber offensive to a temporary halt in the autumn of 1943. But the lull was only temporary, and when the raids resumed the B-17s continued to drop their lethal cargoes through to the end of World War Two in Europe.

LEFT: The city of Cologne, Germany, was devastated by repeated Allied bombing raids during World War Two. Public Domain T4c. Jack Clemmer US Department of Defense

NORDEN BOMBSIGHT

RIGHT: This example of the famed Norden bombsight resides in the Computer History Museum in Mountain View, California. Creative Commons Allan J. Cronin via Wikimedia Commons

FAR RIGHT: This photo of the nose of the B-17 bomber *Liberty Belle* was taken at a New Orleans air show in 2005. The Norden bombsight is shown in position. Creative Commons Nolabob via Wikimedia Commons

The state-of-the-art Norden bombsight was a cornerstone of the US precision daylight strategic bombing offensive in World War Two. The advent of the Norden made the US doctrine more plausible in that it promised to deliver explosive payloads with unprecedented accuracy, allowing for a more efficient expenditure of bombs, planes, and airmen than area bombing, which was practiced at night by the partner Royal Air Force.

The Norden bombsight was a sophisticated machine, in fact a computer in itself and a functioning system for placing ordnance on time and on target, and it consisted of more than 2,000 individual components. As a bomber approached the target, the bombardier fed data on wind speed and direction along with the bomber's airspeed and altitude into the analogue computer incorporated into the Norden. Stabilised by an internal gyroscope that permitted the use of its telescopic sight with diamond-etched crosshairs at high altitude, the bombsight made calculations accounting for wind drift and derived the appropriate aiming and release point. In cooperation with the Sperry C-1 autopilot, the Norden bombsight delivered a new level of accuracy; however, it required level flight for optimum performance and was regularly hampered by cloud cover, smoke that obscured a target, and the unavoidable shuddering of the aircraft due to nearby blasts of enemy flak.

During its development and deployment, the Norden bombsight was shrouded in mystery, and its very existence was initially cloaked as 'secret', or of such sensitivity that its possession by an enemy would in fact endanger US national security. As World War Two progressed, the level of confidentiality was lowered as well. Inevitably, examples of Nordens would fall into German hands during the course of the air war, even though they were likely damaged, and both the US Navy and US Army issued specific instruction in how to destroy one thoroughly in the event of loss in combat. In actuality, the Germans had the Norden plans in hand before the outbreak of the war, as agent Herman W. Lang, an employee of the Carl L. Norden Company, provided details of its design. Lang was apprehended when the FBI later busted the famed Duquesne Spy Ring, and he was sentenced to a lengthy prison term.

The genesis of the Norden bombsight actually began with the US Navy Bureau of Ordnance, which ordered an accurate design to replace existing tools. Carl Norden, a Dutch engineer who emigrated to the US in 1904, was given the contract in 1920. The prototype was delivered in 1931, and the first Norden bombsight was tested in April 1939 at Fort Benning, Georgia, when four B-17s 'attacked' a simulated battleship measuring 600ft by 105ft and placed 10 of 12 bombs on target. The Norden was subsequently adopted as the Mark 15 by the US Navy and the M-9 series by the Army Air Forces. In 1941, one optimistic civilian observer opined: "The Norden bombsight is considered to be the principal single factor of superiority which the air forces of this country possess over those of potential enemy countries.

Fantastic claims of its accuracy surrounded the implementation of the Norden bombsight, and the press hyped the capability of the new technology to drop a bomb into a pickle barrel from an altitude of 20,000ft. However, contemporary bomb assessment produced mixed results, due in part to inexperienced bombardiers, varying weather conditions, and improperly calibrated sights that were used while in need of overhaul because of the rough handling they incurred. The true effectiveness of the Norden bombsight remains a subject of debate among historians to this day.

During the course of World War Two, nearly 90,000 Norden bombsights were produced at a cost of roughly $13,000 each, and the cost of the entire program topped $1bn. Despite mixed evaluations, it remained in use with the US armed forces into the Vietnam era.

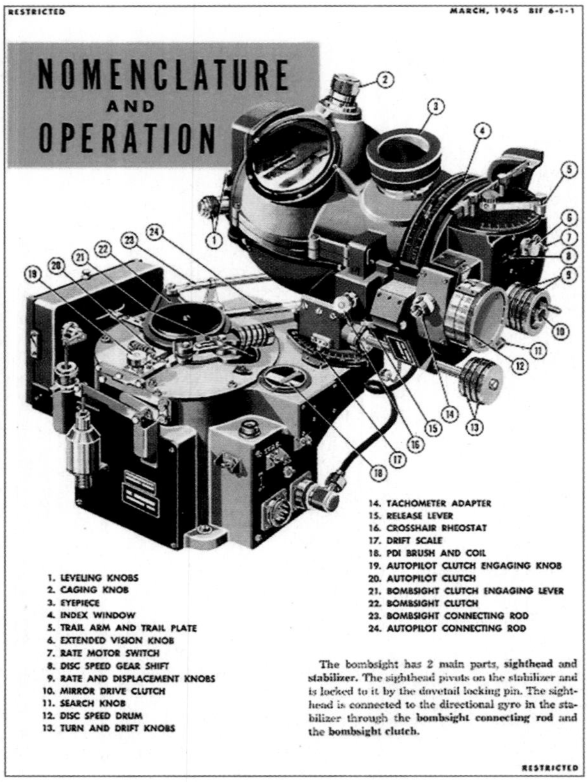

RESTRICTED MARCH, 1945 BIF 6-1-1

NOMENCLATURE AND OPERATION

1. LEVELING KNOBS
2. CAGING KNOB
3. EYEPIECE
4. INDEX WINDOW
5. TRAIL ARM AND TRAIL PLATE
6. EXTENDED VISION KNOB
7. RATE MOTOR SWITCH
8. DISC SPEED GEAR SHIFT
9. RATE AND DISPLACEMENT KNOBS
10. MIRROR DRIVE CLUTCH
11. SEARCH KNOB
12. DISC SPEED DRUM
13. TURN AND DRIFT KNOBS
14. TACHOMETER ADAPTER
15. RELEASE LEVER
16. CROSSHAIR RHEOSTAT
17. DRIFT SCALE
18. PDI BRUSH AND COIL
19. AUTOPILOT CLUTCH ENGAGING KNOB
20. AUTOPILOT CLUTCH
21. BOMBSIGHT CLUTCH ENGAGING LEVER
22. BOMBSIGHT CLUTCH
23. BOMBSIGHT CONNECTING ROD
24. AUTOPILOT CONNECTING ROD

The bombsight has 2 main parts, **sighthead** and **stabilizer**. The sighthead pivots on the stabilizer and is locked to it by the dovetail locking pin. The sighthead is connected to the directional gyro in the stabilizer through the **bombsight connecting rod** and the **bombsight clutch**.

RESTRICTED

BELOW: This page extracted from the *Bombardier's Information File* (BIF) and marked 'restricted' conveys the complexity of the Norden bombsight. Public Domain US Government via Wikimedia Commons

GENERAL HENRY 'HAP' ARNOLD

The budget for the long-range heavy bomber had been approved by Congress. It was 1934, and after the idea of strategic bombing had taken hold with the leaders of the US Army Air Corps, the quest for the machine to execute that mission was at last gaining traction – but the funding was a relative pittance compared to what was needed to make the enterprise truly viable and pit an air fleet against a future foe.

Nevertheless, it was a victory, and largely responsible for it were a group of air officers that included Carl A. 'Tooey' Spaatz, George C. Kenney, Hugh K. Knerr, Frank M. Andrews, and Henry 'Hap' Arnold. Each of these officers was destined to achieve general rank and play a key role in the development of US Army air power in the years leading up to and including World War Two. Still, the road would be long. Setbacks would occur.

In 1940, then General Arnold stated: "The Air Corps is committed to a strategy of high-altitude precision bombing of military objectives." He remained a steadfast advocate of the strategic bombing campaign and the development of the Boeing B-17 Flying Fortress, the weapon that some believed would be decisive in the war that was then raging in Europe if the US became involved. When the first B-17s were built primarily for defensive purposes to guard the coastlines of the United States out to 100 miles, it was Arnold who championed revisions that would turn the Flying Fortress into an offensive weapon, including increased armour protection, heavier armament, self-sealing gasoline tanks, and other equipment.

Early B-17 production was but a trickle, and in 1938 Congress cut a budgetary request for 50 new aircraft. Not until 1941 did production pick up substantially, and only American entry into World War Two really energised US assembly lines to their potential in turning out the big bombers. Despite the assertion by many historians that the B-17 was already obsolete when it was being manufactured in massive numbers, the Flying Fortress and the Consolidated B-24 Liberator developed into the strategic aerial sledgehammer that American air power wielded, and the B-17 became a legend in wartime. In later years, Arnold confirmed his long-held belief, declaring that the B-17 "had only one predecessor of equal importance in air history." That, he said, was the rickety biplane the Wright Brothers flew at Kitty Hawk, North Carolina, in 1903.

Like other air power advocates, Hap Arnold had been devoted to the ascension of the aircraft as a primary weapon of war. Earlier in his career, he had become a disciple of General Billy Mitchell, whose zeal in advocating aerial bombing had led to court martial in 1925. At the time, Arnold was a mere major, but his support of Mitchell would require much of the junior officer. Mitchell was accused of eight counts of insubordination, and Arnold was called to testify during the proceedings. Although he was well aware that doing so might place his own career in jeopardy, Arnold was true to his convictions and followed through. When Mitchell was found guilty, those who had supported him were squarely in the crosshairs, and retribution followed. »

LEFT: General Henry 'Hap' Arnold was a driving force in the development of the B-17 and senior commander of the US Air Forces in World War Two. Public Domain US Air Force via Wikimedia Commons

LEFT: Young Henry Arnold sits at the controls of a Wright Model B airplane in 1911. Public Domain US Air Force via Wikimedia Commons

BELOW: In 1934, Arnold led a historic round-trip flight from Washington, DC, to Anchorage, Alaska. The aircrews flew the Martin B-10 twin-engine bomber. Public Domain US Air Force via Wikimedia Commons

ABOVE LEFT: The 1925 court martial of General Billy Mitchell was a worldwide spectacle and nearly cost Hap Arnold his military career. Public Domain US Air Force via Wikimedia Commons

ABOVE RIGHT: Following his promotion to General of the Army, Hap Arnold wears the five-star rank earned in wartime. Public Domain US Department of Defense via Wikimedia Commons

When Major Arnold was offered the choice of resigning his commission or facing a court martial of his own, he chose the latter and forced the hand of the senior army officers involved. Instead of another high-profile trial, they decided to banish Arnold to Fort Riley, Kansas, to command the 16th Observation Squadron. It was a backwater assignment, far away from the nexus of power where decisions on the future of the Air Corps were made. At the same time, Major Arnold's personnel file was documented with the damning pronouncement: "In an emergency he is liable to lose his head."

At a professional crossroads, Arnold chose to serve his time in virtual exile and compiled an admirable record in due course. His determination led to emergence from obscurity and trauma to become one of the most influential military air officers of the 20th century. In the twilight of his career, he was promoted to five-star General of the Army rank, and later assumed the same with the US Air Force, becoming the only officer ever to achieve the rank in two branches of service.

Born on June 25, 1886, in Gladwyne, Pennsylvania, Hap Arnold was a well-known individual in his hometown even before he took the entrance examination to the US Military Academy at West Point after his brother refused to do so and profoundly disappointed their father, a prominent local physician. Although his academic record was not remarkable, Hap graduated in 1907 and received a commission as a 2nd lieutenant. Conjecture surrounds the origin of his nickname, some historians asserting that was simply short for 'Happy', while others say his wife, Bee, was responsible, or that it originated while he worked in silent films during the 1920s.

In a short time, Arnold found that he did not like the infantry and secured a transfer to the fledgling aviation section of the Signal Corps. He completed pilot training under Orville and Wilbur Wright, the Kitty Hawk aviation pioneers, himself a trailblazer of sorts, receiving pilot certificate No. 29 and military aviator certificate No. 2. The fact that he remained an aviator was remarkable since he actually developed a fear of flying early in his career following the death of fellow pilot Al Welsh in a crash in June 1911.

Arnold began to doubt his own skills as a pilot. In the wake of the Welsh tragedy, he crashed a plane into Massachusetts Bay when it was buffeted by high winds, learned of another friend's death in a crash, and survived another accident during an artillery spotting exercise. At the nadir of his self-confidence, the young officer took a leave of absence, collected himself and conquered his fears, returning to make his first solo flight in five years in November 1916. From there, he trained new pilots and set aerial records as first to carry US mail by air and first to fly over the US capitol building. He established a new altitude mark at 3,260ft. With the outbreak of World War One, he held staff positions in Washington, DC, and the Panama Canal zone before traveling to France. He contracted influenza and recovered just in time to arrive at the Western Front on November 11, 1918, the day the war ended.

With the controversy that surrounded Billy Mitchell resulting in a tremendous career setback, Arnold applied himself dutifully and found support in his quest for professional rehabilitation in Major General James E. Fechet, chief of the Army Air Corps. An accomplished author, Arnold wrote numerous magazine articles related to air power. As he progressed, fitness reports took a decidedly positive tone, describing him as an intelligent, driven officer with potential for higher command. This was

RIGHT: A formation of B-17 Flying Fortresses wings its way toward a target in 1944. Hap Arnold's advocacy of the B-17 was key in its production and deployment in World War Two. Public Domain National Museum of the US Air Force via Wikimedia Commons

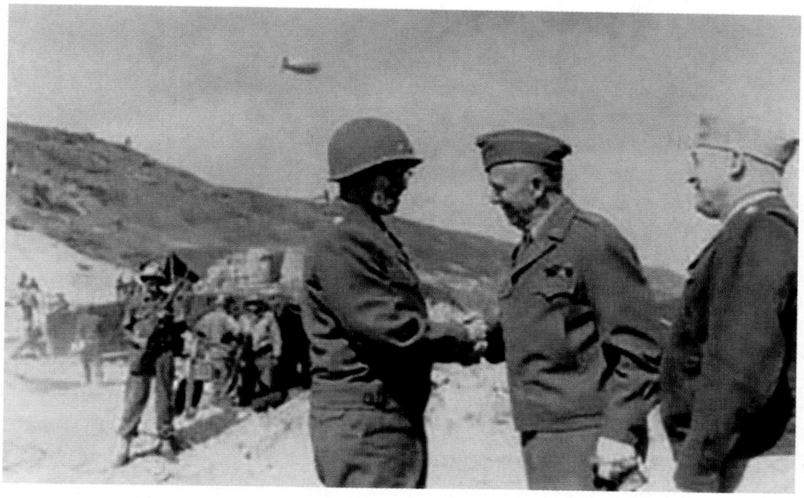

RIGHT: During his wartime travels, General Arnold (right) and Army Chief of Staff General George C. Marshall greet General Omar Bradley, commander of 12th Army Group, in Normandy, 1944. Public Domain United States Army Center of Military History via Wikimedia Commons

evidenced by his recommendation to the Command and General Staff School at Fort Leavenworth, Kansas, and his graduation in 1929.

In 1931, Lieutenant Colonel Arnold was given command of March Field, California, and he took responsibility for mail delivery in three operational zones. In the pivotal year of 1934, he not only participated in securing funding for the embryonic B-17 construction programme but also led a flight of 10 Martin B-10 bombers on a historic round-trip flight from Washington, DC, to Anchorage, Alaska. The twin-engine B-10 was the first fully enclosed American monoplane bomber. Promoted brigadier general in 1935, Arnold's rise from the veritable ashes was remarkable. He was given command of the 1st Wing of General Headquarters at March Field and all the while continued to advocate for the development of a well-trained and equipped bomber force. His tireless promotion of the B-17 proved essential in producing the number of aircraft necessary to prosecute the strategic bombing offensive in World War Two.

In 1936, Hap Arnold became assistant chief of the Air Corps, and two years later he was named to overall command with the rank of major general. Shortly after the US entered World War Two, his title was revised to chief of the Army Air Forces, and he was elevated to lieutenant general. With responsibility for all Army Air Forces operations during the conflict from 1941 to 1945, the forces under his command grew from a mere to 22,000 people and 3,900 aircraft to 2.5 million men and women in uniform and 75,000 combat, transport, and auxiliary planes. Arnold also made key appointments to execute the organisation and deployment of American air power. Among these was General Spaatz, the first commander of the legendary Eighth Air Force in England, and General Ira C. Eaker, the first head of Eighth Bomber Command and later the Eighth Air Force. Arnold also promoted General Jimmy Doolittle, leader of the famed April 1942 raid on Tokyo, to key command roles in the Mediterranean and England.

During the course of the war, General Arnold became well known for his willingness to take risks, to endure the losses incurred in the skies over Nazi-occupied Europe, and to remove officers who were deemed incompetent or ineffective. Among his most controversial appointments was that of General Curtis LeMay to lead the Twentieth Air Force in the Pacific theatre. LeMay had been a bomber commander in Europe and was credited with innovative tactics to assist in getting bomber formations to and from their assigned targets with improved results. LeMay subsequently laid waste to Japanese cities via a committed firebombing strategy, raising questions regarding the necessity of such devastating raids and the inevitable civilian casualties that occurred.

The tremendous stress of senior command took its toll on Arnold's health during the war years. He was plagued by gastric ulcers and suffered four heart attacks between 1943 and 1945. He remained relentless despite the setbacks and travelled regularly, attending strategic conferences with the Allied heads of state, and inspecting facilities and equipment at air bases across the globe. One lengthy tour covered an astounding 35,000 miles. In 1943, he was promoted to four-star full general rank. Three years later, a bout of cardiac arrhythmia forced the cancellation of a South American tour and compelled him to retire. He was elevated to five-star general rank in 1946 and was delighted to witness the creation of the US Air Force as a separate arm of the American military the following year.

Arnold, the author of several books, spent his last years at his ranch in Sonoma, California, and as his memoir *Global Mission* went to press in 1948, he suffered his fifth heart attack. He died at his home on January 15, 1950, at the age of 63 and was buried at Arlington National Cemetery. In retrospect, it is apparent that he had sacrificed his own health and vigour in the cause of Allied victory.

RIGHT: Colonel Henry Arnold is shown while stationed at the War Department in Washington, DC, in the spring of 1918. Public Domain National Archives and Records Administration via Wikimedia Commons

RIGHT: General Arnold stands at centre among Allied civilian and military leaders at the Cairo Conference in 1943. Public Domain collection database of the Australian War Memorial via Wikimedia Commons

GENERAL FRANK M. ANDREWS

When the experimental Boeing Model 299, also known as the XB-17, crashed, and burned during a test flight at Wright Field, near Dayton, Ohio, on October 30, 1935, the future for the heavy, four-engine bomber, considered by some observers to be the most technologically advanced military aircraft of its time, appeared bleak.

The XB-17 was the largest aircraft intended for land operations that had been designed and reached the prototype stage up to that time, and it had held promise for acting Brigadier General Frank M. Andrews. Andrews was the commander of General Headquarters Air Force, the combat component of the US Army Air Corps, based at Langley Field, Virginia, and had been since March 1, 1935. A staunch advocate of an independent air force, he had also envisioned the potential of strategic bombing as a war-winning enterprise.

Born in Nashville, Tennessee, on February 3, 1884, Andrews was a 1906 graduate of the US Military Academy at West Point and a veteran of World War One, having spent 11 years in the cavalry before assignment to the Aviation Section of the Signal Corps in 1917. By the time the United States entered World War Two, he had served in the Army for 35 years in various command posts, and his views on strategic air power were well known.

When Andrews took command of GHQ Air Force, he consolidated available aircraft into nine combat groups across the United States. Each group, designated bombardment, tactical, or pursuit was assigned to one of three composite wings and theoretically would fulfil the role of the Air Corps in air defence, tactical, and strategic missions during wartime. General Hugh Drum, Army Deputy Chief of Staff, had summed up the rationale for selecting Andrews as leader of GHQ Air Force, writing: "We all feel he will be able to meet the situation and develop the force along the lines contemplated. Furthermore, in addition to being an efficient flyer, he has been in harmony with all the War Department has been trying to do."

ABOVE: General Andrews stands second from left with General George C. Marshall, far left, General Henry 'Hap' Arnold, and General Oliver P. Echols at Wright Field, Ohio. Public Domain US Department of Defense via Wikimedia Commons

FAR LEFT: The bodies of General Andrews and other victims are removed from the B-24 crash site in Iceland in May 1943. Public Domain US Army via Wikimedia Commons

LEFT: General Frank Maxwell Andrews was a pioneer in the development of strategic bombing in the US Army Air Corps and in the proliferation of the B-17. Public Domain US Air Force via Wikimedia Commons

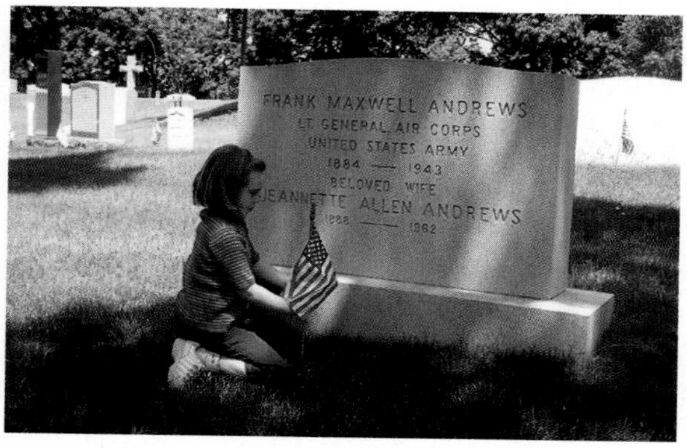

ABOVE: A child straightens the flag placed on the grave of General Andrews and his wife in Arlington National Cemetery, 2004. Creative Commons E.ThomasWood via Wikimedia Commons

Andrews did initially face a major challenge in that he had no long-range bomber to carry out the strategic component of his command. However, he knew that Boeing had its XB-17 on the drawing board, and when the first big bomber was constructed, the time was ripe to demonstrate its worth. Then came the October crash, which was later determined to have been caused by a ground crew failure to release the flight control gust locks that prevented damage to control surfaces while the aircraft was on the ground.

Nevertheless, Andrews's effort to confirm the XB-17 as the big American bomber of the future suffered a serious setback when the less-capable, twin-engine B-18 was chosen as the primary Air Corps bomber, a condition which would persist for the next five years. Andrews, though, maintained his advocacy of the four-engine bomber and persuaded Major General Oscar Westover, Chief of the Air Corps, and numerous sceptics in the War Department to approve the purchase of 13 XB-17s for research and experimentation purposes. The first operational B-17s reached the 2nd Bomb Group at Langley Field, on March 1, 1937. Under the command of Lieutenant Colonel Robert Olds, the group was designated to put the B-17 through its paces, evaluating the new strategic weapon and familiarising crews with its operational capabilities.

Andrews regularly promoted the B-17 with demonstrations of its aerial prowess. In February 1938, six of the big bombers flew 5,225 miles on a promotional tour that took them to far away Buenos Aires, Argentina, and then back to Langley. During joint war games with the US Navy in May, he took advantage of the opportunity to show the B-17's ability to find an enemy 'aircraft carrier' at sea. Actually, the Italian passenger liner *Rex* had served as a stand-in, but the bombers found their quarry more than 700 miles off the US east coast. Still, detractors downplayed the effectiveness of the B-17, some stating that the four-engine bomber was 'Andrews's Folly'.

Andrews had put his career on the line. Along the way, he was promoted to acting major general, but he ruffled influential feathers and was passed over for appointment as Air Corps Chief when Westover died in a plane crash in Burbank, California, in September 1938. It was said that his push for the XB-17 had cost him the job. In fact, he was offered the prestigious post in return for dropping his campaign for acceptance of the bomber but declined to accept under such circumstances.

Meanwhile, the situation had become even more difficult with the appointment General Malin Craig as Army Chief of Staff, succeeding General Douglas MacArthur, in October 1935. Craig believed that the role of the air forces was to support troops on the ground. He disagreed with the concept of a heavy bomber such as the new Boeing type, as well as any movement toward an autonomous and independent Air Corps. On the eve of the outbreak of World War Two in Europe, the situation had become critical as Andrews continued to press for the augmentation of the American air forces despite the fact that Secretary of War Harry Woodring had decided that additional production of the new B-17 Flying Fortress should be cancelled.

Just as Andrews' hopes for the strategic future of the B-17 had been further dimmed, he found an influential ally in General George C. Marshall, head of the US Army War Plans Division and future US Army chief of staff. Andrews intended to build American air supremacy around the cornerstone of the Flying Fortress, and he was convinced that large numbers of the planes were capable of defeating an enemy in the air and destroying its capacity to wage war through heavy bombing of infrastructure and military targets. The two officers met for the first time in »

RIGHT: Airmen of the 322nd Bombardment Group pose at RAF Andrews in 1944. Public Domain Collections of the Imperial War Museums

RIGHT: Workers tend the airfield at RAF Andrews, while a B-17 sits in the background. The field was named in honour of General Frank Andrews after his death. Public Domain US Army Air Forces via Wikimedia Commons

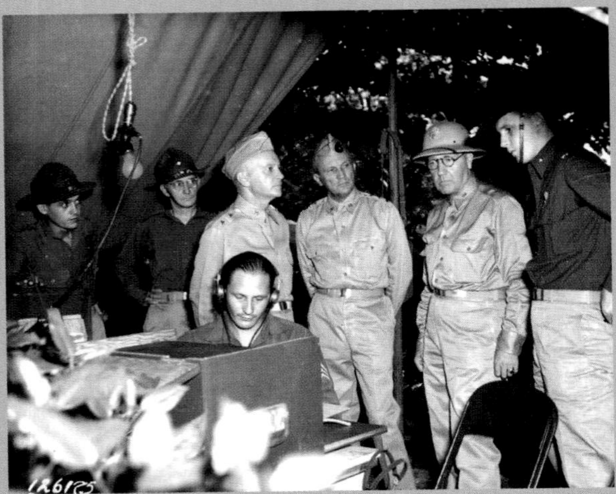

ABOVE: General Frank M. Andrews, centre, visits a command post during army manoeuvres in Puerto Rico, 1941. Public Domain US Army Center of Military History via Wikimedia Commons

FAR RIGHT: General George C. Marshall, Army Chief of Staff, was a friend and benefactor of General Frank Andrews. Public Domain US Army Center of Military History via Wikimedia Commons

August 1938, and Andrews explained his perspective, noting ominously that the United States already lagged behind other nations in the augmentation of its air forces.

Marshall was impressed and agreed to tour airfields and aircraft production facilities across the US. For nine days, Andrews presented the state of the air forces and elaborated on his vision, often personally piloting the plane that carried the two men across the country. At last, a high-ranking officer whose point of view had previously been from the ground only had gained insight into the importance of developing American air power. Marshall appreciated Andrews' comprehensive approach during a period in which he had been charged with preparing the army for the coming of another world war, and Marshall became convinced that the B-17 was a crucial component of US military plans.

Andrews impressed on Marshall the urgency of a buildup in air power, particularly in strategic bombing capability. He had already boldly stated: "If it takes three months to train an artilleryman and 10 months to build a cannon, then you have got to have a reserve cannon. But when it takes a year to build an airplane and up to three years to train the crews to operate and maintain that airplane, then there is not quite such a big argument for a reserve of airplanes, particularly where aeronautical advancement in types is as rapid as it is today. We cannot afford to equip the air force of tomorrow with the airplanes of yesterday."

After the tour, Marshall wrote to Andrews: "I want to thank you again…for the splendid trip you gave me, and for your personal efforts to make it a pleasant one and highly instructive. I enjoyed every minute of the trip and my association with you, and I really think I acquired a fair picture of military air activities in general. A little study will help me to digest something of all I saw…With warm regards."

It was the beginning of a firm friendship, and a significant bond of trust developed between the two officers.

Still, it appeared that Andrews would pay a personal price for his B-17 advocacy. When his term in charge of GHQ Air Force ended in March 1939, the vindictive Craig sent him into virtual exile in San Antonio, Texas, as air officer to the VIII Army Corps, reverting to his permanent rank of colonel. Marshall intervened. Named Army Chief of Staff on September 1, 1939, he called Andrews to Washington, D.C., to serve as Assistant Chief of Staff for Operations and Training with the permanent rank of brigadier general. From there, Andrews advanced steadily to higher command. At the same time, he had promoted the B-17, Andrews had played a key role in the eventual formation of the Army Air Forces in 1941 and later the US Air Force.

In 1940, Andrews was ordered to the Panama Canal Zone to prepare air defences there, and he subsequently headed Caribbean Defense Command. He soon rose to command US Middle East Forces, and during the Casablanca Conference of January 1943, he was named commander of all US forces in the European Theatre of Operations. The latest appointment was made largely on the recommendation of his friend General Marshall.

Andrews was poised to have direct influence and control over the coming American daylight precision bombing campaign in Europe. But it was not to be. At the height of his prestige and power, he embarked on a tour of bases under his command. On May 3, 1943, he was flying to Meeks Field in Iceland, one of the most distant from his new headquarters in England and near the Icelandic capital of Reykjavik. That afternoon, Andrews was killed in the crash of the Consolidated B-24 Liberator bomber he was aboard when the plane slammed into fog shrouded Mount Fagradalsfjall on the bleak island. He was 59 years old.

The death of General Andrews, who would certainly have reached the rank of four-star general had he lived, was a severe blow. His talent and vision had contributed significantly to the capability of American air forces to embark on the long road to victory in World War Two, while his energy had shaped the future organisation of the air forces as well.

General Marshall spoke at Andrews's funeral, commenting: "No army produces more than a few great captains. General Andrews was undoubtedly one of these."

BELOW: Joint Base Andrews was named in honour of General Frank Andrews. In this photo a former *Air Force One*, aircraft of the US president, is shown on display at the base. Creative Commons Acroterion via Wikimedia Commons

GENERAL CARL 'TOOEY' SPAATZ

RIGHT: The Fokker aircraft *Question Mark* is refuelled in the air during the historic flight of 1929. Public Domain US Air Force

The highest-ranking US air officer in the European theatre throughout American involvement in World War Two, General Carl 'Tooey' Spaatz was a man of few words. But when asked about the Flying Fortress, he quickly asserted: "Without the B-17, we might have lost the war."

Spaatz was an air pioneer, a veteran fighter pilot of World War One credited with shooting down three German aircraft. Born on June 28, 1891, in Boyertown, Pennsylvania, he was a 1914 graduate of the US Military Academy, gaining the nickname 'Tooey' for his striking resemblance to another cadet, an upperclassman named F.J. Toohey. After brief service with the infantry, he was assigned to the Aviation Section of the Signal Corps and flew with the punitive expedition against Mexican bandit Pancho Villa led by General John J. Pershing in 1916.

After World War One, Spaatz was a leader in endurance flights that tested the methodology of midair refuelling. He commanded Kelly Field in Texas and led the 1st Pursuit Group among several other posts. In January 1929, Spaatz, Eaker, and future USAAF General Elwood 'Pete' Quesada set a record for remaining aloft in an aircraft named Question Mark. While being refuelled in the air, Question Mark stayed airborne for more than 150 hours.

Spaatz was a friend and follower of General Henry 'Hap' Arnold, chief of the Army Air Forces (USAAF), and, therefore, a staunch advocate of airpower and its ability to transform the face of modern warfare. Spaatz had been a supporter of General Billy Mitchell during the famous court martial in the mid-1920s, helping the visionary accused of "insubordination to the War Department" to prepare his defence and then testifying on his behalf at the risk of his own career.

With the mindset of the American bombing doctrine, that heavily armed bombers could attack targets in precision daylight raids without fighter escort, ward off enemy fighters, and make their way to and from a target while sustaining losses that were 'acceptable', Spaatz went to England in the summer of 1942 to command the Eighth Air Force, while his deputy, General Ira C. Eaker was to lead VIII Bomber Command. Spaatz had already witnessed the evolution of aerial bombardment in 1940, when he had been detailed to London as a military observer during the desperate Battle of Britain.

Following the initial Eighth Air Force raid on Nazi-occupied Europe against rail marshalling yards at Rouen, France, Spaatz wrote to Arnold in Washington, DC: "It is my opinion and conviction that the B-17 is suitable as to speed, armament, armor, and bomb load. I would not exchange it for any British bomber in production."

Arnold then forwarded the communication directly to President Franklin D. Roosevelt with an additional endorsement: "The above more than vindicates our faith in the Flying Fortresses and precision bombing." »

RIGHT: General Carl Spaatz was the commander of US Strategic Air Forces in the European theatre. Public Domain US Air Force via Wikimedia Commons

FAR RIGHT: Future General Carl Spaatz is shown as a West Point cadet in 1914. Public Domain West Point Howitzer Yearbook via Wikimedia Commons

RIGHT: General Carl Spaatz stands at centre with General Henry 'Hap' Arnold and General Hoyt Vandenberg in Luxembourg on April 7, 1945. Public Domain US Air Force Historical Research Agency via Wikimedia Commons

Although both officers were enthusiastic, the hard lessons to come would alter their conclusions surrounding daylight precision bombing. Time and experience required the modification of the original doctrine, especially when the horrific losses of the autumn of 1943 over Regensburg and Schweinfurt sounded the death knell of unescorted heavy bombing raids deep into the Third Reich. At that point, the USAAF had temporarily lost the battle for air supremacy in Europe. The heavy bombing campaign was suspended as the senior American airmen acknowledged the need for long-range fighter escorts to fend off the aggressive attacks of Luftwaffe fighters that ravaged bomber formations with regularity.

Though British air leaders had been sceptical of daylight precision bombing from the beginning, the Americans persisted, but then it was up to Arnold and Spaatz to adapt. Spaatz had been instrumental in developing the early plans of the Air Corps and then the USAAF for war. In 1938, Arnold had called him to Washington to serve as chief of plans in the event that the United States should be drawn into the conflict that was inevitable in Europe. By 1941, Spaatz was promoted chief of the air staff, and when he came to Britain in 1942, he emphasised the American commitment to daylight precision bombing.

In February 1943, Spaatz was designated to command Allied air forces in North Africa and then the Mediterranean, including the Northwest African Air Force and the US Twelfth and Fifteenth Air Forces. By early 1944, he was back in England as commander of US Strategic Air Forces in Europe. Eaker, previously commanding the Eighth Air Force, was promoted, and given command in the Mediterranean, while Spaatz brought the already famous General James H. 'Jimmy' Doolittle with him from North Africa to command the Mighty Eighth.

By this time, the revised American perspective on daylight bombing acknowledged the need for long-range fighter escorts. Although additional fuel drop tanks had been added to Lockheed P-38 Lightning and Republic P-47 Thunderbolt fighters, their range remained inadequate. However, with the introduction of the North American P-51 Mustang in late 1943, the Americans finally had their true long-range air superiority fighter.

While the original priorities for the Combined Bomber Offensive identified by Allied leaders during the Casablanca Conference of January 1943 remained valid as codified in the Casablanca Directive and implemented in the orders of Operation Pointblank, Doolittle and Spaatz understood that air superiority in the skies over Europe was a prerequisite to the success of the Allied D-Day landings set for June 6, 1944, in Normandy.

Doolittle suggested that the Allied fighters would win that air superiority by forcing the Luftwaffe into the air to confront American bomber formations in daylight. The Germans, he reasoned, had no choice but to concentrate their fighters in defence of vital infrastructure, including rail and transportation centres, aircraft and armour assembly plants and the factories that produced their components, and oil and synthetic oil production facilities.

Therefore, the waves of American bombers would not only deliver their devastating cargoes, but also serve as bait to lure Luftwaffe fighters into the air where they would be systematically destroyed by overwhelming numbers of Allied fighters. The Germans would not only lose vital fighter aircraft, but their experienced pilots would inevitably be shot down, killed, wounded, or captured. Doolittle put his plan forward, asserting that American fighter pilots should be allowed to range ahead of the bombers and engage the Germans wherever possible in the air and on the ground. Spaatz gave his support and approval, as did Arnold.

During 'Big Week', also known as Operation Argument, February 20-25, 1944, nearly 4,000 Allied bombers and hundreds of fighters hit a dozen aircraft manufacturing facilities across Nazi Germany. During these few days of heavy air combat, the Allies lost 357 bombers and only 28 fighters. German losses totalled more than 260 fighters destroyed and 150 damaged, many of their pilots to never fly again. The onslaught broke the back of German fighter opposition, and only a relative handful of sorties were

BELOW LEFT: Exercising General Spaatz's emphasis on German oil production facilities at Ploesti, Romania, burn after a 1943 raid by US B-24 Liberator bombers. Public Domain Library of Congress Department of Defense via Wikimedia Commons

BELOW RIGHT: General Spaatz is shown seated at far right during the Nazi surrender ceremonies at Reims, France, May 7, 1945. Creative Commons musée de la reddition de Reims via Wikimedia Commons

flown against the D-Day landings in June. At the same time, the monthly loss rate for Eighth Air Force heavy bombers dropped from 5.1% in 1943 to 1.9% in 1944.

Spaatz and Doolittle agreed that losses had moderated to the point that in July 1944 they increased the number of bombing missions required to complete an airman's tour of duty from 25 to 35. German fighter production was reportedly set back two months during the Big Week raids. Although it did recover later in 1944, and the number of new fighters increased substantially, the upper hand gained in the spring was crucial to the success of D-Day.

In addition, Spaatz broadened the scope of the new tactic to include the target prioritisation of German oil production facilities. In March 1944, he proposed to General Dwight D. Eisenhower, Supreme Allied Commander in Europe, his 'Oil Plan' for bombing the Nazi armed forces into a state of paralysis. The response from Eisenhower and other senior officers was initially lukewarm. Other targets remained high on the Allied list through D-Day and beyond. These included transportation and rail hubs, as well as the sites where V-1 buzz bombs and V-2 rockets, Nazi terror weapons that hit British cities, were launched.

A long debate between advocates of the 'Transportation Plan' and the 'Oil Plan' led to the implementation of both as air forces were available. A pair of large raids against oil production facilities prior to D-Day was followed by a strike at the major rail terminal at Hamm, Germany, and attacks on the V-1 and V-2 launch sites. By the autumn of 1944, however, Allied intelligence and bomb damage assessment concluded that the greatest impact had been achieved by the raids on synthetic oil facilities. The information raised the priority of these targets, validating Spaatz's insight. As a result, the Germans eventually felt the sting of fuel shortages so acute that air training flights were suspended for lack of fuel. New fighter planes sat without deployment because of the fuel shortage, and German army ground units were so short of fuel that their armoured units often rolled to a halt or remained idle.

The crippling of the German oil industry was essential to the eventual Allied victory in Europe. In 1945, General Eisenhower credited Spaatz and General Omar Bradley, commander of the US XII Army Group, as the two senior American officers who had made the greatest contribution to the defeat of Nazi Germany.

In July 1945, Spaatz was reassigned as commander of US Strategic Air Forces in the Pacific. He reported directly to Arnold's Washington headquarters and led the final months of the strategic bombing campaign that devastated Japan. He was present for the surrender of German forces on May 7, 1945, at Reims, France, the surrender to the Soviet Red Army hours later in Berlin, and the Japanese surrender in Tokyo Bay on September 2, 1945, the only Allied general present at all three proceedings.

Spaatz was appointed commanding general of the Army Air Forces in 1946 and following the creation of the US Air Force the next year, he was named its first chief of staff. He retired in 1948 with the rank of four-star general after 44 years of service and died at the age of 83 in 1974.

ABOVE: General Spaatz, centre, and General Jimmy Doolittle attend a briefing conducted by General J. Lawton Collins of the US VII Corps in France, November 1944. Public Domain US Army via Wikimedia Commons

LEFT: After victory in Europe in World War Two, General Carl Spaatz was ordered to the Pacific. Public Domain US Air Force via Wikimedia Commons

LEFT: General Carl Spaatz and other senior officers await the return of the B-29 Superfortress *Enola Gay* to its base at Tinian in the Marianas after dropping the atomic bomb on Hiroshima, August 6, 1945. Public Domain US Air Force via Wikimedia Commons

GENERAL IRA C. EAKER

FAR LEFT: Experienced in fighter aircraft, General Ira C. Eaker was nevertheless chosen to establish Eighth Bomber Command in January, 1942. Public Domain US Army Air Forces via Wikimedia Commons

LEFT: Between the world wars, Captain Ira Eaker stands with a Boeing P-12 biplane. Eaker was a record-setting pilot. Public Domain US Air Force via Wikimedia Commons

Following the first American heavy bomber raid against Nazi-occupied France on August 17, 1942 - an attack by a dozen B-17 Flying Fortresses against a railroad marshalling yard near Rouen - General Ira C. Eaker, head of Eighth Air Force Bomber Command, wrote an assessment of the big plane to his superior, Eighth Air Force commander General Carl 'Tooey' Spaatz.

"I think it is a great airplane," Eaker commented, adding that it possessed "…excellent defensive firepower. It is too early in our experiments in actual operations to say that it can definitely make deep penetrations without fighter escort and without excessive losses. I can definitely say, however, that it is my view that the German fighters are going to attack it very gingerly."

Like Spaatz and General Henry 'Hap' Arnold, commander of the US Army Air Forces (USAAF), Eaker was a staunch supporter of the American doctrine of daylight precision, high altitude bombing. The B-17, after its initial combat test, might be an ideal weapon, he believed. A month after the Rouen raid, Eaker repeated his position. "There are enough airdromes now built and building to accommodate all the Allied air forces need for the destruction of Germany," he told a group of British reporters in September 1942. "I believe it is possible to destroy the enemy from the air. By destroying his aircraft factories, you can put an end to his air force. By destroying his munitions plants and communications, you can make it impossible for him to build submarines. There is nothing that can be destroyed by gunfire that cannot be destroyed by bombs."

Through the course of the air war in Europe, Eaker, Spaatz, and Arnold were among the senior Allied air commanders who came painfully to the realisation that precision daylight bombing was a prohibitively costly affair, that heavy bombers like the B-17 and its cohort, the Consolidated B-24 Liberator, were highly vulnerable to Nazi fighter attack despite bristling with defensive machine guns, and that the war could not, in fact, be won solely via a strategic bombing campaign.

Nevertheless, as the air war progressed, American belief in daylight precision bombing persisted. When General Arnold got wind on the eve of the January 1943 Casablanca Conference that British Prime Minister Winston Churchill intended to strongly petition President Franklin D. Roosevelt to end the Eighth Air Force's daylight bombing and join RAF Bomber Command in its nocturnal area bombing effort, Arnold dispatched Eaker to win over the prime minister and dissuade him from derailing the American strategy.

Eaker was up to the task. Eloquent and highly intelligent, he wrote a succinct, single-page memorandum explaining the daylight rationale and met with Churchill over lunch. The Prime Minister especially appreciated Eaker's brevity, as well as his deftness in the writing craft. Eaker won Churchill over with the phrase: "If the RAF continues night bombing and we bomb by day, we shall bomb them round the clock and the devil shall get no rest."

In the combined bombing offensive that followed, USAAF bombers suffered tremendous losses through much of 1943, due in large part to the inability of the Allies to provide long-range fighter escort for the bombers streaming into enemy airspace. With the introduction of the North American P-51 Mustang fighter late in the year, the situation improved considerably. Still, the losses in men and planes had been agonising, and with them perished the notion that the heavily-armed bomber – without escort – would always 'get through'.

Despite the sobering experience, the Allied bombing of the Third Reich

BELOW: A Boeing B-17 comes in for a landing in England. General Eaker flew on the first Eighth Air Force bombing mission against Nazi-occupied Europe. Public Doman US Air Force via Wikimedia Commons

no doubt contributed to the eventual victory in Europe. And Eaker stands tall among contemporaries as a key player in the organisation and development of the Eighth Air Force into the legendary 'Mighty Eighth'." In February 1942, he had arrived in England with six other officers. They were tasked with organising the American bombing effort and set to work establishing the Eighth Air Force headquarters. The work was done initially on a shoestring with virtually no planes, personnel, or even office furniture in the beginning.

Due largely to Eaker's leadership and organisational skills, the Eighth Air Force grew from a fledgling force to more than 4,000 aircraft and 185,000 personnel by the end of 1943. All the while, Eaker had been under mounting pressure from Arnold and Spaatz to get American bombers into the air as soon as possible. He accomplished that order with the Rouen Raid of August 1942, and displayed personal courage at age 47 by flying along in the lead B-17 of the 414th Bombardment Squadron, 97th Bomb Group.

"I don't want any American mothers to think I'd send their boys someplace where I'd be afraid to go myself," he told a friend. And he insisted through a directive that his staff officers should fly "sufficient operational missions in order to be cognizant of the problems facing combat crews."

Clarence Ira Eaker was born to a tenant farming family in Llano County, Texas, on April 13, 1896. He earned a Bachelor of Science degree at a teaching college and enlisted in the US Army in 1917, attending Officer Training Camp and receiving a 2nd lieutenant's commission in the infantry reserve. Three months later, he was transferred to the aviation section of the Signal Corps and began flight training. He qualified as a fighter pilot but did not see action during World War One, earning his wings in 1919.

During the interwar years, Eaker gained a reputation as one of the most respected and capable officers in the Air Corps. He held several posts in the United States and the Philippines, including command of Mitchel Field, Long Island, New York, while studying law at Columbia University. He served in the office of the chief of the US Air Service in Washington, DC, and participated in the defence of General Billy Mitchell during the celebrated court martial of the pioneer aerial bombing advocate. While temporarily detached from the service, he piloted a Pan American Airways »

ABOVE: Major General Ira Eaker greets King George VI and Queen Elizabeth at Duxford in the spring of 1943. Public Domain collections of the Imperial War Museums via Wikimedia Commons

FAR LEFT: Shortly after arriving in England, General Ira Eaker takes a moment with pipe and pup. Public Domain US Air Force via Wikimedia Commons

LEFT: General Eaker, left, confers with officers of the US Army and Air Forces in 1944. Public Domain US Army via Wikimedia Commons

ABOVE LEFT: A dashing Captain Ira Eaker is shown in the open cockpit of an aircraft. Public Domain National Company Collection Library of Congress via Wikimedia Commons

ABOVE RIGHT: During ceremonies on April 1, 1985, Eaker receives the fourth star denoting full general rank. Public Domain G. Dennis Plummer National Archives and Records Administration US Air Force

plane during a goodwill flight, covering an astounding 22,065 miles from December 1926 to May 1927, and receiving the Distinguished Flying Cross.

Eaker returned to duty and subsequently set an aerial refuelling record while piloting a Fokker C-2A monoplane that remained aloft for 150 hours and was refuelled 43 times, flying 11,000 miles while circling above Los Angeles, California. He also tested aircraft at Bolling Field and made the first transcontinental flight with mid-air refuelling in 1930. Eaker graduated from the Army Command Tactical School at Maxwell Field, Alabama, in 1936, and then made a transcontinental flight guided solely by instruments as the canopy of his aircraft was hooded.

Eaker became close friends with both Spaatz and Arnold and co-wrote three books with Arnold before and after US entry into World War Two, including *The Flying Game*, *Winged Warfare*, and *Army Flyer*. In one of those books, he put forward his personal leadership philosophy writing: "No man should plan air battles who has not fought in a flying machine... Great leaders in the air and on the ground do not send men. They lead them."

He worked in the office of General James E. Fechet, chief of the Army Air Corps, and reached the rank of colonel prior to being ordered to Britain as an observer in the summer of 1941. He gained intimate knowledge of the RAF victory in the Battle of Britain the previous year along with insights into Fighter Command tactics.

Promoted to the rank of brigadier general in January 1942, Eaker returned to the United States and was chosen to lead Eighth Bomber Command. Astounded, he commented: "But I've been in fighters all my life!" Both Spaatz and Arnold had advocated for the appointment, and Arnold responded, "I know. We want the fighter spirit in bombardment aviation."

During the coming days, Eaker forged solid working relationships with Churchill and Air Chief Marshal Sir Arthur 'Bomber' Harris, head of RAF Bomber Command. He spent his first three months in Britain as Harris's house guest while laying the foundation for the future of the Eighth Air Force. Eaker shouldered the responsibility for the establishment of a force significant enough in size, training, and aircraft to mount a bomber campaign and strove to manage the expectations of his contemporaries and superior officers regarding a realistic timetable. When the American air campaign commenced, he worried over the losses incurred.

Spaatz was ordered to the Mediterranean theatre in late 1942, and with his departure, Eaker assumed command of the entire Eighth Air Force with the rank of major general in December. Despite his best efforts and the repeated diversion of assets originally intended for Eighth Air Force to other areas, the pace of Eaker's progress continued to concern General Arnold, who decided change was necessary. By January 1944, Spaatz was again in Britain to head the US Strategic Air Forces in Europe. At the same time, General Jimmy Doolittle, famed leader of the April 18, 1942, raid on the Japanese capital of Tokyo, arrived to replace Eaker as commander of the Eighth Air Force.

Receiving the third star of lieutenant general rank and being named commander of Allied Air Forces in the Mediterranean theatre were some solace to Eaker, who felt that to an extent he had been 'kicked upstairs'. Regardless, he capably discharged his Mediterranean duties through to the end of World War Two in Europe. In the spring of 1945, he was named deputy commander of the Army Air Forces and chief of the Air Staff. He retired from active duty on August 31, 1947, and his three-star rank was made permanent on the retired list the following year. The magnitude of his contribution to the Allied victory in Europe is undeniable.

In civilian life, Eaker held executive posts with both Douglas Aircraft and Hughes Aircraft. Among numerous other activities, he wrote a syndicated column that appeared in 180 newspapers. He was promoted to four-star full general rank (retired) during the administration of President Ronald Reagan in 1985 and died at the age of 91 on August 6, 1987.

RIGHT: Captain Ira Eaker, right, poses with General James Fechet, chief of the Army Air Corps, in 1925. Public Domain National Company Collection Library of Congress via Wikimedia Commons

ABOVE: Flying Fortresses accompany the Italian passenger liner *Rex* in 1938 after Lieutenant Curtis LeMay demonstrated his extraordinary navigational skills. Public Domain US Air Force via Wikimedia Commons

GENERAL CURTIS E. LEMAY

The citation for the Distinguished Service Cross read succinctly: "Brigadier General Curtis Emerson LeMay, United States Army Air Forces, for extraordinary heroism in connection with military operations while serving as pilot of a B-17 Heavy Bomber…while participating in a bombing mission on 17 August 1943, against enemy ground targets in the European Theater of Operations. General LeMay, fully realizing the extent of the hazards involved, although not required to participate through obligation or reason of duty, undertook the responsibility of directing this mission…."

LeMay was at the head of the Regensburg portion of the twin raids against the Messerschmitt aircraft assembly plant there and the ball bearing facilities at Schweinfurt, Germany, on that day of heavy losses. While commanding the USAAF 4th Bombardment Wing, he did not hesitate to go where his courageous airmen had been sent.

General Curtis LeMay was a driven, purposeful, and some would say ruthless leader of men in war. He had risen from the tough existence of a poor family, sometimes itinerant as his handyman father sought work. Born in Columbus, Ohio, on November 15, 1906, LeMay was a product of the city's public schools. When his effort to obtain an appointment to the US Military Academy at West Point was thwarted, he worked his way through college, obtaining a civil engineering degree from the Ohio State University and a commission in the US Army Air Corps Reserve in 1929 through the university's Reserve Officer Training Corps (ROTC) programme.

In early 1930, LeMay's commission as a 2nd lieutenant transferred to the active US Army Air Corps. First flying fighters, he became a bomber navigator in 1937, one of the earliest officers to receive specific training in aircraft navigation. He distinguished himself during combined air and naval exercises, serving as lead navigator in flights of large B-17 formations from the US to South America in 1937 and 1938, the latter effort receiving the coveted Mackay Trophy for outstanding aerial achievement. He famously navigated the lead B-17 of three Flying Fortresses in the exercise to locate the Italian passenger liner *Rex* more than 700 miles off the Atlantic seaboard in May 1938, effectively demonstrating the ability of the heavy bombers to defend the US coastline. In doing so, he helped secure the future of the Flying Fortress amid scepticism from top army brass.

LeMay was a major serving as operations officer of the 34th Bombardment Group when war broke out in Europe, and when the US entered World War Two, he was commanding the 305th Bombardment Group. Promotion came rapidly in wartime, and along with it LeMay displayed significant insight regarding precision bombing tactics. He organised and trained the 305th and moved with it in September 1942 to RAF Grafton Underwood, Northamptonshire, and then RAF Chelveston in December. By mid-1942, he had risen to colonel, and in September 1943, he had earned the rank of brigadier general. Along the way, he demonstrated personal bravery while leading the 305th Bombardment Group in combat and received promotions to command of the 4th Bombardment Wing and 3rd Air Division.

LeMay's reputation for toughness grew right along with his command responsibilities. He constantly trained his people and told them: "You fight as you train!" His command style was effective and earned him the nickname 'Iron Ass' during the course of his career.

When future US Secretary of Defense Robert McNamara, who served with the USAAF Office of Statistical Control during the war, commented in a report on the level of aborted »

FAR LEFT: General Curtis LeMay was an innovative bomber commander during World War Two. Public Domain US Air Force via Wikimedia Commons

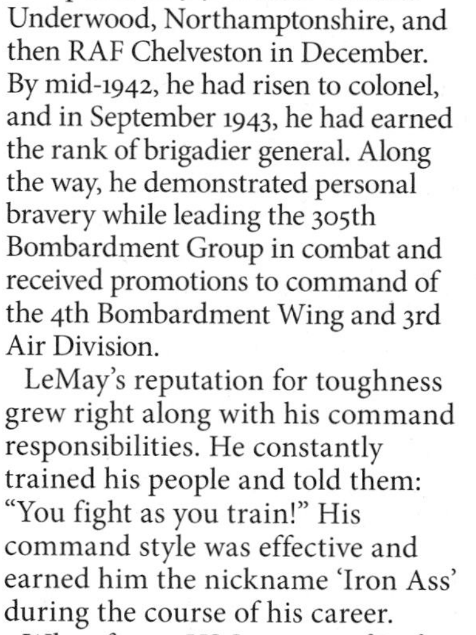

LEFT: Curtis LeMay is shown in 1929 with the rank of lieutenant. He went on to become one of the youngest general officers in the US military. Public Domain US Air Force via Wikimedia Commons

RIGHT: Colonel Curtis LeMay congratulates a B-17 crew of the 305th Bombardment Group at RAF Chelveston. Public Domain Collections of the Imperial War Museums via Wikimedia Commons

air missions in the European theatre, he observed of LeMay: "He was the finest combat commander of any service I came across in war. But he was extraordinarily belligerent, many thought brutal. He got the report. He issued an order. He said, 'I will be in the lead plane on every mission. Any plane that takes off will go over the target, or the crew will be court martialled.' The abort rate dropped overnight. Now that's the kind of commander he was."

At the same time, LeMay was innovative.

Early in the Eighth Air Force precision bombing campaign, wedge formation flying had been employed. However, the notion of zig-zagging over target areas to reduce the effectiveness of German anti-aircraft fire had resulted in a lack of formation cohesiveness, sub-optimal bombing results, and rising aircraft losses due to both flak and Luftwaffe fighter attacks. Any mutual protection offered by the interlocking fields of fire from a group of Flying Fortresses' .50-calibre machine guns was diminished with the loose formations as well.

LeMay brought a fresh perspective both to formation flying and to bombing accuracy. In the case of the latter, he advocated that bombers fly straight and steady over their target and release their bombs in concert. He identified the most proficient bombardiers and made them the lead men. When the lead bombardiers released their bombs above the target, other bombardiers in formation would follow suit, improving accuracy with the state-of-the-art Norden bombsight. While accuracy improved, the straight flight actually minimised the bombers' time over the target and therefore their exposure to German flak.

On November 23, 1942, B-17s of the 305th Bombardment Group joined in a raid against the U-boat pens at St. Nazaire, France. LeMay remembered that his Flying Fortresses were over the target area for seven long minutes. "I told my outfit that I was going straight in," he said, "and that I thought we could get away with it, and that I would be flying the lead aircraft. We made the longest, straightest bomb run which had ever been made by B-17s over the continent of Europe." None of LeMay's bombers were lost in the raid.

In regard to formation flying, a study conducted in 1943 revealed that approximately half of the bombers lost to enemy fire were those that broke formation when a pilot took evasive action or lost his nerve, or a bomber suffered battle damage. Single bombers were often easy pickings for Luftwaffe fighter pilots. LeMay is credited with using the 305th Bombardment Group to demonstrate improvements to existing bomber formations with the introduction of a staggered formation, or combat box. With aircraft flying at different altitudes, as much as 3,000ft between high and low, the bombers were less susceptible to exploding enemy anti-aircraft shells. The staggered formation also maintained the integrity of the bombers' mutually supporting fields of defensive machine-gun fire.

The staggered combat box often included up to 12 squadron bombers in the vertical and horizontal arrangement in lead, high, and low elements. While three squadron boxes made up a group box, three groups comprised a combat wing box of up to 108 aircraft. In the squadron box, the lead element flew ahead with the high element above, to the right, and behind. One low element flew below, to the left, and behind the lead element, while the second low element flew directly below and behind the lead. In the group box, the lead squadron formation flew ahead with the high squadron formation above, behind, and to the right. The low squadron flew below, behind, and to the left of the lead squadron formation. In the wing box, the lead group formation of 36 aircraft flew ahead with the high group box above, behind, and to the right, and the low group box below, behind, and to the left of the lead formation.

Variations of the combat box were used throughout the war, and though there were improvements in both offensive and defensive respects, the

BELOW LEFT: General Curtis LeMay confers with General Joseph Stilwell in China in 1944. Public Domain Library of Congress via Wikimedia Commons

BELOW RIGHT: General Curtis LeMay stands at left with other officers of the US Army Air Forces in the autumn of 1945. General Henry 'Hap' Arnold stands third from left. Public Domain US Air Force via Wikimedia Commons

RIGHT: Boeing B-29 Superfortress bombers under the command of General Curtis LeMay rain incendiary bombs on the city of Yokohama, Japan, May 29, 1945. Public Domain National Park Service via Wikimedia Commons

FAR RIGHT: B-17s of the 493rd Bombardment Group are shown flying in a combat box formation. Public Domain US Army Air Forces via Wikimedia Commons

time required for bombers to form up was substantial. The formations did increase the exposure of the bombers to anti-aircraft fire while engaged in the actual bomb run since no evasive action could be taken without disrupting bombing accuracy. The most vulnerable combat box position was at the rear of the lowest or highest element, where the protective convergent machine-gun coverage was limited. These so-called 'Tail End Charlies' were also often the first to attract the attention of Luftwaffe fighter pilots.

LeMay displayed personal courage, innovation, and innate skill as a pilot during his time in England, and such attributes inevitably came to the attention of General Henry 'Hap' Arnold and other senior USAAF officers. In August 1944, Major General LeMay was transferred to the China-Burma-India theatre, where he led XX Bomber Command. In January 1945, he was reassigned to lead XXI Bomber Command in the Pacific based on Guam in the Marianas Islands, and then given command of all US strategic air forces in theatre.

Analysing the course of the bombing campaign against the Japanese home islands, LeMay revised the tactics employed by the heavy Boeing B-29 Superfortress bombers under his command. The big planes were initially used as high-altitude precision bombers, but the results had not been favourable. Weather conditions often precluded accurate high-level bombing, as did the high winds of the prevailing jet stream.

Rather than bombing from altitudes of 20,000ft or more, LeMay ordered the B-29s to make their runs at lower altitudes, bombing from 9,000ft or lower and at night. LeMay ordered machine guns and other gear stripped from the bombers and crammed the maximum payloads of incendiary bombs aboard. He knew that Japanese cities were largely constructed of wood and combustible materials, and the incendiaries set off raging fires.

The most famous – or infamous – of the firebombing raids carried out by B-29s under LeMay's orders against nearly 70 population centres in Japan was the March 9, 1945, raid on Tokyo that killed approximately 100,000 Japanese and reduced 15.8 square miles of the capital city to rubble and ash. LeMay was unapologetic. After all, it was war. He did once comment: "I suppose if I had lost the war, I would have been tried as a war criminal." Historians debate the justification of the firebombing raids that devastated Japan to this day.

With the end of World War Two, LeMay took the controls of a B-29 and flew it non-stop in a record trek from the Japanese island of Hokkaido to Chicago, Illinois. As commander of US air forces in Europe, he organised the Berlin Airlift of 1948-1949. He then led US Strategic Air Command during a critical transition from propeller-driven aircraft to modern jet bombers and amid the introduction of intercontinental ballistic missiles to its arsenal.

In 1957, LeMay was named vice chief of staff of the US Air Force, and four years later he became chief of staff. He served in that capacity during the ever-increasing US involvement in Vietnam and vigorously disagreed with Secretary McNamara and President John F. Kennedy during the Cuban Missile Crisis of October 1962, arguing that launching sites for medium-range Soviet ballistic missiles in Cuba should be bombed. He retired in 1965 with the rank of four-star general and 36 years of service. In 1968, former Alabama Governor George Wallace sought the presidency of the United States and persuaded LeMay to run alongside for the office of vice president. The bid was controversial and unsuccessful.

General LeMay, a legendary air commander of the 20th century, died on October 1, 1990, at the age of 83.

Throughout his career, LeMay's admiration for the Flying Fortress never wavered. He once said: "It was the first of our four-engine bombers and, in many ways, the greatest…I fell in love with the 17 at first sight."

BELOW: This diagram depicts a 12-plane squadron combat box formation employed by US bombers in World War Two. Creative Commons Anynobody via Wikimedia Commons

GENERAL JAMES H. 'JIMMY' DOOLITTLE

ABOVE: Jimmy Doolittle piloted this Curtiss floatplane racer to win the Schneider Trophy in 1925. Public Domain Great Images in Nasa via Wikimedia Commons

RIGHT: The famous Granville GeeBee Super Sportster sits in a hangar in 1932. No Restrictions San Diego Air and Space Museum Archives via Wikimedia Commons

RIGHT: General Jimmy Doolittle received the Medal of Honor and led major air forces, including the Eighth Air Force in England, during World War Two. Public Domain US Air Force via Wikimedia Commons

The sign, hanging on the wall of the Eighth Air Force fighter commander's office for months read simply: "The first duty of the Eighth Air Force fighters is to bring the bombers back alive."

When General James H. 'Jimmy' Doolittle arrived in England to take command of the Eighth Air Force, he ordered the sign taken down immediately. It was replaced with one that read: "The first duty of the Eighth Air Force fighters is to destroy German fighters."

Make no mistake, Doolittle was a bomber pilot at heart. But he knew that the aerial war of attrition raging in the skies of Nazi-occupied Europe in daylight would drag on interminably if the Nazi Luftwaffe remained capable of sending veritable clouds of Messerschmitt and Focke-Wulf fighters aloft to shoot down American B-17 and B-24 bombers. In an ironic twist, Doolittle knew the best defence was a stout-hearted offense. The best way to protect the 'big friends' was for the 'little friends' to take the fight to the enemy, shooting them from the sky in pitched dogfights, rather than staying close to the bomber formations.

Of course, when word of the new tactic spread through the ranks of the Eighth Air Force, the bomber crews were dismayed. They howled their disapproval and believed they were being left to fend for themselves. On the contrary, Jimmy Doolittle was right. While American Republic P-47 Thunderbolt, Lockheed P-38 Lightning, and later North American P-51 Mustang fighter planes ranged from the bomber boxes, picking fights with Luftwaffe pilots, the losses the American fighters took could be replaced. However, the Germans were hopelessly unable to replace the experienced pilots lost to the marauding American fighter jockeys. Therefore, the bombers did benefit as contact with the enemy was often made at distance. When their escort missions were completed, the American fighter pilots were often allowed to enhance their influence on the air and ground battle, strafing enemy airfields and other targets of opportunity.

German fighter losses mounted steadily. A shocking 30% loss occurred in January, another 30% in February, and a staggering 56% in March, an attrition rate of well over 100%. By the end of June 1944, a total of 2,262 German fighter planes had been shot from the sky, many of their skilled pilots killed or wounded in action.

Doolittle went on to command the Eighth Air Force through the end of World War Two in Europe and then transferred with the Mighty Eighth to the island of Okinawa in the Pacific in anticipation of an invasion

RIGHT: A Boeing B-17 Flying Fortress of the 97th Bomb Group, Fifteenth Air Force, based at Foggia, Italy, flies over the Alps. General Doolittle commanded the Fifteenth Air Force. Public Domain US Air Force via Wikimedia Commons

RIGHT: Lieutenant Colonel Jimmy Doolittle, second from left, stands with his bomber crew before the raid on Tokyo. Public Domain US Air Force via Wikimedia Commons

RIGHT: On the deck of the aircraft carrier USS *Hornet*, Lieutenant Colonel Doolittle ties a medal from the Japanese government to the tail fin of a bomb destined for Tokyo. Public Domain US Navy via Wikimedia Commons

of the Japanese home islands that never took place.

By the time he reached England in 1944, Jimmy Doolittle was already a national hero. A recipient of the Medal of Honor for leading 16 twin-engine North American B-25 Mitchell medium bombers on a daring raid against the Japanese capital of Tokyo on April 18, 1942, he had baled out of his bomber in China and evaded capture to reach safety and continue one of the most storied careers in the history of US military aviation.

The so-called Doolittle Raid had taken place a scant four months after the Japanese attack on Pearl Harbor plunged the United States into World War Two. The seemingly far-fetched idea to strike a blow against Japan and bolster the morale of the American people involved the Army Air Corps medium bombers, the only such aircraft with the range to reach the home islands, and the only ones capable of taking off from the pitching deck of a US Navy aircraft carrier. To any casual observer, the mission looked like a suicide run.

Fearful that a Japanese patrol craft had discovered the presence of the naval task force transporting the Doolittle raiders on the morning of April 18, the intrepid American airman, then holding the rank of lieutenant colonel, proved his mettle in a meeting with the naval commanders, Admiral William F. 'Bull' Halsey leading the task force and Admiral Marc Mitscher, commanding the aircraft carrier USS *Hornet*. The three men weighed their options and agreed to launch the bombers from *Hornet* well beyond their intended departure point rather than abort the mission. Sometime prior to taking off, Doolittle had assembled his men and fastened to the fins of a bomb meant for the Japanese a medal he had received from the enemy government during the years between the world wars. It was to be a new type of air mail and 'return to sender'.

The Doolittle raiders completed their mission, so startling the Japanese high command that its strategic plan for World War Two in the Pacific was significantly altered. The Japanese changes led to defeats at the Battle of the Coral Sea in May 1942 and the epic Battle of Midway, the turning point in the Pacific war, the following month.

After returning from the raid, Doolittle rose rapidly in rank. He transferred to the European theatre and took command of the strategic arm of the Allied Northwest Africa Air Force, under General »

LEFT: General Jimmy Doolittle, left, stands with General Curtis LeMay in Britain in 1944 just as he took command of Eighth Air Force. Public Domain US Department of Defense via Wikimedia Commons

Carl 'Tooey' Spaatz, from March to November 1943, then the Fifteenth Air Force, the strategic bombing arm of the Allied Mediterranean Air Forces, based at Foggia, Italy, from November 1943 to January 1944, when his tenure with the Eighth Air Force began. He reached the rank of temporary lieutenant general in March 1944.

Jimmy Doolittle, slight in stature but a daredevil of a man, had achieved some measure of fame prior to the outbreak of World War Two. Born December 14, 1896, in Alameda, California, he spent five of his early years in Alaska. When the family returned to California, he was eight years old and began an educational journey in the Los Angeles public schools. He took up boxing and gained a reputation as a formidable bantamweight along the length of the US west coast. Doolittle considered a career as a mining engineer, but after attending an air show in 1910, his course was altered. He became enamoured with flight, and when World War One broke out he halted his pursuit of a degree in mine engineering and joined the Army Signal Corps Reserve as a flying cadet.

In March 1918, Doolittle received a commission as a 2nd lieutenant in the Signal Corps Aviation Section. Disappointed that he did not see combat, the young officer served as a flight and gunnery instructor at Camp Dick, Texas, Wright Field, Ohio, and other bases. Two weeks after the Great War ended, he made his debut as a barnstorming stunt pilot at an air show in San Diego, California. Remaining in the air service, he received his academic degree from the University of California in 1922 and then embarked on a string of hazardous cross-country flights. By the mid-1920s, he had received his Doctor of Science degree from the prestigious Massachusetts Institute of Technology.

Doolittle remained active in the air, performing as a stunt pilot while his need for speed led to competitive air racing. In 1925, he borrowed a US Navy Curtiss R3C2 floatplane and won the Schneider Cup international races. On leave of absence from the military, he survived a crash in 1926 but broke both ankles. Undeterred, he continued making cross-country flights and became the first pilot to complete the dangerous outside loop aerial manoeuvre. In 1930, he resigned his active duty commission and went to work for the Shell Oil company. He did retain his major's commission in the Reserve Officer Corps and continued racing.

The young airman won the Bendix Trophy in 1931, flying an average speed of 225mph, and also captured the Harmon Trophy. He piloted the 800hp stubby-winged GeeBee Super Sportster to win the Thompson Trophy with an average speed of 250mph and retired from racing in 1933. In 1940, he was elected president of the Institute of Aeronautical Sciences. A year later as war clouds gathered, he was recalled to active duty with the Army Air Corps with the rank of major.

When Doolittle reached senior air command, he was a dynamo. One officer who served with him in North Africa called him 'the little man who is everywhere'. He was regularly seen at the far reaches of his command, flying hundreds of miles a day aboard his personal B-17 Flying Fortress. He was known to keep a couple of bombs aboard, stowed in the bomb bay, as one officer said: "just in case he should see something to drop them on."

Another officer who served under Doolittle in the Mediterranean commented: "I wish the general would stay put long enough for me to talk to him. If he's here, he never stands still, but paces all over the place, and I have to talk and run at the same time. If I turn my back, he's off to Oran, or Algiers, or Casablanca, or somewhere else, before I can get hold of him."

When he came to the Eighth Air Force, Doolittle brought experience, drive, and vigour to his command. No doubt, his refocus of fighter tactics brought greater success to the bombing formations of B-17s and B-24s flying over enemy territory and even saved the lives of many bomber crews.

After World War Two, Lieutenant General Doolittle maintained his Air Force reserve status and returned to work for Shell Oil. He retired from both in 1959, and in his later years made numerous public appearances and speeches regarding his remarkable career. In 1985, he was promoted to the rank of four-star full general on the retired list. He died at the age of 96 on September 27, 1993, an aviation pioneer whose career spanned more than a half century from the earliest days of flight to the Space Age.

FAR LEFT: Major General Jimmy Doolittle autographed this photo taken at his desk during World War Two. Public Domain US Department of Defense via Wikimedia Commons

LEFT: General Jimmy Doolittle, under whose leadership Eighth Air Force in England gained air superiority in Europe during World War Two, posed for this photo in 1986. Public Domain Garfield Jones US government via Wikimedia Commons

ANATOMY OF A MISSION

They flew almost daily from bases across England, from East Anglia to the Midlands and other RAF supplied locales. The airmen who boarded the big bombers of the Eighth Air Force, in concert with their partners of the Royal Air Force, experienced combat in World War Two thousands of feet in the air, the prospect of instant destruction always with them, either at the hands of a Luftwaffe fighter pilot or from the blast of enemy flak. The same was true of B-17 crewmen in all theatres of the war, from the deserts of North Africa to the Mediterranean and the expanse of the Pacific.

The day of the mission, start to finish, included a somewhat choreographed series of events. The time in the air was interwoven with extended periods, sometimes several hours, of mind numbing boredom as the four engines of the Flying Fortresses droned toward their assigned target, the waiting abruptly punctuated with moments of sheer terror. Regularly, the doldrums were swiftly shattered with the puff and pounding of anti-aircraft fire. The sight of a group of enemy fighters forming up to make firing passes and then slashing through the bomber formations made adrenalin pump and anxiety peak.

But it was their job, and the men of the US Army Air Forces were everywhere equal to the call, to the sacrifice. Their courage has, some observers assert, remained unsurpassed in the experience of any other combat endeavour on land, sea, or air.

Usually roused from fitful sleep at three or 4am, airmen groaned as the sergeant whose title was 'Charge of Quarters' pounded down the hallway of the quarters hut, threw open the door and shouted the names of those slated to fly the day's mission. The men sat up, scratched their heads, and made their way to the latrines and through their morning ablutions. They donned uniforms and then headed to the mess hall, young men in their teens and 20s, circuiting the line and sitting down to a breakfast that regularly consisted of powdered eggs, sausage, and hot coffee.

The requisite briefing followed. "Dressed in our flying clothing and carrying our gear, we climbed into trucks that took us to headquarters," remembered Captain Frank Murphy of the 100th Bombardment Group in his book *Luck of the Draw.* "A vigilant MP wearing a white helmet and a white armband checked us in. We filed into the briefing room and took our seats elbow to elbow on narrow wooden benches like playgoers »

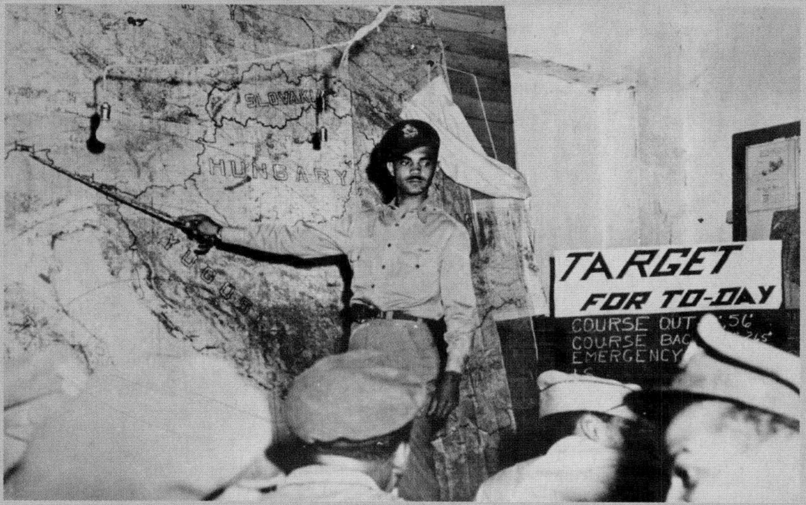

LEFT: An officer uses a pointer to describe the 'target for today' during a briefing of air personnel in England. Public Domain US National Archives and Records Administration via Wikimedia Commons

LEFT: An officer briefs aircrews of the 303rd Bombardment Group at RAF Molesworth prior to a bombing mission on October 9, 1944. Public Domain US Army Air Forces via Wikimedia Commons

BELOW: This beautifully restored B-17 lifts into the air at Buchanan Field, Concord, California, reminiscent of a combat mission take-off. Creative Commons Bill Larkins via Wikimedia Commons

ABOVE LEFT: A B-17G of the 452nd Bombardment Group flies through heavy German flak over a target in Europe. Public Domain US Army Air Forces via Wikimedia Commons

ABOVE RIGHT: Crewmen of the 401st Bombardment Group pause in front of their B-17F *Fancy Nancy IV* at RAF Deenethorpe. Public Domain US Army Air Forces via Wikimedia Commons

at an oversold stage production. Curtains hid the wall behind the rostrum. A lectern stood on the left side of the dais, and to our right, we saw an easel covered by a large cloth, obviously to prevent us from getting a premature look. In the front of the room, a small table held a gadget for projecting photos and flimsies on a screen. It was a dramatic setting."

Murphy continued, "At the cry of 'Ten-hut!' that signalled the start of every group military meeting I ever attended, we shuffled to our feet. A team of senior officers strode briskly down the center aisle and took their places along the front row. One of them was Major Minor Shaw, a veteran of the First World War, who was chief of S-2 (intelligence). He immediately stepped to the lectern, barked, 'At ease', and motioned for the curtains to be opened. As they were swept aside, we saw a huge color map of the British Isles and western Europe almost completely covering the wall behind the stage. On the face of the map, a string of red yarn fastened with pins traced a line from an assembly point near Thorpe Abbotts to a departure point on the south coast of England, then stretched south across the channel to a point in France. It finally came back to England, showing us our return route. Referring to the map with a pointer, Major Shaw solemnly intoned, 'Gentlemen, your target for today is the Gnome and Rhône engine works at Le Mans, France.' Silence."

RIGHT: A B-17E Flying Fortress is shown with bomb bay doors open during an attack on a Japanese airfield at Lae, New Guinea, in June 1942. Public Domain US Army Air Forces via Wikimedia Commons

Once the main briefing concluded, pilots, navigators, and bombardiers met to gather information related specifically to their jobs. The airmen were driven by truck or jeep to the hardstands where their respective bombers squatted. They clambered aboard and took their various stations, and pre-flight procedures commenced. Usually, a crew of 10 men flew aboard the B-17, but sometimes that number was reduced to nine.

Engines coughed to life, and the initial sputter mounted to a deafening crescendo as the bombers taxied into position for take-off, lifted into the sky burdened by their cargo of bombs, fuel tanks that were topped off, and the weight of the crew. Climbing into formation was a hazard in itself, particularly in weather conditions that were less than ideal. Collisions on the ground or in mid-air were all too common. Once in formation, the bombers headed along their assigned course to target.

As the Flying Fortresses gained altitude, the effects of numbing cold and thin air took hold. The B-17 did not have a pressurised cabin like the later B-29 Superfortress that saw action in the Pacific theatre. When planes reached altitudes of more than 20,000ft, temperatures could dip below -400 Fahrenheit. Electrically heated flight suits and gloves were worn to protect flesh, which would suffer near-instantaneous frostbite if exposed. One airman remembered that if bare skin touched a metal surface at high altitude, it would immediately adhere. Long missions meant relieving one's self was problematic. A toilet was located near the rear fuselage, but circumstances often precluded its use. A funnel and tube, opening to the outside, were also located near the bomb bay.

Oxygen was required at altitudes above 10,000ft, and each airman was provided with an oxygen mask that was attached to the onboard system. Portable 'walk around' oxygen tanks were available to allow the crew to move about the B-17, but these only lasted a few minutes. They were, however, critical to survival in the event that a crewman had to bale out. At high altitude without oxygen, it was likely that a parachuting man would be rendered unconscious before he could pull the cord to open his parachute.

Concerns such as oxygen and creature comfort were ever present, but most often they were accepted, much less of a problem than the deadly business at hand. Quite often the first encounter with the enemy might be a telltale blot of anti-aircraft fire against the sky at some distance. Soon enough, the pace and accuracy of the flak might pick up, and bombers were wounded or stricken, sometimes falling out of formation to become stragglers.

The onslaught of enemy fighters was to be expected. Rarely did a mission over Nazi-occupied Europe, for example, begin and end without interference from the Luftwaffe. Every man aboard the B-17, except the pilot and co-pilot, had access to a defensive machine gun, either as a primary or secondary responsibility, as in the case of the bombardier and navigator. The German fighters regularly approached American

LEFT: Trailing smoke from a damaged no. 3 engine, a B-17 limps toward home following a bombing raid. Public Domain US Air Force via Wikimedia Commons

bomber formations at speeds in excess of 300mph. Although many gunners aboard the bombers claimed kills against attacking enemy fighters and a number were actually credited as aces with five or more confirmed victories, the gunners were often unsure of the accuracy of their fire.

One waist gunner, though, remembered a vivid shootdown. Eighteen-year-old Sergeant Jack Novey, who survived 25 combat missions aboard a B-17 nicknamed *Black Hawk*, recounted an experience during a mission in September 1943 in his book *The Cold Blue Sky: A B-17 Gunner in World War II*. "...All of a sudden, right in front of me appeared an Me-109...I let loose a burst of fire from my .50-caliber machine gun, and shells exploded around the cockpit. The pilot blew his canopy and ejected...His suit was on fire. His parachute opened up, burned away in an orange-yellow blaze, and he came out mouthing a scream. I'll never forget that image freezing in front of me in slow motion...I can only hope the pilot was dead before he started to fall in flames – but I don't think he was."

More often, however, it was the experience of the B-17 crews to see their fellow airmen shot down, bombers spinning out of control or exploding in the air, devastated by enemy machine-gun and cannon fire or a disabling hit from heavy flak. When a bomber was going down and the heat of the ordeal permitted, crewmen aboard surrounding planes would count the parachutes of those exiting the stricken bomber. The tension was incredible, and inevitably such sights took their toll on the psyche of an individual who witnessed the earthward plunge or sudden end of a B-17 that was likely crewed by men he knew well.

Through fighters and flak, the heavy bombers pressed on, flying straight as the bombardier took control of the aircraft to make an accurate drop of the ordnance. Staying in formation was critical to the effectiveness of the release, and those agonising moments were the most vulnerable for the B-17s. There was no way to avoid enemy flak. The drama simply had to be endured. Meanwhile, during raids over western Europe and the Third Reich itself, Luftwaffe fighters usually broke off their attacks temporarily as bombers reached their targets to avoid their own anti-aircraft fire.

But they weren't finished.

Often the German pilots touched down at nearby airfields, refuelled and replenished ammunition to hit the bombers on their return to base. Once the bombers were within range of Allied fighters, the situation improved somewhat. However, it was not until the introduction of the P-51 Mustang in late 1943, that bomber formations had fighter escort throughout missions into Germany.

When returning to their airfields, bombers with casualties aboard would discharge flares to signal ground personnel and alert ambulances or firefighting vehicles. As bombers approached their airfields, ground crewmen began counting the returning numbers. After landing, pilots and crewmen were debriefed, often asked questions about the accuracy of the bombing, the intensity of flak or fighter opposition, types of enemy aircraft encountered, and any distinctive markings that might indicate that a certain enemy squadron had been active.

For most, rest and limited recovery from the harrowing mission experience followed, but there was always the lingering realisation that another mission was soon to come. During World War Two, combat soldiers on the ground experienced a ratio of three to four wounded infantrymen for every one killed. During the air war, the converse was true. For every airman wounded in action, statistics revealed that three were killed.

LEFT: Luftwaffe officers inspect the wreck of the B-17F *Miss Ouachita* of the 91st Bombardment Group shot down over Germany in February 1944. Creative Commons Bundesarchiv Bild via Wikimedia Commons

LEFT: This restored B-17 resides at the Museum of Flight, Boeing Field, Seattle, Washington, and is open for tours daily. Creative Commons InSapphoWeTrust via Wikimedia Commons

THE B-17 AND THE MEDAL OF HONOR

Often at dizzying altitudes and amid numbing cold, not to mention the ominous thud or crackle of shrapnel from enemy anti-aircraft fire or the impact of a bullet or shell, American airmen discharged their duties as best they could aboard the fighters and bombers of the US Army Air Forces in World War Two.

At times, the act of courage exhibited by a single airman was remarkable – above and beyond the call of duty – as it is usually described. And at times such conduct was worthy of the highest recognition the United States could bestow upon one of its fighting sons, the Congressional Medal of Honor. Seventeen men serving aboard the Boeing B-17 Flying Fortress heavy bomber distinguished themselves in such a manner as to merit the Medal of Honor, according to witnesses, recommendations, and the close scrutiny of authorities who took very seriously their responsibility to reserve the medal for those most deserving. Eleven of the recipients of the Medal of Honor aboard the B-17 in World War Two received their medals posthumously, having given their lives in their displays of incredible heroism.

The first recipient of the Medal of Honor for service aboard the Flying Fortress was 1st Lieutenant Jack W. Mathis, of the 359th Bombardment Squadron, 303rd Bombardment Group. A native of San Angelo, Texas, 21-year-old Mathis was a bombardier who flew 14 combat missions, the last a bombing raid against Bremen, Germany, on March 18, 1943. Mathis was the bombardier of the lead B-17, and his release of bombs was to guide the accuracy of his entire squadron.

As his B-17 flew straight and level, at its most vulnerable, to allow maximum accuracy of the Norden bombsight, a flak burst seriously damaged Mathis's bomber. Shards of shrapnel tore into the young aviator, shattering his right arm and gouging into his abdomen. In terrible pain and knowing that the wounds were life threatening, Mathis dragged himself back to his post, propped up against the bombsight, found the appropriate drop point, and released his bombs. He died aboard the aircraft during the return flight. Jack's brother Mark, also an aviator, was waiting at RAF Molesworth when the B-17 carrying his brother's body touched down. Mark gained a transfer to Jack's former crew and served with it until it had completed its tour of duty. Afterward, Mark remained in a combat squadron and was killed in action when his bomber was attacked over the North Sea in May 1943.

ABOVE: First Lieutenant Jack W. Mathis stands in the second row far right with his flight crew in this 1942 photograph. Public Domain US Air Force via Wikimedia Commons

On June 16, 1943, over the island of Bougainville in the Solomons archipelago, South Pacific, Major Jay Zeamer, and 2nd Lieutenant Joseph Sarnoski, members of the same crew aboard the B-17 nicknamed *Old 666* both received the Medal of Honor, Sarnoski posthumously. Normally a bombardier, Sarnoski volunteered to fly that fateful mission as a crewman. Zeamer, the pilot, was executive officer of the 65th Bombardment Squadron, 43rd Bombardment Group, Fifth Air Force.

Old 666 was designated to fly an arduous 1,200-mile reconnaissance mission to photomap the west coast of Bougainville and a Japanese airstrip on the small island of Buka in preparation for possible American amphibious landings on Bougainville. Bad weather postponed the mission for two months, but in mid-June clearing conditions permitted take-off. Zeamer piloted the big bomber into the sky at 4am on the morning of June 16. Twice Zeamer had bucked the Buka leg of the mission, concerned that Japanese fighters were swarming the area.

LEFT: Major Jay Zeamer's B-17, *Old 666*, sits at an airfield in the southwest Pacific. Public Domain US Army Air Forces via Wikimedia Commons

RIGHT: Major Jay Zeamer survived the June 16, 1943, mission and received the Medal of Honor. Public Domain US Army Air Corps via Wikimedia Commons

When the aircraft arrived over Bougainville too early to begin the aerial mapping chore, he asked to crew to decide on either performing the Buka reconnaissance or killing the time by flying over the open Pacific. When the crew voted to perform the reconnaissance, he was aware that enemy fighters, most likely the proficient Mitsubishi A6M Zero type, might be thick in the vicinity of Buka. He went in anyway, and soon his biggest worry was confirmed. At least eight Zeros and at least one floatplane fighter pounced on the lone B-17.

The Japanese pilots made pass after pass against the single American bomber, firing away. The first Zero fired its 20mm cannon, blasting Sarnoski several feet from his machine-gun position and mortally wounding the airman. Nevertheless, Sarnoski struggled back to his weapon and fired directly at the second attacking Zero, forcing it to break away. Four more 20mm shells slammed into the B-17, smashing the instrument panel and breaking Zeamer's left leg while shrapnel tore a gaping hole in his left thigh. Zeamer was also wounded in both arms, his right leg, and right wrist.

Three other crewmen of *Old 666* were wounded, and a fire had broken out when oxygen tanks ruptured. Despite his wounds, Zeamer managed to ward off more attacks by turning into the Zeros to minimise their ability to target the B-17. After 40 minutes, the enemy fighters finally headed back to base. Zeamer continued to fly the plane, allowing the co-pilot to tend the other wounded men until the co-pilot took the controls for an emergency landing at Dobodura, New Guinea. The plane was badly damaged, and four men were seriously wounded.

RIGHT: Major Jay Zeamer receives the Medal of Honor from General Henry 'Hap' Arnold as his parents look on in 1944. Public Domain National Museum of the US Air Force via Wikimedia Commons

Sarnoski had died after heroically returning to his .50-caliber machine gun. His posthumous Medal of Honor citation credited the 28-year-old officer with shooting down two enemy fighters. Zeamer was initially thought to have died due to blood loss. However, he recovered to receive his Medal of Honor from General Henry 'Hap' Arnold, chief of the US Army Air Forces, in 1944. He spent 15 months recovering from his wounds, rose to »

RIGHT: Second Lieutenant Joseph Sarnoski, who was killed in the June 16, 1943, B-17 mission, is shown on the second row far right in this crew photo. Pilot Jay Zeamer is second from left on the back row. Public Domain US Army Air Forces via Wikimedia Commons

ABOVE: This image illustrates the 1944 version of the Medal of Honor presented to US Army personnel. Public Domain US Army Institute of Heraldry via Wikimedia Commons

RIGHT: Brigadier General Kenneth Walker is shown at right with Fifth Air Force commander General George Kenney in August 1942. Public Domain US Army Air Forces via Wikimedia Commons

the rank of lieutenant colonel, and was discharged from the service in January 1945. Zeamer died in 2007 at age 88.

In 1942, Brigadier General Kenneth Walker was named to lead V Bomber Command, Fifth Air Force in the southwest Pacific. With such an important command role, he might have avoided actual combat. Instead, General Walker decided to personally lead a small air raid against the Japanese base at Rabaul on the island of New Britain. In fact, Walker frequently flew combat missions. He had already received the Silver Star for gallantry during four raids over Port Moresby, New Guinea, when intelligence reports indicated a Japanese reinforcement effort would be undertaken from Rabaul to troops at Lae, New Guinea.

Walker scraped together six B-17s and six B-24 Liberator bombers to attack the Japanese movement. He decided to fly aboard the lead Flying Fortress, *San Antonio Rose I* of the 64th Bombardment Squadron, 43rd Bombardment Wing, while Lieutenant Colonel Jack Bleasdale, the 43rd's executive officer would pilot the bomber. When the attackers reached the vicinity of the convoy, they found plenty of targets, but the majority of the Japanese convoy had sailed two hours earlier than expected.

The Americans also met a wall of Japanese anti-aircraft fire and determined enemy fighters. They dropped 500 and 1,000lb bombs from altitudes below 9,000ft and claimed hits on nine enemy transport craft. Postwar records indicate that one Japanese ship was sunk and an escorting destroyer damaged. Two B-17s were lost in the raid, and one of them was *San Antonio Rose I*. The bodies of those aboard were never recovered. The crew of the other B-17 shot down was located and rescued.

Fifth Air Force commander General George Kenney was furious when he learned that Walker had flown on the hazardous mission. Kenney told theatre commander General Douglas MacArthur that he would reprimand Walker and send him to Australia for a time as punishment. MacArthur replied: "All right George, but if he doesn't come back, I'm going to send his name in to Washington recommending him for the Congressional Medal of Honor." After his death, Walker did receive the coveted medal posthumously.

Second Lieutenant David R. Kingsley gave his life and received the Medal of Honor for selflessly handing his own parachute to another crew member and caring for wounded men aboard a B-17 during a raid on the oil production facilities at heavily-defended Ploesti, Romania, on June 23, 1944. Kingsley served as bombardier aboard a Flying Fortress of the 97th Bombardment Group, Fifteenth Air Force, based in Italy.

After the B-17 was hit by enemy flak, three Luftwaffe Messerschmitt Me-109 fighters peppered the crippled bomber further, and both the tail gunner and radio operator were seriously wounded. Eight more Me-109s joined the attack, inflicting more damage and wounding the ball turret gunner. When the pilot ordered the crew to bale out, Kingsley assisted the wounded men into their chutes. Then, without hesitation, Kingsley gave his own parachute to the tail gunner, Staff Sergeant Michael Sullivan, whose gear had been lost in the chaos of the moment. The B-17 flew for a few more minutes and then plunged into the ground, killing 25-year-old Kingsley whose body was later recovered from the wreckage. The Medal of Honor was presented to his brother, Thomas Kingsley, on April 9, 1945.

Brigadier General Frederick W. Castle was a 1930 graduate of the US Military Academy at West Point. He was among the group of officers led by General Ira C. Eaker that established the Eighth Air Force in Britain in 1942, and later assumed command of the 94th Bombardment Group. Charged with improving the group's morale, he personally led a raid against the Focke Wulf aircraft assembly plant at Oschersleben, Germany, on July 28, 1943, and received the Silver Star for the mission. In April 1944, he was promoted to command the 4th Combat Bomb Wing, receiving his brigadier's star at age 36.

Bad weather hampered Allied air operations after the Germans initiated their Ardennes Offensive in mid-December 1944, but when conditions had slightly

RIGHT: Brigadier General Kenneth Walker personally flew numerous combat missions aboard the B-17 Flying Fortress. Public Domain US Army via Wikimedia Commons

FAR LEFT: Second Lieutenant David R. Kingsley was killed during a B-17 mission against oil facilities at Ploesti, Romania, on June 23, 1944, and received a posthumous Medal of Honor. Public Domain US Army Air Forces via Wikimedia Commons

LEFT: First Lieutenant Donald J. Gott was killed in action piloting a B-17 on November 9, 1944. Public Domain US Government via Wikimedia Commons

improved, Castle decided to fly as co-pilot aboard a Flying Fortress nicknamed *Treble Four* of the 487th Bombardment Group on Christmas Eve, 1944. The bombers took off from RAF Lavenham in weather that was less than ideal, actually causing the formations to miss their rendezvous with escorting P-51 Mustang fighters.

As the bombers droned toward their target, a Luftwaffe airfield at Babenhausen, Germany, *Treble Four* began experiencing engine problems. Compounding the difficulties, German fighters attacked the slowed B-17 while it was over Belgium, causing it to fall out of formation. Two more clutches of German fighters attacked *Treble Four*, and both engines on the bomber's right wing caught fire. The plane momentarily spun into a dive, but the pilot recovered control long enough to allow seven crewmen to bale out. Seconds later, the pilot was seen attaching his parachute while Castle flew the bomber and bought precious time for the others. Abruptly, *Treble Four* exploded in a ball of fire, but five crewmen had survived the shootdown. The gallant General Castle was interred at the American Cemetery and Memorial, Henri-Chapelle, Belgium.

During a November 9, 1944, bombing mission of the 729th Bomb Squadron, 452nd Bombardment Group, pilot 1st Lieutenant Donald J. Gott and co-pilot 2nd Lieutenant William E. Metzger, Jr., earned posthumous Medals of Honor side by side. The two airmen were flying a B-17 mission over Saarbrücken, Germany, when their Flying Fortress was seriously damaged by enemy fire. The bomb run was completed, but several crewmen were seriously wounded, and both the 21-year-old pilot and 22-year-old co-pilot realised that the most seriously injured member of the crew needed care that would probably not be available if he were parachuted over enemy territory. They decided to risk flying their crippled bomber back to Allied airspace and to attempt a crash landing.

When the damaged B-17 was sufficiently over Allied territory, the two pilots stayed aboard the plane with the seriously wounded man and maintained control while the others baled out. As Gott and Metzger attempted to crash land their bomber, flames streaking across its fuselage, the aircraft exploded just prior to reaching the ground. All three airmen aboard were killed.

On May 16, 1945, six months after their deaths, the brave pilot and co-pilot each received the Medal of Honor.

These are just a few of the many acts of bravery and intrepidity recorded by US airmen who flew aboard the B-17 Flying Fortress in World War Two that were deemed worthy of the Medal of Honor. Other posthumous recipients of the pale blue ribbon during the conflict include 2nd Lieutenant Robert Femoyer, Sergeant Archibald Mathies, 1st Lieutenant Walter E.Truemper, and Captain Harl Pease. First Lieutenants William R. Lawley, Edward Michael, and John C. Morgan, Staff Sergeant Maynard H. Smith, and Technical Sergeant Forrest L. Vosler survived their trials aboard the Flying Fortress to receive their medals for heroism.

LEFT: Staff Sergeant Maynard H. Smith receives the Medal of Honor from Secretary of War Henry L. Stimson. Public Domain US Air Force via Wikimedia Commons

LEFT: Second Lieutenant William E. Metzger, Jr., died alongside Donald Gott in the crash of their B-17 on November 9, 1944. Public Domain US Department of Defense via Wikimedia Commons

THE SAGA OF *MEMPHIS BELLE*

LEFT: The crew of *Memphis Belle*, 324th Bombardment Squadron, 91st Bombardment Group is shown in England after completing 25 missions. Public Domain media. defense.gov/2004/May/28/2000591581/-1/-1/0/021001-O-9999J-010.JPG via Wikimedia Commons

On May 19, 1943, the B-17F Flying Fortress *Memphis Belle*, 324th Bombardment Squadron, 91st Bombardment Group, lurched to a halt on the runway of its base at RAF Bassingbourn, Cambridgeshire. The big bomber had just completed its 25th mission against targets in continental Europe, a raid on U-boat pens and harbour facilities at Kiel, Germany, on the coast of the Baltic Sea.

B-17s that survived the ravages of the air war to complete 25 missions during World War Two were exceptional, and *Memphis Belle*'s accomplishment was significant to say the least. However, two other B-17s, *Hell's Angels* of the 303rd Bombardment Group and another bomber of the 91st Bombardment Group, *Delta Rebel No. 2* of the 323rd Bombardment Squadron, accomplished the feat earlier. *Delta Rebel No. 2* reached 25 missions on May 1, 1943, and *Hell's Angels* on May 13.

So why was *Memphis Belle* so celebrated? Nothing diminishes the heroism of the bombers' crews; however, circumstances contributed to the elevation of *Memphis Belle* to legendary and virtually mythical status, representative of the service, heroism, and sacrifice of all airmen of the Eighth Air Force and other US air forces that fought the Axis powers.

Memphis Belle was, in fact, the first B-17 to complete 25 missions and return to the United States. Its story would provide a substantial public relations opportunity for the Army Air Forces, and so the plane was sent on a war bond and recruiting tour across the country to stoke the patriotic fire of the citizenry.

Hell's Angels remained in action in the European theatre and completed 48 combat missions without serious damage or the loss of a crewman. Returning to the United States on February 10, 1944, *Hell's Angels* toured aircraft assembly plants around the country to inspire workers and encourage productivity. In 1945, this historic B-17 was sold for scrap.

Delta Rebel No. 2 came to a tragic end during a 91st Bombardment Group raid on the city of Gelsenkirchen, Germany, on August 12, 1944. The B-17 was damaged by a Luftwaffe fighter flown by a Hauptmann Naumann of JG 26 and then shot down by Oberfeldwebel Adolf Glunz, another JG 26 pilot, flying a Focke Wulf Fw-190 fighter. Four crewmen were killed in action, and the six survivors were taken prisoner.

By the time *Memphis Belle* had completed its 25th mission, the B-17 was already on its way to becoming famous. The 1944 release of the film documentary *Memphis Belle: A Story of a Flying Fortress* was coming up. Acclaimed Hollywood director William Wyler, serving in the First Motion Picture Unit, US Army Air Forces, with the rank of major, and his film crew flew several missions aboard B-17s, two of them with *Memphis Belle*, while capturing actual 16mm colour combat footage that was used in the making of the movie, including moments from *Memphis Belle*'s final mission. First Lieutenant Harold J. Tannenbaum,

LEFT: The B-17F *Memphis Belle* is shown at Patterson Field, Ohio, during its war bond tour. Public Domain US Air Force via Wikimedia Commons

BELOW: The famed B-17 *Memphis Belle* is shown in flight during its journey home for a war bond tour in 1943. Public Domain US Air Force via Wikimedia Commons

one of the three cinematographers working with Wyler, was killed in action on April 16, 1943, while filming aboard another bomber that was shot down over St. Nazaire, France. In 1990, nearly half a century after the end of World War Two, the feature film *Memphis Belle* further enhanced the story of the famed B-17.

Memphis Belle, worthy of remembrance in its own right, survived World War Two, and after years on loan to the city of Memphis, Tennessee, in 2005 the Flying Fortress was relocated to the National Museum of the United States Air Force at Wright-Patterson Air Force Base near Dayton, Ohio. Following an extensive and painstaking 13-year restoration project, *Memphis Belle* was placed on permanent display at the museum in May 2018, marking the 75th anniversary of the completion of its 25th mission.

Both *Memphis Belle* and *Hell's Angels* were candidates for adulation in the press and useful as public relations tools for recruiting and war bond drives. The officers of VIII Bomber Command looked at the records of both B-17s. *Memphis Belle* had flown its first combat mission on November 7, 1942, against the port of Brest, France, while *Hell's Angels* had followed just 10 days later with a mission to St. Nazaire. The crew of *Hell's Angels* had participated in all 25 missions intact. However, *Memphis Belle*'s original crewmen had flown as many as 21 missions aboard the bomber and crewed other B-17s while *Memphis Belle* was undergoing repairs after sustaining damage. A replacement crew had actually flown *Memphis Belle*'s 25th mission, and members of the original crew had completed their 25th mission on May 17, 1943, two days earlier than the famous bomber, having participated in a raid on the U-boat pens and port facilities at Lorient, France.

Weighing the best option, VIII Bomber Command concluded that *Memphis Belle* would serve first in the public relations role. On June 9, 1943, the pilot, 24-year-old Captain Robert Morgan, and crew flew from England aboard *Memphis Belle* for the United States. The crew headed stateside was actually assembled from airmen who had flown some missions aboard *Memphis Belle*, but the original crew had experienced some turnover between November 1942 and May 1943. Taking license, during the war bond tour the Army Air Forces presented the crew that it considered the most representative of completing 25 missions with *Memphis Belle*.

Records reveal, for example, that Captain James Verinis served as pilot for a single mission aboard *Memphis Belle* and flew a total of six with the famous B-17. Verinis completed 20 other missions aboard other B-17s, 19 as pilot of *Connecticut Yankee* and one aboard *Our Gang*. Verinis, though, was presented as the co-pilot of *Memphis Belle* throughout the 31-city war bond tour. The Army Air Forces even published a brochure that stretched the truth with the statement, "With its distinguished crew, which has remained intact since its formation 10 months ago, the ship has been returned to the United States for another – and no less important – mission."

Memphis Belle was completed at the Boeing facility in Seattle, Washington, in 1942 as B-17F-10-BO with manufacturer's serial number 3470 and Army Air Corps serial number 41-24485. The bomber was named after Captain Morgan's girlfriend, Margaret Polk. *Memphis Belle* received significant combat damage for the first time on its ninth mission, an attack on Lorient on January 23, 1943. During its tour of duty, the B-17 sustained damage on at least two other occasions, and engine problems that necessitated returning to base before dropping its bombload occurred as well.

Following the war bond tour, *Memphis Belle* returned to duty as a trainer at MacDill Airfield, Florida. With the end of the war, it appeared that the historic aircraft's days were numbered. Flown to Altus Army Airfield, Oklahoma, in anticipation of its being scrapped along with hundreds of other surplus warplanes, the B-17 received an unexpected reprieve when Mayor Walter Chandler of Memphis, Tennessee, authorised a payment of $350 for the plane that bore his city's name. Placed in storage until 1949, *Memphis Belle* was later on public display at the local National Guard armoury.

By the 1980s, the bomber's condition had deteriorated due to exposure to the elements and the ravages of souvenir hunters. Though the city had returned ownership to the US Air Force a decade earlier, the military allowed Memphis to retain the aircraft with the expectation that it would be restored. *Memphis Belle* was moved to indoor storage from time to time but remained in poor condition.

Finally, the National Museum of the US Air Force took possession and embarked on the lengthy restoration project. The plane was refurbished and painted in its original combat colour scheme. While its story is an amalgamation of myth, legend, fact, and fiction, the *Memphis Belle* is visited by thousands annually, providing a tangible and awe-inspiring visual testament to the men who flew in wartime many years ago.

ABOVE: Crew members of *Memphis Belle* are shown as luncheon guests at the US House of Representatives. Public Domain National Archives and Records Administration via Wikimedia Commons

ABOVE LEFT: Captain Robert Morgan is remembered as the pilot of *Memphis Belle* and also flew the B-29 Superfortress in the Pacific. Public Domain Jack1956 at English Wikipedia via Wikimedia Commons

LEFT: The restored B-17F *Memphis Belle* is shown on permanent display at the National Museum of the US Air Force at Wright-Patterson Air Force Base near Dayton, Ohio. Public Domain US Air Force National Museum of the US Air Force via Wikimedia Commons

MEMORABLE FLYING FORTRESS MISSIONS

The B-17F *Piccadilly Lily* was the lead plane in the low squadron, 17th to take off that morning of October 8, 1943. The target was Bremen, Germany, and the mission had been delayed twice by stubborn cloud cover.

On board was crew no. 22, considerably altered in makeup since its formation at Gowen Field, Idaho, on January 2, 1943. Actually, a couple of men had completed their combat tours while others had been reassigned for various reasons. One had been injured in an accident at the 100th Bombardment Group's base, Thorpe Abbotts, Norfolk.

Three crewmen, pilot Captain Thomas E. Murphy, navigator Charles Sarabun, and bombardier Floyd Peterson, were members of the original crew. Ironically, they had been reassigned before this mission only to be abruptly recalled when, for reasons that remain unclear, their replacements were delayed. The three did not grumble; they simply retrieved the flight gear they had turned in earlier that morning. A late addition to the crew was Captain Alvin Barker, the 351st Bombardment Squadron's operations officer. *Piccadilly Lily* carried 11 men when the big bomber finally lifted off sometime after 11:30am, and Barker flew in the co-pilot's seat.

While flying over the coast of Nazi-occupied Europe, navigators quipped warnings to be alert for Luftwaffe fighters. A few minutes later, a German Focke Wulf Fw-190 came flashing through the 100th. A bright orange fireball marked the fighter's collision with a B-17 in mid-air. But the sky was full of fighters and flak. There was little time to contemplate what had happened.

The anti-aircraft fire over Bremen was intense, and just after *Piccadilly Lily* had lined up – at its most vulnerable moment during the entire mission – a heavy flak burst shook the big bomber. The nose and radio compartments were hit, and two crewmen were killed outright. Murphy, however, stayed on course as no mortal damage had been inflicted to the aircraft itself. When the lead B-17 released its bombs, the others in

ABOVE: A B-17G Flying Fortress undergoes restoration to flight capability at the Planes of Fame Museum in Chino, California, before being named *Piccadilly Lily II*. Creative Commons Tomas Del Coro via Wikimedia Commons

LEFT: **The B-17 *All American* returns to base with extensive damage to its aft fuselage after a collision with a German fighter in North African skies in 1942.** Public Domain US Air Force via Wikimedia Commons

LEFT: This close-up photo reveals the heavy damage suffered by the B-17 *All American* in a collision with a German Focke Wulf Fw-190 fighter. Public Domain US Air Force via Wikimedia Commons

formation followed suit. Then, a second massive blast of flak struck as *Piccadilly Lily* lifted upward, lightened after jettisoning nearly 4,000lb of bombs.

Murphy and Barker fought the controls, buying time for the others to attempt to bale out. The no. 3 engine nacelle burned furiously. Before they could extricate themselves, *Piccadilly Lily* exploded in a ball of fire, smoke, and debris. Marshall Lee, the listed co-pilot for the mission, was also still aboard. All three perished immediately. In all, six men were killed in action, while five became prisoners of war. The 100th Bombardment Group lost seven Flying Fortresses that day over Bremen. Seventy-two men were missing, 31 of whom were later confirmed as killed in action.

Though tragic, the terrible end of *Piccadilly Lily* was not, in itself, uncommon during the combat journey of the 'Bloody Hundredth' Bombardment Group. But *Piccadilly Lily* can rightly lay claim as one of the most famous B-17s of World War Two. In a sequence of the famous film *Twelve O'Clock High*, one of the bombers flying in formation is clearly emblazoned with the name of *Piccadilly Lily.* Former Thorpe Abbotts ground crewman John Herman, who had waited vainly for *Piccadilly Lily* to return from the Bremen mission, left a 1949 screening of the acclaimed film deeply moved.

Herman wrote a letter to Beirne Lay, Jr., co-author of the book and of the screenplay that inspired the movie *Twelve O'Clock High*, and he was startled to read the reply he received. "You're darn right," it read in part, "…The *Piccadilly Lily* in 'TWELVE O'CLOCK HIGH' was named after your B-17. I put it into the script for sentimental reasons…." Lay had visited Thorpe Abbotts in 1943 and flown into combat aboard *Piccadilly Lily.*

The 414th Bombardment Squadron, 97th Bombardment Group was based at Biskra, Algeria, in early 1943, and on February 1, the B-17F *All American* took to the air in formation with

others to attack the port facilities at the cities of Bizerte and Tunis, Tunisia. Bursts of flak shook *All American*, and German fighters whizzed through the bomber formations, but the payloads were delivered. As *All American* turned for home, however, the ordeal was far from over. Messerschmitt Me-109 fighters harassed the Flying Fortresses on their return flight, and just as it appeared the melee was dissipating, a pair of enemy pilots pressed in for one last pass.

One of the Me-109 pilots made a head-on attack at the lead B-17, while the second came straight for the nose of *All American.* Concentrated fire sent the first Me-109 spinning toward the ground and trailing smoke. The second, probably piloted by Feldwebel Erich Paczia, an ace with 16 victories, began to peel away, but with the Paczia evidently killed or wounded the Me-109 did not complete the manoeuvre and evidently passed within inches of a full mid-air collision. As it was, the fighter gashed the B-17's fuselage and clipped off its left horizontal stabiliser. The bomber vibrated heavily, and it appeared that the remainder of the tail section might twist apart at any time. The crew donned parachutes and waited.

Miraculously, *All American* returned to base, landing without its tail wheel, which had been torn away. The aircraft was repaired and continued to serve as a utility, or hack, aircraft until March 1945.

Colonel Robert Rosenthal, pilot of the only 100th Bombardment Group B-17 of 13 that took off to bomb Münster on October 10, 1943, later survived the shootdown of his bomber in a September 1944 mission. He was badly injured, with a broken nose and right arm, but evaded capture with the help of the French resistance.

On February 3, 1945, Rosenthal piloted the lead Flying Fortress on a raid against the Nazi capital of Berlin. His B-17 was hit by flak and in flames, but the pilot stayed in formation to drop his bombs and then remained at the controls while the rest of the crew baled out. Rosenthal got out just before the plane exploded only 1,000ft above the ground. He was rescued by a unit of the Soviet Red Army and again made it back to England. That particular raid hit administrative buildings in Berlin and killed fanatical Judge Roland Freisler, notorious for his persecution of Germans, military and civilian, who opposed the Nazi regime.

After the war, Rosenthal, an attorney, interrogated former Luftwaffe chief Reichsmarschall Hermann Göring and served as an assistant prosecutor at the Nuremburg Trials.

One of the most incredible individual survival stories of World War Two occurred on January 3, 1943, when the B-17 *Snap! Crackle! Pop!* of the 360th Bombardment Squadron, 303rd Bombardment Group attacked the Nazi U-boat pens and port installations at St. Nazaire, France. It was the seventh combat mission for Staff Sergeant Alan Magee and just days before his 24th birthday.

German flak inflicted significant damage on the Flying Fortress, and Magee was forced to abandon his position in the now useless ball turret. He quickly discovered that his parachute had been shredded, and then a second blast of flak blew off a portion of the bomber's right wing. As the plane »

LEFT: General Robert Travis led the costly bombing mission to Stuttgart, Germany, on September 6, 1943. Public Domain US Air Force via Wikimedia Commons

BELOW LEFT: The B-17 *Big Yank* taxies while on a runway in England. Note the missions recorded on its nose. Public Domain National Archives and Records Administration

BELOW RIGHT: The nose of the B-17 *Big Yank* bore a portrait of President Franklin D. Roosevelt. Public Domain National Archives and Records Administration via Wikimedia Commons

RIGHT: A Messerschmitt Me-262 jet fighter is shown in the gun camera of a US P-51 Mustang fighter. B-17 gunner Babe Broyhill shot down a pair of Me-262s on a single bombing mission. Public Domain US Air Force via Wikimedia Commons

nosed down into a death spiral, Magee lost consciousness due to a lack of oxygen. He had moved from the bomb bay to the radio room and was somehow ejected from the plane. In freefall for roughly 21,000ft, an altitude of four miles, Magee came to earth after falling through the roof of the St. Nazaire railroad station. He had plunged through the station's glass ceiling, which probably slowed his descent enough to survive impact with the floor.

Taken prisoner, Magee was treated for broken bones, the traumatic near-amputation of his right arm, and injuries to his nose, lungs, and kidneys. He was liberated from a German prison camp in May 1945 and visited St. Nazaire on the 50th anniversary of the unforgettable raid in 1993, when statue was unveiled to memorialise the crew of *Snap! Crackle! Pop!*

On September 6, 1943, the Eighth Air Force target for the day was the Bosch manufacturing complex at Stuttgart, Germany, where an estimated 90% of the magnetos and fuel injection nozzles for engines were being manufactured. A total of 388 Flying Fortresses from 16 bomber groups took to the air that day, and for those who participated the raid was one of the most harrowing experiences of the air war in Europe. Mission No. 91 covered 1,200 miles and seven hours in the air. Thick cloud cover prevented many of the B-17s from hitting the primary target, and 45 B-17s were shot down with 335 men listed initially as killed in action or missing.

The cloud cover had rolled in unexpectedly, and the Flying Fortresses at 25,000ft were ordered to circle the target by General Robert Travis, the commander of the mission. Travis wanted better bombing conditions, but the aircrews were ravaged continually by Luftwaffe fighters and intense anti-aircraft fire as they complied with the order. Three passes were made, and a half hour was spent over the target before bombs were released. Many of the planes that returned had sustained damage during the extended manoeuvre, and precious fuel had been expended to the extent that some planes came back to base with little left. Needless to say, such missions brought morale among the bomber crews to a nadir, some questioning the sanity of the air commanders. One bomber crewman lamented: "We began to wonder if they were trying to kill all of us."

General Travis completed 35 combat missions during World War Two. Among his awards were the Distinguished Service Cross, Silver Star, Distinguished Flying Cross, and Purple Heart. He died of injuries received in a plane crash in 1950.

Twenty-year-old Lincoln 'Babe' Broyhill sat in the tail gunner's position aboard the B-17 *Big Yank* of the 840th Bombardment Squadron, 483rd Bombardment Group, on March 24, 1945. The target for the day was the Daimler-Benz tank factory located on the outskirts of Berlin, and the area was vigorously defended by Luftwaffe fighters, many of them the revolutionary jet Messerschmitt Me-262.

As the German fighters mounted their attacks, Broyhill started firing his .50-calibre machine guns and became a record setter. "The first made a pass at 200 yards, and my tracers were going right into its fuselage," he later recalled. "Suddenly, it went down in flames. The second came into my sights after the first had dropped. I kept shooting away because he was getting into my hair. Suddenly, it also spiralled down."

The Me-262 was the most advanced fighter plane of World War Two, and Broyhill's remarkable feat was one of several. Another gunner on *Big Yank* was credited with a jet, and the B-17 set the wartime record for Me-262s shot down in a single mission. The 483rd Bombardment Group also claimed a record six enemy jet fighters that day. Broyhill survived the war to become a successful real estate developer in Virginia. He died in 2008 at age 83.

The last B-17 shot down during World War Two was actually participating in Operation Chowhound, a mission of mercy. On May 7, 1945, hours before the German surrender, the bomber was shot down by a flak battery while dropping much-needed food to starving civilians in the Netherlands, their flow of supplies cut off by the Nazis in retaliation for Dutch resistance operations. The Flying Fortress belonged to the 95th Bombardment Group, which flew 270 missions during the war, 214 of them over Germany.

Two of the 10 crewmen parachuted from their burning B-17 on that fateful mission. The remaining men died in the crash. Ironically, the last Flying Fortress lost to enemy fire had gone down trying to save lives.

RIGHT: A German Messerschmitt Me-262 jet fighter sits at an airfield late in World War Two. Babe Broyhill and a fellow gunner aboard his B-17 shot down three jets in one mission. Public Domain Government of Japan 1899 Copyright Act of Japan via Wikimedia Commons

RIGHT: A B-17 Flying Fortress airdrops food to the starving people of the Netherlands during Operation Chowhound. Creative Commons Dutch Ministry of Defence vial Wikimedia Commons

REPORTERS RIDE ALONG

An enterprising Army Air Forces public relations officer had dubbed them the 'Writing 69th', a pun referencing the US Army's 69th Infantry Regiment, which had earned a reputation for excellence in ground combat and a lineage that included the Great War and stretched back even to the American Civil War.

The Writing 69th, however, was quite a different outfit. Rather, more specifically, these men were eight journalists working for various news agencies and reporting on World War Two in Europe. As America's military commitment to the conflict expanded, war correspondents were provided with special status. They were treated as officers, although without rank, and wore a sleeve badge emblazoned with the letter 'C' for correspondent.

In early 1943, the Writing 69th was busy covering the air war in Europe, particularly the growing presence of the US Eighth Air Force. The group's roster included Andy Rooney of the Army newspaper *Stars and Stripes*, Walter Cronkite of United Press, Gladwin Hill of the Associated Press, William Wade of the International News Service, Homer Bigart of the *New York Herald Tribune*, Robert Post of the *New York Times*, Paul Manning of CBS radio, and Denton Scott of *Yank*, the US Army's own weekly magazine.

Based in England, the reporters of the Writing 69th were given access to the crews of Eighth Air Force bombers, who had returned from missions over Nazi-occupied Europe and the Third Reich itself. Their stories and broadcasts were popular reading with military personnel and the American public back home. The group was among the trailblazers who defined the role of the journalist in modern wartime. Decades after the war, Rooney achieved fame as an editorial commentator on the CBS television news magazine *Sixty Minutes*. Cronkite would go on to anchor the CBS Evening News and achieve esteem seldom realised among news reporters. For 19 years he ended his nightly broadcasts with "And that's the way it is..." and he earned the moniker of the "most trusted man in America."

Rooney and Cronkite became close friends, and with the other journalists of the Writing 69th, they circulated among the young airmen who were risking their lives day in and day out in the burgeoning bombing campaign. "Every time there was a raid, we would split up and each go to a different bomber group," he told an interviewer years later. "Then, when the crews came back, we would interview them. And sometimes they didn't come back. We, on the other hand, went back to our flats in London and lived quite a comfortable life.

"After a while," Rooney continued, "we saw so many people we had gotten to know who were shot down, taken prisoner, or killed that we all began to feel guilty about covering this war the way we were. It just seemed wrong to us. I don't know who decided to do it, but we decided we'd better go on a bombing raid ourselves. Though correspondents were never supposed to man a gun or carry any kind of a weapon, we were all forced to go to gunnery school; we practiced gunnery in case they needed us in the air."

That so-called 'guilt' motivated the reporters. They did undergo a week of intensive training, which also covered aircraft identification, operating a parachute, adjusting to high altitudes, and other basic skills required of combat airmen. Of course, handling any weapon was a violation of the Geneva Convention, but this was war, and such a detail was apparently dismissed without much concern.

When the day arrived, the reporters were each assigned to a particular plane and crew, some of them aboard Boeing B-17 Flying Fortresses, and others aboard Consolidated B-24 Liberators. February 26, 1943, would be unforgettable. Seventy-six B-17s and 17 B-24s from six bombardment groups were assigned to attack the Focke Wulf aircraft assembly plant at Bremen, Germany. However, thick cloud cover obscured the initial »

LEFT: Journalists of the Writing 69th suit up during flight training. Walter Cronkite is at centre. Public Domain US Army Air Forces via Wikimedia Commons

LEFT: Andy Rooney, photographed in 2008, flew aboard a B-17 during the combat mission of February 26, 1943. Creative Commons Stephenson Brown via Wikimedia Commons

LEFT: Walter Cronkite, shown in 1983, wrote a vivid account of his experience over Wilhelmshaven. Creative Commons Bernard Gotfryd photograph collection Library of Congress via Wikimedia Commons

target, and an alternate choice, the port facilities at Wilhelmshaven, was bombed instead. There was no fighter escort that would accompany the bombers all the way to their target and back. The limited range of the available Supermarine Spitfires, Republic P-47 Thunderbolts, and Lockheed P-38 Lightnings meant that the big bombers would fly at least part of the way to and from the target on their own.

"The raid we went on was only the second raid into Germany," said Rooney. "It was on Wilhelmshaven. I got in my bomber, and I thought to myself, 'Why am I doing this? I'm scared to death. I mean, I don't have to risk my life' – except that I felt so bad for all the men who did have to risk their lives all those times that it just seemed like it was the honest thing to do."

No doubt, the other reporters felt the same pangs of genuine loss and a determination that in order to really report on the experience of air combat they would have to live it.

The B-17s and B-24s lifted into the grey skies over England and made their way toward enemy airspace. The raid was redirected, and the bombs were dropped. After action reports indicated the 59 B-17s reached Wilhelmshaven, while only six of the B-24s were assessed to have effectively hit the target during the raid. Claims of Luftwaffe fighters shot down appear wildly inflated at 21 destroyed, nine probables, and five damaged. Records indicate that when the air fight was over 13 American bombers failed to return to their bases.

Rooney recalled the preparation for take-off. "I remember we had these heavy flak jackets. A B-17 is not like a modern airliner. Wires and everything were all over, and getting through the bomb bay to the back – which would be the cabin in a passenger plane now – was very difficult. If you had a parachute on, it was tough to get past all the wires without getting snagged on everything. So I didn't wear my flak jacket. I stood on it. I had this feeling that I didn't want to be hit from underneath, but of course what happened was the flak exploded in the air around you and didn't necessarily come from below."

Cronkite clambered aboard a B-17 of the 303rd Bombardment Group, flying from RAF Molesworth in Cambridgeshire. When German fighters were encountered, he was given an opportunity to fire a machine gun at the enemy. In his 1996 book *A Reporter's Life*, he wrote, "I fired at every German fighter that came into the neighborhood. I don't think I hit any, but I'd like to think I scared a couple of those pilots…I could hardly get out of the plane when we got back – I was up to my hips in spent .50 caliber shells…."

A short while later, Cronkite sat down to type his story for United Press. His perspective had been obviously altered after experiencing the crucible of combat. "American Flying Fortresses have just come back from an assignment to hell," he wrote, "a hell 26,000 feet above the earth, a hell of burning tracer bullets and bursting gunfire, of crippled Fortresses and burning German fighter planes, of parachuting men

ABOVE: A B-17 of the 303rd Bombardment Group drops its bombs. Walter Cronkite flew with the 303rd against Wilhelmshaven on February 26, 1943. Public Domain US Army Air Forces via Wikimedia Commons

LEFT: A B-17 of the 359th Bombardment Squadron 303rd Bombardment Group, flies over its base at RAF Molesworth. Public Domain US Air Force via Wikimedia Commons

LEFT: Walter Cronkite fired a B-17's .50-calibre machine guns at Luftwaffe fighters like this Focke Wulf Fw-190 during the mission of February 26, 1943. Public Domain National Museum of the US Air Force via Wikimedia Commons

RIGHT: In his article on the mission to Wilhelmshaven, Andy Rooney described the cramped interior of the B-17 Flying Fortress. Creative Commons Duch via Wikimedia Commons

RIGHT: A B-17 takes off in this 2010 image. Writing 69th participants in the raid on Wilhelmshaven carried the memory for the rest of their lives. Creative Commons Bill Larkins via Wikimedia Commons

and others not so lucky. I have just returned with a Flying Fortress crew from Wilhelmshaven…Actually the first impression of a daylight bombing mission is a hodge-podge of disconnected scenes. Things like bombs falling past you from the formation above, a crippled bomber with smoke pouring from one engine thousands of feet below. A Focke Wulf peeling off somewhere above and plummeting down shooting its way through the formation."

For the *New York Herald Tribune*, Bigart wrote: "A mission to Germany is a nasty experience. Apart from the very real danger to life and limb, there is the acute discomfort of enduring sub-zero temperatures for hours at a stretch and taking air through an oxygen mask. The altitude can affect your sinews, your kidneys, even the fillings of your teeth. You are very tired when you return. If you are a delayed-reaction type, you are likely to feel slightly under par for a couple of days. I must be crazy, but I should like to go again."

Rooney told the story that he believed was the best of all. In the pages of *Stars and Stripes*, he had written of flak damage to his B-17. He noted that pilots might manoeuvre to avoid flak until the moment that the final bombing run began, and the plane had to fly straight and steady.

"That plane was a perfect target for the gunners from underneath, and that was the frightening part of it – you just had to sit there," Rooney commented. "…I was up in the nose of the plane, and a shell came in and took a small piece of the Plexiglas nose off. The bombardier, who was in front of me, panicked and tried to stuff something in the hole. At seventeen or eighteen thousand feet the air coming in is subzero, and he took his gloves off. His hands froze and it was terrible."

Rooney continued: "I looked across at the little desk that the navigator used. His oxygen tube had been pierced and he lost his oxygen, and at eighteen thousand feet he collapsed. So I got to the pilot intercom and I asked him what to do. He said, 'Well, we have emergency air in oxygen bottles up behind me. Take some deep breaths and come back up behind me and get the oxygen bottle; bring it back down and hook him up to that.' Well I didn't know how to do any of this and here I was, with somebody's life at stake, and I didn't know how long you lasted once you took your oxygen mask off. But I took some deep breaths, I took my oxygen mask off, and went through this alleyway up behind the pilot. There I got an oxygen bottle and hooked up the navigator, who was a much more experienced flyer than the bombardier. He regained consciousness and got the bombardier quieted down. So I had by far the best story to tell of all the correspondents who went out that day."

One of the correspondents, Post of the *New York Times*, failed to return. The B-24 which he was aboard was hit by German flak and exploded in midair, killing Post and several members of the crew. His death officially ended the Army Air Force's sanctioning of correspondents flying into combat. Some men of the Writing 69th who missed the mission of February 26, 1943, were said to have made flights on their own afterward.

The lives of those journalists who had joined bomber crews in the embattled skies over Europe were forever changed.

BELOW: This B-17 Flying Fortress of the 359th Bombardment Squadron, 303rd Bombardment Group, made a belly landing at RAF Molesworth after a mission in 1943. Public Domain US Air Force via Wikimedia Commons

OPERATION APHRODITE

It had been quite an experiment. But ultimately, the idea of remotely controlled B-17 Flying Fortress bombers, filled to the brim with British Torpex high explosive half again as powerful as TNT, and crashing into high value targets in Nazi-occupied Germany had failed.

Dubbed Operation Aphrodite, the project was undertaken in the spring of 1944 by the US Army Air Forces alongside a US Navy effort code named Operation Anvil. The high-tech endeavour was born of two circumstances – first, the frustration of Allied air planners surrounding the destruction of some hard targets such as Nazi U-boat pens and V-1 and V-2 terror weapon launch sites, and second, the realisation that the Germans had surpassed the Allies in the development and deployment of unmanned, radio-guided weaponry.

General Jimmy Doolittle, commander of the US Eighth Air Force in Britain, is credited with the concept of Operation Aphrodite and received approval to proceed, assigning the 3rd Bombardment Division with preparations to launch 'war weary' Flying Fortresses, bombers that had essentially been worn out from lengthy use and were in their last days of effective service, against targets across the European continent. While the army was to employ B-17s, the navy contributed some of its equally worn out Consolidated PBY Catalina flying boats, and the Consolidated B-24 Liberator bomber was also eventually used. Subsequently, the 562nd Bomb Squadron based at RAF Honington in Suffolk was chosen to train and execute the program.

In theory, the B-17s, designated BQ-7s, were to be stripped of all unnecessary equipment and armament, reducing their weight, and allowing a high explosive 12,000lb payload weighing significantly more than the normal bomb-carrying capacity of the Flying Fortress to be packed aboard. The aircraft, or drone, was to be flown by a pilot and co-pilot or flight engineer who would parachute from the plane at the appropriate time, turning over control to personnel aboard an accompanying mother ship, the CQ-4, after arming the explosives and activating the autopilot and remote control equipment along with two cameras, primitive television apparatus recently developed by the Radio Corporation of America (RCA). The drone would then be deliberately flown into the target to detonate on impact. Pilots and crewmen involved in Aphrodite were all volunteers, and their charge was to take the drone to 2,000ft prior to transferring control to the mother ship.

The relatively primitive nature of the remote control and television equipment contributed to the necessity of the pilot and co-pilot flying the drone aircraft for a period of time during each

LEFT: An RAF Handley Page Halifax bomber flies over the artillery emplacements at Mimoyecques on July 6, 1944. When conventional bombing failed, the target was given to Operation Aphrodite. Public Domain collections of the Imperial War Museums via Wikimedia Commons

LEFT: US Navy Lieutenant Joseph P. Kennedy, Jr., lost his life while piloting a drone during Operation Aphrodite. Public Domain John F. Kennedy Presidential Library and Museum via Wikimedia Commons

BELOW: This B-17F, nicknamed Careful Virgin, completed 80 missions with the 323rd Bombardment Squadron and was then detailed as expendable to Operation Aphrodite. Public Domain US Air Force via Wikimedia Commons

RIGHT: A radio-controlled B-17 Flying Fortress bomber takes off during tests of Operation Aphrodite at RAF Fersfield. Public Domain US Air Force via Wikimedia Commons

mission. Needless to say, these missions would be fraught with risk. The drones were susceptible to German fighter attack, flak, and the instability of their substantial explosive cargoes. Further, the human crew would compensate for the risk that the drone might become uncontrollable and crash into a residential area or military base in Britain with catastrophic results.

At first, the long runway at RAF Woodbridge seemed ideal for the Operation Aphrodite launch site; however, the real possibility that incoming damaged aircraft might collide with drones caused the programme to be relocated to RAF Fersfield, home of the 38th Bomb Group, a more secluded location in Norfolk.

The first Aphrodite missions were flown on August 4, 1944, and involved four B-17s slated to hit Nazi V-1 bunkers at Siracourt in French Calais, a complex of 150mm artillery weapons positioned at Mimoyecques in northern France and with range to hit targets in Britain, and the bunkers of the V-2 rocket launch facilities at La Coupole, Wizernes, in the Pas-de-Calais.

One of the drone aircraft was armed and exited by its pilot and engineer but spun out of control before reaching its target at Mimoyecques. The B-17 intended for Siracourt experienced control problems from the outset and crashed into a wooded area near Sudbourne, killing the pilot. Two B-17s scheduled to hit Wizernes were both lost, the first crashing near Orford after one of the crewmen managed to bale out, its blast devastating an area of more than two acres. Both airmen died. The second Wizernes plane crashed an estimated 1,500ft from its intended target after apparent cloud cover obscured the view from its nose.

Three days later, more Aphrodite missions were mounted with similar dismal results. Two B-17s crashed into the English Channel, while a third was shot down by enemy fire over Gravelines, France. A crewman aboard another B-17 was killed as he attempted to bale out. That aircraft continued toward its target in German Heligoland in the province of Schleswig-Holstein but was lost to enemy fire before reaching its objective. On September 3, 1944, a single B-17 was sent aloft to hit the U-boat pens at Heide, a German village on the coast of Heligoland. The US Navy controller mistakenly guided the drone to crash on nearby Düne Island, causing no appreciable damage. A week later, another attempt was made to strike the U-boat pens. The drone came close to its target but was shot down by ground fire.

The attack on Wizernes was perhaps the closest an Operation Aphrodite aircraft came to succeeding in its task. Scarcely more than a dozen attempts were made between August 1944 and the suspension of Aphrodite in early 1945 as Allied troops overran many of the erstwhile intended targets and the programme was proving difficult to maintain. On January 27, General Carl 'Tooey' Spaatz, commander of US Strategic Air Forces in Europe, ordered Doolittle: "Aphrodite babies must not be launched against the enemy until further notice."

Operation Aphrodite is best known for claiming the life of Lieutenant Joseph P. Kennedy, Jr., the scion of a wealthy and politically involved New England family. Kennedy, the son of the former US Ambassador to Great Britain, and his flight engineer, Lieutenant Wilford J. Willy, were detailed for another try at Mimoyecques on August 12, 1944. They climbed aboard a modified PB4Y1, the navy variant of the B-24 Liberator bomber, its nose and fuselage packed with more than 21,000lb of Torpex, and took off.

As their aircraft approached the coastline near Halesworth, the crewmen turned over control to their Lockheed Ventura mother ships. Willy activated the television equipment, while Kennedy armed the explosives. For a moment, everything seemed to proceed according to plan. At 6:20pm, however, tragedy struck. A massive explosion destroyed the drone aircraft and killed both Kennedy and Willy.

The death of Lieutenant Kennedy punctuated the high risk associated with Operation Aphrodite. The award of the Navy Cross, Distinguished Flying Cross, and Air Medal to both men was little consolation for their families. The Kennedys had hoped to see their young naval officer pursue a postwar political career that would include a run to the White House. As events turned out, that lofty ambition was left for the second son, John F. Kennedy, a naval hero in his own right, to achieve in 1960.

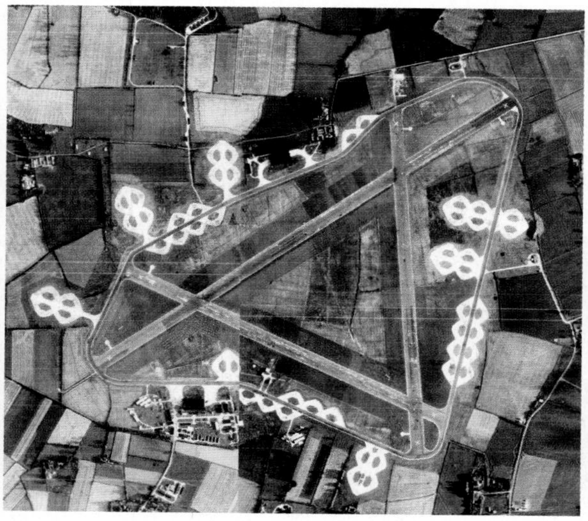

BELOW LEFT: This aerial view taken shortly after World War Two depicts RAF Fersfield, where Operation Aphrodite was centred. Public Domain United Kingdom Government via Wikimedia Commons

BELOW RIGHT: This last known photo of Joseph P. Kennedy, Jr., was taken the day he died before the mission of August 12, 1944, during Operation Aphrodite. Public Domain a scan of the original photo taken by Earl P. Olsen via Wikimedia Commons

OPERATION FRANTIC

RIGHT: B-17s of the 97th and 99th Bombardment Groups return to their airfield at Amendola, Italy, during Operation Frantic in 1944. Public Domain US Air Force via Wikimedia Commons

It was an unusual sight. On the afternoon of June 2, 1944, the first of 129 US Army Air Forces B-17 Flying Fortress bombers began to arrive at the airbase at Poltava in central Ukraine and two other locations not far away. The bombers were accompanied by 64 US fighter planes serving as escort, and together these were the vanguard of Operation Frantic, a programme that had been long considered and painstakingly put together in cooperation with the Soviet Union.

Operation Frantic, if successful, would allow American bombers of the Eighth and Fifteenth Air Forces to conduct long-range missions, striking targets in eastern Germany and across eastern Europe, then land at Soviet airfields to refuel and rearm before setting out to bomb enemy targets on the return flights to their home airfields in England and Italy. Senior American air commanders considered the idea of shuttle bombing valid for several reasons. Luftwaffe air defences would be stretched to defend high-priority targets as the D-Day invasion approached, while heavy bombing would more easily reach locations in eastern Europe. Shuttle bombing would reinforce the common cause of the US and the Soviet Union in the defeat of the Nazis and might lead to future agreement in using bases in Siberia to bomb the home islands of Japan.

RIGHT: Soviet General Alexander Perminov welcomed the B-17s of the first Operation Frantic combat mission at Poltava. Creative Commons novayagazeta.ru/articles/2020/04/27/85125-krylom-k-krylu via Wikimedia Commons

When the Americans first proposed the idea to the Soviets in mid-1942, the response was lukewarm at best. The subject was raised again during the Moscow Conference of October 1943; however, little progress was made until President Franklin D. Roosevelt approached Soviet Premier Josef Stalin directly at the Tehran Conference in November 1943. Stalin gave the go-ahead in February 1944.

Three bases, Poltava, Piryatin, and Mirgorod, each within 50 miles of one another and located about 450 miles southwest of Moscow, were selected, and Poltava became the eastern headquarters of Operation Frantic. American command was handed to General Carl 'Tooey' Spaatz, head of US Strategic Air Forces in Europe. The first combat mission was accompanied by some ceremony on June 2, 1944. General Ira C. Eaker, commander of Allied Air Forces in the Mediterranean, arrived aboard one of the B-17s and pinned the American Legion of Merit medal to the chest of welcoming Soviet General Alexei Perminov. Handshakes, cigars, and bouquets of flowers were exchanged, and Averill Harriman, US Ambassador to the Soviet Union, was on hand to impress upon the always suspicious Soviets the importance the Americans were placing on the cooperative endeavour.

Although it was undertaken with high hopes, Operation Frantic was destined to fail, lasting only four months, and encompassing a handful of offensive shuttle bombing raids and fighter sweeps. At least 10 B-17 bombardment groups, including the 95th, 96th, 100th, 388th, 390th, and 452nd of the Eighth Air Force flying from England and the 2nd, 97th, 99th, and 483rd of the Fifteenth Air Force flying from Italy, took part.

Four days after arrival in the Soviet Union, American bombers took off from their airfields and attacked the enemy air base at Galati, Romania. They returned to the Soviet bases until June 11, when they struck other targets in Romania on their flights back to Italy. The second shuttle mission occurred on June 21, when a heavy raid against the Nazi capital of

BELOW: After the destructive Nazi raid on the airfield at Poltava, the remains of a burnt out B-17 lie crumpled. Public Domain US Air Force via Wikimedia Commons

Berlin included 22 bomber groups of the Eighth Air Force. When the bulk of the bombers and fighters turned back toward England, 140 Flying Fortresses and 65 North American P-51 fighters earmarked for Operation Frantic continued to Poltava and Mirgorod, touching down after a gruelling 11 hours in the air.

Unknown to the Americans, they had been shadowed by a German Heinkel He-177 long-range bomber used in a reconnaissance role. The bases at Poltava and Mirgorod were photographed, and the intelligence set the stage for a terrible blow to the future of Operation Frantic. Shortly after 11pm on the night of June 21, a force of 150 German Heinkel He-111 and Junkers Ju-88 bombers swept over Poltava and wreaked havoc, dropping 110 tons of bombs. The raid lasted one hour and 40 minutes, and the destruction was widespread. Forty-seven B-17s were assessed as 'destroyed or damaged beyond economical repair'.

Every other Flying Fortress on the field, as well as other aircraft, had sustained some degree of damage. Roughly 2,000 bombs, 400,000 rounds of .50-calibre ammunition, and 200,000 gallons of precious aviation fuel had been consumed. Miraculously, only two American airmen were killed, while the Soviets suffered 34 dead and more than 60 wounded. A second Luftwaffe raid struck Mirgorod the following night, and substantial ordnance was lost along with another 200,000 gallons of aviation fuel, and more aircraft were destroyed on the ground.

In the wake of the Poltava debacle, Operation Frantic continued from the unscathed base at Piryatin, as well as the wounded Poltava and Mirgorod, when 72 B-17s bombed the oil refinery at Drohobycz in Nazi-occupied Poland on June 26. Every bomber safely returned to base in Italy. Still, Poltava inevitably created an increasing air of mistrust between the Americans and their Soviet hosts. Each side blamed the other for an intelligence failure, the lack of a coordinated response to

LEFT: Soviet soldiers stand with a B-17 Flying Fortress damaged during Operation Frantic at the Poltava airfield, June 22, 1944. Public Domain US Air Force via Wikimedia Commons

the German air raids, and even the ability of the Soviets to adequately protect American bombers with sufficient anti-aircraft assets.

Operation Frantic fighter sweeps were conducted in support of advancing Red Army ground troops, while air bases in Hungary were bombed. On August 6, mission Frantic V unleashed 76 Flying Fortresses and their escort of 64 Mustangs against an aircraft assembly plant at Gdynia, Poland. Two German planes were shot down, and there were no American losses. Bad weather hampered air operations for several weeks, and the advancing Red Army captured territory that eliminated the need for further bombing in the area.

On September 11, Eighth Air Force bombers raided an armaments factory at Chemnitz, Germany. They followed up two days later, bombing the steel fabrication facilities at Diosgyor, Hungary, on their return flight, first to Italy and then to Britain. Fighter sweeps maintained some momentum for Operation Frantic in the weeks that followed, but the Warsaw Uprising that had commenced on August 1, 1944, contributed to the eventual demise of the enterprise.

Urgent requests to allow Frantic B-17s to fly arms to the Poles battling the Nazis in the streets of Warsaw were angrily denied by Stalin, who hoped that the Germans would eliminate Polish resistance that could pose a problem to Soviet domination of eastern Europe after the end of World War Two. One largely humanitarian airdrop was allowed on September 18. Dubbed Frantic VII, it involved more than 100 B-17s carrying 1,284 parachuted containers of food, medicine, and some weapons and ammunition. Stalin was aware, however, that the Red Army – holding territory that included much of the designated drop zone – would receive the bulk of the supplies intended for the Poles.

The final major Operation Frantic raid took place on September 19, 1944, as 93 B-17s and 55 P-51s struck the railroad marshalling yards at Szolnok, Hungary. Afterward, the raison d'etre for Operation Frantic steadily faded as Allied troops, both east and west, overran many of its slated targets. The last American air personnel departed the Soviet Union in June 1945, weeks after the war had ended. The cooperative shuttle bombing effort, undertaken with optimism, had proven a strategic disappointment, and perhaps the frosty relations engendered provided a foreshadowing of the coming Cold War.

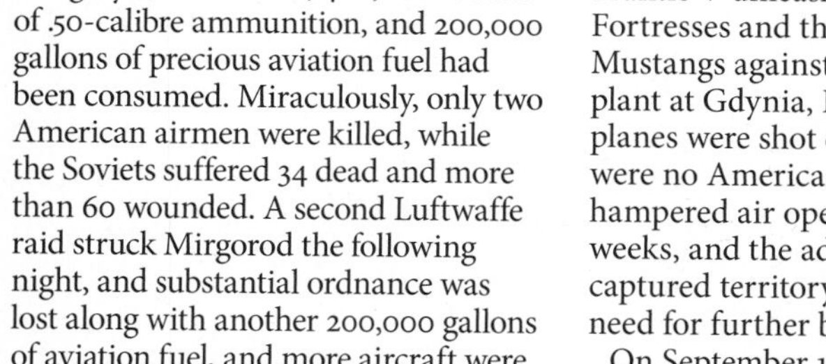

FAR LEFT: An American airman participating in Operation Frantic stands with two Soviet counterparts in front of a Lend Lease Bell P-39 Airacobra fighter of the Red Air Force. Creative Commons FOTO: Fortepan ID 15947 via Wikimedia Commons

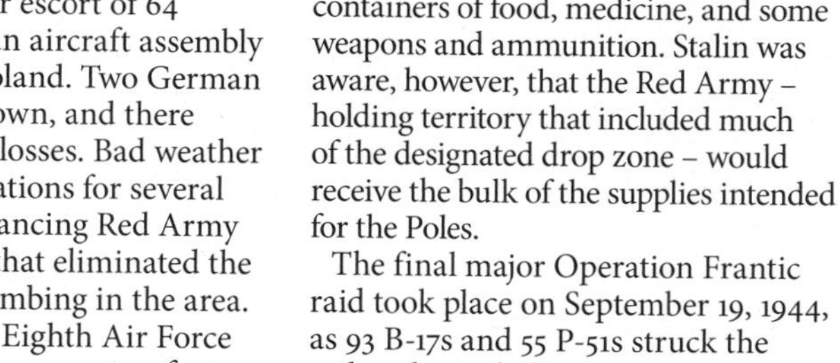

LEFT: The crew of a 95th Bombardment Group B-17 nicknamed *Sarkcsillag* poses for a photograph during Operation Frantic. Creative Commons Foto: Fortepan ID 15948 via Wikimedia Commons

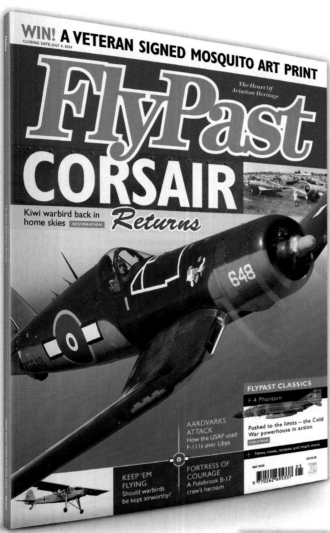

THE DEATH OF THE BALL TURRET GUNNER

FAR LEFT: An air crewman demonstrates the process of climbing into a ball turret aboard an Allied bomber. Public Domain collections of the Imperial War Museums via Wikimedia Commons

LEFT: This view depicts the top of a ball turret from the interior of a B-17 Flying Fortress bomber. Creative Commons Mark Wagner via Wikimedia Commons

Perhaps the most curious and frightening position aboard some variants of the B-17 Flying Fortress was that of the ventral ball turret. The smallest member of the bomber crew typically manned the cramped quarters of the ball turret, intended to add firepower in defence against enemy fighter aircraft.

American poet Randall Jarrell, a native of Nashville, Tennessee, graduate of Vanderbilt University, and professor at the University of Texas in Austin from 1939-1942, left the academic world temporarily and enlisted in the US Army Air Forces in the latter year. According to biographical information, he became a flying cadet and later a 'celestial navigation tower operator', a job title he considered the most poetic in the air force. Apparently, he was deemed too old to serve as a combat pilot but spent months as an instructor. His experience in the military prompted Jarrell to write numerous poems on the topic of war. One of them, a haunting poem of five lines, stands out from the others.

The Death of the Ball Turret Gunner was released in 1945. It reads:

From my mother's sleep I fell into the State,
And I hunched in its belly till my we fur froze.
Six miles from earth, loosed from its dream of life,
I woke to black flak and the nightmare fighters.
When I died, they washed me out of the turret with a hose.

The imagery of Jarrell's words is stark, and they no doubt resonated with the veterans of the air campaigns of World War Two who read them, particularly those who experienced missions while occupying the ball turret of a B-17 or B-24 Liberator bomber in the skies above war-torn Europe.

Jarrell described the ball turret in detail writing: "A ball turret was a Plexiglas sphere set into the belly of a B-17 or B-24, and inhabited by two .50 caliber machine guns and one man, a short small man. When this gunner tracked with his machine guns a fighter attacking his bomber from below, he revolved with the turret; hunched upside-down in his little sphere, he looked like the fetus in the womb. The fighters which attacked him were armed with cannon firing explosive shells. The hose was a steam hose."

Jarrell's work has been the topic of much analysis and literary criticism. After World War Two, he returned to teaching and suffered from extended bouts of depression. He became the 11th consultant in poetry to the US Library of Congress, known today as the Poet Laureate or Official Poet of the United States. After attempting suicide, Jarrell returned to work at the University of North Carolina in the autumn of 1965. While walking along a highway near the town of Chapel Hill, North Carolina, he was struck and killed by an automobile on October 14 of that year. Questions surrounded the circumstances of his death, whether it was accidental or suicide.

The Death of the Ball Turret Gunner remains a thought provoking work of profound brevity. It served as the basis for a play of the same title written by Anna Moench, which made its debut in New York City in 2008.

LEFT: This historical marker in Nashville, Tennessee, pays tribute to poet Randall Jarrell. Creative Commons Michael Rivera via Wikimedia Commons

CLARK GABLE AND THE FLYING FORTRESS

By the time the United States was plunged into World War Two with the Japanese surprise attack at Pearl Harbor on December 7, 1941, Clark Gable was the 'King of Hollywood'.

Literally, more than 20 million people had voted in a national poll, and Gable had been chosen by a wide margin. After all, he had won an Academy Award for the 1934 film *It Happened One Night*, while other box office smashes, including the epic *Gone With The Wind*, were among his notable acting credits. He was handsome, at the peak of his popularity, and married to the love of his life, actress Carole Lombard.

Sure. Gable was a womaniser and hard drinker. Lombard was his third wife, as well. But there was something different about their relationship. The man might drift slightly, but his heart was always tethered to the woman he affectionately referred to as 'Ma'. She, in turn, understood him and called Gable, 'Pa'. Both pet names were in reference to starring roles they shared in the 1932 film *No Man of Her Own*.

The story goes that Gable had no intention of joining the service in late 1941. In fact, he told fellow actor Jimmy Stewart, who enlisted in the Army Air Forces: "You know you're throwing your career away, don't you? You won't catch me doing that, but I wish you godspeed."

At the same time, Gable was willing to do what he could to help the war effort, and he did even cable President Franklin D. Roosevelt with a pledge of full support and asking what he could do for the war effort. FDR responded: "You are needed where you are." Lombard was, perhaps, behind Gable's first overture and wanted him to join the army in some capacity. She was a zealous supporter of the war effort, determined to raise funds through bond drives and possibly even join the Red Cross.

Two weeks after Pearl Harbor, Gable became the chairman of the Screen Actors Division of the Hollywood Victory Committee. Lombard was a native of Indiana, and when it came time to kick off a bond drive in her home state, Gable encouraged her to go to the rally. She never returned, dying in the fiery crash of her Douglas DC-3 airliner on January 16, 1942, just after take-off from Las Vegas after a stopover en route to Burbank, California.

Gable was devastated. And it was soon afterward that his life became entwined with the wartime saga of the B-17 Flying Fortress bomber. Gable was 41 years old, but he decided to volunteer for the Army Air Forces after growing despondent and losing 20 pounds during the months following Lombard's death. On August 12, 1942, he enlisted, and quite probably it was his broken heart speaking when he told a friend: "I'm going in, and I don't expect to come back, and I don't really give a hoot whether I do or not."

With the intent to train as a gunner aboard a big bomber, Gable undertook the army's 13-week officer candidate training course and emerged as a 2nd lieutenant qualified in aerial gunnery and as a photographer. He received a promotion to captain, and General Henry 'Hap' Arnold, chief of the Army Air Forces, approved a special task for the King of Hollywood. Gable was attached to the First Motion Picture Unit, under command of Lieutenant Colonel Jack Warner, erstwhile film executive with Warner Bros Studios. Other Hollywood luminaries associated with the unit included Ronald Reagan, Van Heflin, and Alan Ladd. Gable was one of the few who was designated for duty in Britain, and his 'special task' was to produce aerial film footage for a propaganda movie titled *Combat America*. It was hoped that the film would energise recruiting for aerial gunners, a »

LEFT: Clark Gable offers a rakish smile in this 1940 publicity photo. Public Domain movie studio via Wikimedia Commons

LEFT: Clark Gable and Carole Lombard posed for this photo after their honeymoon in 1939. Public Domain studio publicity photo Wikiwatcher1 upload via Wikimedia Commons

FAR LEFT: Actress Carole Lombard, the love of Clark Gable's life, was killed in a 1942 plane crash. Public Domain Paul Hesse via Wikimedia Commons

LEFT: Both in uniform, Major Clark Gable talks with Lieutenant Colonel Jimmy Stewart during World War Two. Creative Commons Bwmoll3 uploaded via en.wikipedia to Wikimedia Commons

job for which it often seemed there was little enthusiasm.

Meanwhile, the 351st Bombardment Group was training at Biggs Army Airfield near El Paso, Texas. One excited clerk wrote to his parents that Gable was soon to arrive and the 351st was sure to be "a pretty nice outfit with me and Clark Gable. Tell the boys hello and tell 'em me and Clark Gable are putting this 351st outfit in shape." In April 1943, the group arrived at Peterborough, England, about 80 miles north of London. The group was widely known by its nickname, Hatcher's Chickens, in reference to its commanding officer, Colonel William Hatcher.

On the day of the group' arrival in England, Nazi radio propagandist William Joyce, better known as Lord Haw Haw, offered an ominous broadcast. "Welcome to England, Hatcher's Chickens. Among whom is famous American cinema star, Clark Gable. We'll be seeing you soon in Germany, Clark. You will be welcome there too." Gable was actually a favourite of Nazi Fuhrer Adolf Hitler, a well-known film enthusiast, and a bounty was said to have been offered to any German who might bring Gable in as a live prisoner of war. When he considered the prospect of being captured by the Nazis, the actor told a friend, "If Hitler catches me, the son of a bitch will put me in a cage like a gorilla and send me on a tour of Germany. If a plane that I'm in ever gets hit, I'm not baling out."

It did not take Captain Gable long to get into the air. During his first mission on May 4, 1943, targeting industrial facilities at Antwerp, Belgium, the bombers encountered waves of German fighters and a veritable wall of flak. Anti-aircraft fire damaged one of the B-17's engines, and then a 20mm cannon shell from a Luftwaffe fighter ripped through the heel of Gable's boot and passed completely through the bomber's aluminium skin, missing his head by just inches. The actor had been hunched near a waist gunner's position, operating his film camera. He didn't notice the damage to his boot until later, but both he and the gunner were lucky to be alive.

In the beginning, some personnel had been sceptical of Gable's real intent. They could not buy into his willingness to go in harm's way. But there are those today who believe the great actor was compelled by a 'death wish' to perish in the fire of a plane crash just as his beloved wife had done, despite later interviews with the screen star that would contradict such a conclusion.

Regardless, Gable earned the respect of every man in the 351st Bombardment Group. By the autumn of 1943, Gable and his associates, another cameraman and a sound engineer, had produced 50,000ft of combat film. Records indicate that he flew five combat missions over Nazi-occupied territory, but some fellow airmen who were there recall that he flew many more. The three-man team was said to have followed the story of a B-17 nicknamed *Ain't It Gruesome* during 24 missions, one of them particularly harrowing as a Luftwaffe Focke Wulf Fw-190 fighter inflicted heavy damage, compelling the aircrew to bale out of the plane above an English pasture when fog made conditions too hazardous to land the stricken bomber. On a mission over the German city of Gelsenkirchen, the bomber Gable was aboard took heavy damage but returned to base.

Gable was also known to have flown two missions with the 91st Bombardment Group aboard a Flying

RIGHT: Famed actor Clark Gable stands beside the tail of a B-17 bomber in Britain in 1943. Public Domain United States Government via Wikimedia Commons

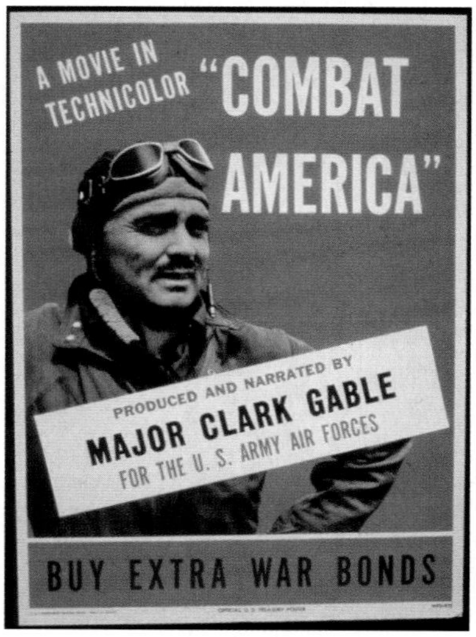

RIGHT: Clark Gable's film *Combat America* was produced in Technicolor and debuted in 1945. Public Domain National Archives and Records Administration via Wikimedia Commons

BELOW: Clark Gable stands with the crew of the B-17 Flying Fortress nicknamed Eight Ball at an airfield in England. Public Domain US Air Force via Wikimedia Commons

Fortress of the 323rd Bombardment Squadron nicknamed *Delta Rebel No.2*, which may well have been the first B-17 to complete 25 missions as recent research suggests. Sometime after one of those missions was completed, Sergeant Steve Perri, the ball turret gunner aboard Delta Rebel No.2, remembered the captain as "a great friend of the enlisted men and a great all around guy."

On more than one occasion, Gable actually took over for .50-calibre machine gunners who had been wounded or killed in action. His B-17 returned from one mission with at least 15 holes from bullets, shells, and shrapnel. He participated in a raid on industrial facilities in Norway, the longest mounted by the Eighth Air Force up to that time, and survived a raid against targets in the Ruhr Valley, the industrial heart of Germany, in which 25 of 330 American bombers participating were shot down. His last recorded mission occurred on September 23, 1943, and a month later he was awarded the Air Medal and the Distinguished Flying Cross for meritorious service.

Gable returned to the United States in November 1943, delivering his reels of aerial combat footage only to find that the recruitment of machine gunners had already increased. Essentially left to his own devices concerning the combat footage, he returned to California and edited the film at MGM Studios. According to sources, he produced five short films relating to the operations of the Flying Fortress. In addition, *Combat America*, 62 minutes long, was released in theatres across America in 1945, and Gable provided the narration.

Promoted to the rank of major in 1944, Gable fully expected to return to combat duty in England or possibly in the Pacific theatre. But no new orders came through. He waited until mid-year, and then at age 42, requested a separation from the US armed forces. The discharge was granted. The rest of the great film star's life is well documented. He never recaptured the immense fame he had known prior to World War Two, but his persona remained strong box office currency.

Although he married twice more, Clark Gable mourned Carole Lombard for the rest of his life. He died of a heart attack in 1960 at the age of 59, much better known as a titan of the silver screen than for his exploits in the US Army Air Forces. Altogether though, the life of Clark Gable, military and civilian, is in itself worthy of a Hollywood script.

ABOVE: On January 15, 1944, actress Irene Dunne christens the liberty ship SS *Carole Lombard*, honouring the deceased actress. Lombard's widower, Clark Gable, stands at left with eyes shut. Public Domain Acme Telephoto via Wikimedia Commons

LEFT: Clark Gable, looking the part of a famous actor, attends a Hollywood party in 1945. Creative Commons US Marine Corps Archives via Wikimedia Commons

THE PIGGYBACK INCIDENT

RIGHT: **This B-17G of the 452nd Bombardment Group is similar to those involved in the famous piggyback incident during the Hamburg raid of December 31, 1944.** Public Domain United States Army Air Forces via Wikimedia Commons

For two B-17 bomber crews of the 100th Bombardment Group based at Thorpe Abbotts in England, the last mission of 1944 was unforgettable. The incredible story defies logic, and even today its retelling has lost none of its lustre.

The two big bombers, *Little Skipper*, piloted by Lieutenants Glenn H. Rojohn and William G. Leek, and *Nine Lives*, flown by Lieutenants William McNab and Nelson Vaughn, participated in the December 31, 1944, raid on a synthetic oil factory in Hamburg, Germany. It was New Year's Eve, but that mattered little in wartime. Another day, another hazardous mission in the works as the aircrews participating were roused from their fitful sleep well before daylight.

The flight path to Hamburg would take the bomber formations over the North Sea to landfall on the European continent. As they droned ahead, the airmen realised to their dismay that the expected fighter escort had not made the rendezvous. Dense fog hampered operations at some airfields, and on the ground the famed Battle of the Bulge was raging. The bombers kept going without escort.

According to records, flak was heavy, and German Messerschmitt Me-109 fighters were quite active, queueing up to make firing passes at the B-17s. A dozen of the 37 bombers were shot down during the mission and 100 crewmen killed, missing, or captured when it was over. Although no mission was 'routine', this one had all the markers to indicate that it would be another of those in which planes were lost, targets were bombed, and the remaining B-17s returned to their bases in England.

However, the routine became extraordinary in a flash. Rojohn's formation dropped their bombs and then began the 1800 turn that would take them back over the North Sea, course set for home. As expected, the German fighters reemerged and began making passes at the bombers, flying at 22,000ft. Rojohn held *Little Skipper* in formation, knowing that the mutual support of every bomber's machine guns might help to ward off the nimble Nazi fighters. Just ahead, Rojohn saw another B-17 erupt in flames and quickly fall away as it streamed smoke and fire.

There was no time to grieve. Rojohn moved his bomber forward and descended to 19,000ft to close some of the gap created when the flaming plane had begun its earthward spiral. Suddenly, the pilot and crew of *Little Skipper* felt a tremendous impact. The B-17 shuddered, and the controls began to feel extremely sluggish. Somehow, the plane had gained tremendous weight. And then, the pilot understood what had happened.

RIGHT: **A B-17 waist gunner peers from his position aboard a bomber. Several crewmen from *Little Skipper* escaped their doomed plane through this position.** No restrictions Robert Yarnall Ritchie SMU Central University Libraries via Wikimedia Commons

BELOW: **A Flying Fortress of the 490th Bombardment Group taxies down a runway prior to take-off.** Public Domain collections of the Imperial War Museums

During the closing manoeuvre another B-17, McNab's *Nine Lives*, had slammed into *Little Skipper*. The two planes were thoroughly fused together.

Rojohn paused to assess the situation. There was no explanation for the mid-air collision, perhaps only that it had occurred in the heat of aerial combat as the two pilots strove with all their might to make it back to their base. One crewman described the odd combination as "like mating dragonflies." The top gun turret of *Nine Lives* had smashed into the underbelly of *Little Skipper*, and simultaneously the ball turret of *Little Skipper* had punched through the upper fuselage of *Nine Lives*. The alignment was amazingly close. Only the tail of *Nine Lives* was slightly askew to the left of *Little Skipper's* tail assembly.

A German antiaircraft battery commander spotted the strangely joined B-17s and noted in his log just prior to 1pm, "Two Fortresses collided in a formation in the NE. The planes flew hooked together and flew 20 miles south. The two planes were unable to fight anymore. The crash could be awaited so I stopped the firing at these two planes."

Other Germans, both military and civilian, watched in awe as the two bombers careened across the sky. Some of them believed that they were witnessing the debut of a new American bomber, one perhaps with double the bombload and defensive capacity of a single Flying Fortress. What they were actually witnessing was a desperate attempt by stunned American airmen to cheat death.

Incredibly, all four engines aboard Rojohn's Flying Fortress were still running, while three of McNab's continued to operate. Still, the immediate threat to the crews was the fourth engine of *Nine Lives*; it was on fire, and tongues of flames licked dangerously close to both bombers. The conjoined bombers were rapidly losing altitude, and neither aircraft could separate itself from the other. Apparently, McNab and Vaughn had been killed or injured either prior to or during impact. Believing the lower B-17 to be out of control, Rojohn cut his engines and rang the bale out bell while trying to hold *Little Skipper* steady.

Fighting to maintain level flight, Rojohn and Leek used all their strength to pull back on their controls, even pressing their feet and legs against the instrument panels in front of them. Rojohn knew that the best hope of survival was to turn back toward Germany, even if that likely meant the capture of any survivors by the Germans. If *Little Skipper* went out of control and began a spinning earthward descent, centrifugal force would trap men inside the plane, rendering them unable to exit. Rojohn motioned to the left, and he and Leek fought to make the turn. Leek prayed loudly and tore off his flying cap. Fire was continuing to engulf *Nine Lives*, and Rojohn could feel the heat of flames that spread dangerously close to *Little Skipper*. The pop-pop of .50-calibre ammunition that rapidly began cooking off was unnerving.

In the ball turret of *Nine Lives*, Staff Sergeant Edward L. Woodall, Jr., was miraculously unhurt in the initial collision. However, the ball turret was the most cramped, uncomfortable, and dangerous position aboard a B-17. Shrapnel had zipped past his head, and he realised that all electrical and hydraulic power had been cut. He was trapped. Meanwhile, crewmen aboard *Little Skipper* who would normally exit the bomber through its belly were unable to do so. Rojohn understood their predicament and ordered the top turret gunner and radio operator, Technical Sergeants Orville Elkin, and Edward G. Neuhaus, to move toward the rear of the fuselage and attempt to parachute from the left waist door. He instructed the bombardier, Sergeant James Shirley, and the navigator, 2nd Lieutenant Robert Washington, to follow them. Tail gunner Staff Sergeant Francis Chase and waist gunner Sergeant Roy Little were in position to bale out. All six men hit the silk and cleared the stricken bombers.

Rojohn ordered Leek to bale out as well, but Leek knew that Rojohn could not maintain control of the bombers without his help. In the spin that would surely follow, Rojohn had no hope of escape, so Leek refused the order and stayed with his pilot. While crewmen freed from the damaged bombers watched from their chutes, Rojohn and Leek fought the controls of *Little Skipper*, and Leek remembered years later: "The ground came up faster and faster. Praying was allowed. We gave it one last effort and slammed into the ground."

Nine Lives exploded on impact, and the force jettisoned *Little Skipper*, which lurched upward and then smashed hard again to the ground. It slid out of control, the left wing slicing into a small wooden building before the bomber came to a stop. Rojohn and Leek were virtually unhurt. The forward section of *Little Skipper* was somewhat intact, but the after portion of the plane was a twisted, smouldering wreck. Immediately after they exited the plane, the two airmen were captured by German troops.

Four of the men who parachuted from *Little Skipper* survived their parachute drop and were taken prisoner. Incredibly, four crewmen from *Nine Lives* also came through the ordeal alive, and ball turret gunner Woodall was one of them. In the years that followed, Rojohn repeatedly credited Leek with the fact that he survived. Both men received the Distinguished Service Cross for their heroism on the day of the mission to Hamburg.

TOP: This mock-up of a B-17 ball turret is housed at a museum at Thorpe Abbotts. Edward Woodall survived the piggyback incident inside the cramped space. Creative Commons William McLaughlin via Wikimedia Commons

ABOVE: A B-17 delivers its bombload on a target in Germany. Both *Little Skipper* and *Nine Lives* had dropped their bombs when the planes collided. Public Domain US Army Air Forces via Wikimedia Commons

LEFT: A B-17 of the 365th Bombardment Squadron touches down safely after sustaining damage in a raid over Nazi-occupied France. *Little Skipper* and *Nine Lives* were both lost on December 31, 1944. Public Domain US Army Air Forces via Wikimedia Commons

THE BLOODY 100th

LEFT: This B-17F of the 350th Bombardment Squadron, 100th Bombardment Group, nicknamed *Badger's Beauty V*, was shot down and crashed in Normandy on October 4, 1943. Public Domain US Air Force via Wikimedia Commons

On October 10, 1943, a formation of 18 Flying Fortress bombers of the 100th Bombardment Group took off from the airfield at RAF Thorpe Abbotts, Norfolk, headed for the railroad lines and marshalling yards at the German city of Münster. They were joined by formations of B-17s from the 390th and 95th Bombardment groups. In addition to the transportation infrastructure at Münster, the quarters for nearly every railroad worker in this region of Germany's Ruhr Valley lived nearby. Hitting these residences would render many of the workers homeless or possibly make them casualties of total war.

The bombers formed up and headed over the North Sea, approaching Münster from the north and crossing the coastline of Europe at approximately 2:30pm south of the Dutch city of Rotterdam. Just moments after take-off, the mission began to go awry. Five B-17s aborted due to mechanical problems, and the escort of Republic P-47 Thunderbolt fighters failed to rendezvous at the appointed time and place. Then, the 313 heavy bombers of the Eighth Air Force experienced a vicious aerial assault. More than 200 Luftwaffe fighters, including Me-109s, Fw-190s, and twin-engine Messerschmitt types pressed home attacks.

As they ran the gauntlet, the B-17s of the 100th Bombardment Group were slaughtered. Twelve of the 13 Flying Fortresses that attempted to bomb Münster were shot down. Only one, nicknamed *Royal Flush* and piloted by Lieutenant Colonel Robert Rosenthal, managed to return to Thorpe Abbotts with heavy damage and several wounded crewmen. Forty-six airmen of the 100th were killed in action that day.

Captain Frank Murphy, navigator with crew no. 31 aboard the Flying Fortress *Aw-R-Go*, remembered the fateful day years after baling out of his stricken bomber and parachuting earthward into a field belonging to a German farmer. In his book *Luck of the Draw*, Murphy recalled that the family was kind to him until the authorities came to take him into custody. Two members of crew no. 31 were killed, and the remaining eight spent nearly 19 months in German captivity.

The moments before his stricken B-17 was abandoned were harrowing for Murphy. "The waiting, previously deployed, Luftwaffe aircraft struck the 100th BG full force at 2:53 p.m.," he wrote. "The fighters came after us in steady waves, climbing and racing out ahead of us in trail, winging over and swarming to the attack with all guns blazing and, at the last second, flying directly through our formation, veering away, or rolling over and making a split-S just yards in front of us to drop away toward the ground. As one element broke away, another turned to the attack far ahead of us... We completed our bomb run, dropped our bombs, and began a long, gradual left turn to our rally point with the 95th and 390th BGs. I looked out my left window and saw a B-17 about five hundred to six hundred feet below us falling away steeply with its left wing enveloped in sheets of red and yellow flames."

The German fighters returned to ravage the surviving B-17s, and moments later Murphy's B-17 was hit. "...As I was firing the left nose gun at the attacking German fighters, a violent explosion just behind me and to my left sent me crashing to the floor," he recalled. "I immediately felt a burning sensation in my left arm and shoulder...I knew I had been hit...I had not heard the alarm bell under the navigator's table go off and saw that my intercom controls were shot away. But I knew. It was all over. We were going down...."

Other 100th Bombardment Group B-17 crews fared terribly. *Slightly Dangerous* had its right wing blown

BELOW: B-17s of the 351st Bombardment Squadron, 100th Bombardment Group, fly in formation. The Flying Fortress at centre right was lost in action in the spring of 1945. Public Domain US Air Force via Wikimedia Commons

ABOVE: A twisted propeller from a B-17 that crashed in England is now a museum piece at the Thorpe Abbotts museum. Creative Commons William McLaughlin via Wikimedia Commons

ABOVE RIGHT: The emblem of the 100th Bombardment Group during World War Two depicts a quartet of eagles. Public Domain US Air Force via Wikimedia Commons

off and exploded in mid-air. An Fw-190 shot down *Invadin Maiden* with cannon fire that destroyed its right inboard engine and wing. *M'lle Zig Zag* had been the first to go down, taking flak to the underside of its fuselage and trailing smoke as it quickly fell out of formation.

Münster was a black day for the 100th Bombardment Group, and some historians claim that the unit received its famous moniker 'The Bloody

RIGHT: Lieutenant Colonel Robert Rosenthal was a highly decorated hero of the 100th Bombardment Group. Public Domain US Air Force via Wikimedia Commons

100th' after the raid. Others assert that the 100th was so named due to the losses endured in the entirety of its deployment with the Eighth Air Force.

Activated on June 1, 1942, the 100th Bombardment Group was not staffed until that October with assignment of an officer cadre from the 29th Bombardment Group at Gowen Field, Idaho. After relocating to Walla Walla Army Air Base, Washington, the group received its first four B-17F bombers from the Boeing manufacturing facility in Seattle, and four initial crews were assigned to the planes. After further training of ground crews in Nebraska and aircrews in Iowa, the 100th Bombardment Group headed for England.

By May 27, 1943, ground and air crews reunited at RAF Podington in northern Bedfordshire before relocating to their permanent base at RAF Thorpe Abbotts, Norfolk. The group flew its first combat mission a month later, against U-boat facilities at the German port of Bremen on June 25, three days after making a diversionary run over the North Sea to distract the enemy from other raids. Three bombers of the 100th were among the 18 lost that day over Bremen, and each plane carried a crew of 10 men.

The group continued to see action in raids on German transportation facilities, airfields, and other targets, taking serious losses. Of the 35 original aircrews that flew from Thorpe Abbotts beginning in the spring of 1943, only 14% completed the 25 missions required for a rotation out of action. The casualty rate among the men of the Bloody 100th is also starkly illustrated by the fact that only four of the group's original 38 co-pilots completed 25 missions.

The number of 100th personnel of killed, wounded, and captured mounted steadily, but the same was true among other Eighth Air Force bombardment groups. On the day before the Münster raid, the 100th had participated in an attack on the Focke-Wulf aircraft assembly plant at Marienburg, Germany, along with B-17s of the 94th and 390th Bombardment Groups. Two Flying Fortresses were shot down and 23 more damaged with 21 airmen initially listed as missing in action, some later confirmed as killed and others as prisoners. During the August 17, 1943, raids on Regensburg and Schweinfurt, the 100th lost six B-17s before the surviving bombers reached their target, Regensburg's Messerschmitt Me-109 assembly facility. Before touching down in Tunisia during that shuttle mission, three more 100th Flying Fortresses were shot down.

The 100th gained a reputation as a hard luck group, and some men openly speculated as to whether the outfit was jinxed. Nevertheless, its men earned a reputation for courage and received two Distinguished Unit Citations, for Regensburg and a series of attacks against the German capital of Berlin in March 1944.

Meanwhile, a number of its leaders became well known personas throughout the Eighth Air Force, including the group commander, Colonel Neil 'Chick' Harding, a West Point graduate and football coach before the war who enjoyed drinking and never cared much for discipline, and squadron commanders Majors Gale 'Buck' Cleven of the 350th and John 'Bucky' Egan of the 418th. Both Egan and Cleven epitomised the swagger and audacity of the military airman, often engaging in raucous behaviour but exuding confidence. Lieutenant Colonel Rosenthal, whose aircraft was the lone 100th survivor of the Münster raid, was a lawyer before the war, flew 52 combat missions, and was shot down twice and evaded capture. 'Rosie' received the Distinguished Service Cross, two Distinguished Flying Crosses, two Silver Stars, and two Purple Hearts.

Although postwar analysis reveals that the loss rate of the 100th Bombardment Group was generally equivalent to that of other groups in the Eighth Air Force, the mission to Münster and others made the 100th 'bloody' and the stuff of legend. The experience of Colonel Beirne Lay, Jr., during five missions with the 100th Bombardment Group provided content for his book *Twelve O'Clock High*, which later became a major motion picture.

RIGHT: RAF Thorpe Abbotts was home to the Bloody 100th during virtually its entire deployment in World War Two. Public Domain United Kingdom Government via Wikimedia Commons

303rd BOMBARDMENT GROUP

ABOVE: The B-17 *Mercy's Madhouse* of the 358th Bombardment Squadron made an emergency landing on one wheel after sustaining damage during a raid in late 1944. Public Domain US Air Force via Wikimedia Commons

The report at times seemed detached, almost clinical as it recited results of the 303rd Bombardment Group's costliest day of the air war in Europe. During World War Two, the group flew 364 missions, more than any other B-17 bombardment group, and dropped 26,346 tons of bombs, second only to the 379th, which claimed to have dropped 26,459 tons.

Mission no. 248 against the Krupp Grusonwerke, A.G., at Magdeburg, Germany, on September 28, 1944, resulted in the loss of 11 Flying Fortresses of the 303rd. Thirty crews were dispatched, the length of the mission was an excruciating seven hours, 50 minutes, and when it was over 68 airmen were killed in action with another 23 taken prisoner.

The report described: "…8/10 to 10/10 swelling cumulus clouds with 16,000 to 18,000 ft. tops and no middle or high clouds. Meager and fairly accurate flak was encountered at Hellendorf and Gardelegen with moderate and accurate flak in the target area…"

In reference to the B-17s that were shot down, the narrative reads: "They were lost to enemy aircraft after a persistent attack of an estimated 40 FW-190s and ME-109s. After a bomber was hit, the enemy pilots continued their attack and followed it down. Attacks were chiefly from five to seven o'clock, from low to level and were concentrated on the low squadron. Friendly fighters arrived to engage the enemy and, during the course of dogfights, sporadic attacks were made. Some crews reported that these attacks were made singly and others felt they were made by as many as six abreast. These tactics utilized by the enemy pilots demonstrated that they were determined, efficient, and experienced…."

The 303rd Bombardment Group's aerial trial was one of shared heroism and shared misery, while they compiled an admirable combat record. Organised at Savannah, Georgia on January 28, 1942, it was activated at Pendleton Field, Oregon, six days later. After training, the group arrived at RAF Molesworth, Cambridgeshire, one of the first four Flying Fortress groups in England. The 303rd flew its first combat mission on November 17, 1942, against Nazi U-boat pens at St. Nazaire, France. On that day, heavy cloud cover obscured the target and the bombers turned for home with full loads. The 303rd was back in the air the next day to hit St. Nazaire after redirecting from its primary target at La Pallice.

Missions against U-boat pens, rail marshalling yards, and airfields in France and the Low Countries were regularly flown as only a single bomber was lost in the group's first six air actions. In early 1943, the 303rd began flying missions into the territory of the Third Reich, and through 1944, the cities of Mannheim and Ludwigshafen were bombed a dozen times with the loss of five B-17s. The industrial and rail centre of Cologne was hit 10 times. Frankfurt was bombed nine times with three Flying Fortresses shot down, a heavily defended airfield at Wiesbaden was hit in August 1944, with the loss of nine B-17s, and the marshalling yards at Hamm were attacked six times with the loss of two bombers to enemy flak.

On January 11, 1944, the 303rd Bombardment Group earned a Distinguished Unit Citation during a mission to bomb an aircraft assembly plant at Oschersleben. When bad weather disrupted the rendezvous with fighter escort, the bombers continued the mission on their own, enduring Luftwaffe fighter attacks to drop their ordnance accurately. The group lost 10 bombers that day.

During the run-up to the D-Day landings of June 6, 1944, the 303rd Bombardment Group struck tactical targets to interdict any substantial German response to the landings in northwest France. The bombers struck bridges, troop concentrations, supply depots, and rail lines to prevent the Germans from reinforcing their positions along the coast of the English Channel and in French Normandy, and

RIGHT: The B-17 *Hell's Angels* of the 358th Bombardment Squadron, 303rd Bombardment Group, was among the first Flying Fortresses to complete 25 missions. Public Domain US Army Air Forces via Wikimedia Commons

FAR RIGHT: This image of the B-17 *Hell's Angels* includes both air and ground crewmen. *Hell's Angels* completed its 25th combat mission on May 13, 1943.

three missions were flown on D-Day alone. During Operation Cobra, the Allied offensive and breakout from the Normandy beachhead, the group participated in heavy raids against the German frontline positions to facilitate the rapid movement of American armoured forces to exploit a gap created by carpet bombing. The group completed its first mission against the Nazi capital of Berlin on March 6, 1944.

In response to the German Ardennes offensive that resulted in the Battle of the Bulge, December 1944-January 1945, the 303rd flew missions to impede German advances despite weather conditions that were far from ideal at times. The bombers were again in the air to support the Allied crossing of the River Rhine, the last natural barrier on the frontier of Germany itself. Meanwhile, missions were flown against German launching sites for the V-1 'Buzz Bomb' weapons that terrorised British cities in the waning months of the war. The 303rd's last mission of World War Two was flown against the Skoda armament works at Pilsen, Czechoslovakia, on April 25, 1945.

In an interesting twist, Captain Werner Goering flew 48 combat missions with the 358th Bombardment Squadron. He claimed to be the nephew of Luftwaffe chief Reichsmarschall Hermann Göring. However, this claim has not been substantiated.

During the war, two aircraft of the 303rd Bombardment Group gained a measure of notoriety. The Flying Fortress nicknamed *Hell's Angels* of the 358th Bombardment Squadron completed 25 missions with a raid against a target in northern France on May 13, 1943, while *Knockout Dropper* of the 359th Bombardment Squadron was first to complete 50 missions on November 16, 1943, and then 75 missions on March 27, 1944, an incredible feat. The apparent record for B-17 missions during the entirety of World War Two, however, belongs to B17G *Nine-O-Nine* of the 323rd Bombardment Squadron, 91st Bombardment Group, which completed an astounding 140 missions between February 1944 and April 1945.

Hell's Angels was in close competition with *Memphis Belle* of the 91st Bombardment Group, and many sources credit *Hell's Angels* as the first B-17 to achieve the 25-mission mark. However, recent research suggests that *Delta Rebel No. 2* of the 91st was actually first to complete 25 missions, as of May 1, 1943.

While *Memphis Belle* received the lion's share of acclaim for the 25-mission achievement, returning to the US for a War Bond tour and as the subject of a 1944 documentary film, *Hell's Angels* continued in service with Eighth Air Force in the European theatre until January 1944, finishing 48 missions without substantial damage or casualties among its crews. *Hell's Angels* did return to the United States in early 1944 and embarked on a tour of aircraft assembly factories across the country. This historically significant Flying Fortress, however, was sold for scrap in 1945.

Knockout Dropper's 50th mission was no. 82 for the 303rd Bombardment Group as 130 Flying Fortresses attacked German mining operations at Knaben, Norway. On its 75th mission, *Knockout Dropper* was one of 28 B-17s flying mission no. 129 for the 303rd. The target was the Luftwaffe airfield and nearby repair and assembly facilities at Chartres, France. First Lieutenant John N. Savage, who piloted *Knockout Dropper* that day, remarked that the plane flew as well as any he had handled despite its lengthy service record.

Knockout Dropper received minor damage as two pieces of shrapnel from German anti-aircraft fire struck the plane, but the ordnance was dropped accurately. Sergeant Raymond N. Dean, waist gunner aboard *Knockout Dropper*, watched with satisfaction as the bombs plummeted earthward: "All of them seemed to be hitting in there. Most of the bombs were dropping on the building on the edge of the field."

Knockout Dropper survived the war and was sold as surplus to an oil company in Stillwater, Oklahoma. According to the American Air Museum, the historic plane was placed on pylons at a gas station in Oklahoma City. When a downtown development project was undertaken sometime later, the aircraft was 'bulldozed and buried', now resting unknown to most beneath a large building that was probably constructed sometime in the early 1950s.

Such was the ignominious end of a noble machine of war which is now remembered primarily as a footnote to the combat history of the famed 303rd Bombardment Group.

TOP: The B-17 *Knockout Dropper*, which completed 75 missions over Nazi-occupied Europe, is shown covered in signatures and congratulatory messages at RAF Molesworth in 1945 after the end of World War Two. Public Domain US Army Air Forces via Wikimedia Commons

ABOVE: Captain Werner Goering is shown with the crew of the B-17 *Fearless Fosdick* of the 358th Bombardment Squadron. Public Domain US Army Air Force

LEFT: This photo of the control tower at RAF Molesworth, home of the 303rd Bombardment Group, was taken on September 28, 1944. Public Domain US Army Air Forces via Wikimedia Commons

97th BOMBARDMENT GROUP

During the course of World War Two, the 97th Bombardment Group became known for a series of 'firsts'.

Activated at MacDill Field, Florida, on February 3, 1942, and subsequently training at Sarasota Army Airfield that spring, the 97th prepared for combat operations and flew numerous anti-submarine patrols along the Florida coastline. In June, the group arrived at RAF Polebrook and RAF Grafton Underwood, Northamptonshire, assigned to the 1st Bombardment Wing of the fledgling Eighth Air Force. The 97th included the first American bomber personnel to reach England and become operational with the B-17 Flying Fortress heavy bomber. Its organic squadrons included the 340th, 341st, 342nd, and 414th.

After inclement weather postponed its baptism of fire, 18 Flying Fortresses of the 97th conducted the first American daylight, high altitude precision bombing raid against Nazi-occupied Europe. Six of the bombers flew a diversionary course, while 12 dropped their payloads on the rail marshalling yards at Sotteville, near the French city of Rouen. General Ira C. Eaker, commander of Eighth Bomber Command, flew aboard the B-17 *Yankee Doodle* as an observer, and though the raid was small it was a harbinger of things to come.

Two days after the inaugural combat mission, the 97th participated in Operation Jubilee, the disastrous large-scale commando raid on the French coastal town of Dieppe. The group completed a diversionary mission against a Luftwaffe airfield at Abbeville, France. Into the autumn of 1942, the 97th flew a total of 247 sorties against a variety of targets in France and the Low Countries. The B-17s hit dockyards and naval facilities, factories, and airfields, dropping 395 tons of bombs. The unit's first combat loss occurred on September 6, when a Flying Fortress was shot down and its six surviving crew members taken prisoner.

On October 21, 1942, orders were received transferring the 97th Bombardment Group to North Africa. The transfer was completed in November, and on the 16th, eight days after Allied troops came ashore in Algeria and Morocco during Operation Torch, the group, assigned to the newly formed Twelfth Air Force under General James H. 'Jimmy' Doolittle, became the first to conduct an air raid against German forces in Tunisia. On that day, six Flying Fortresses of the 340th Bombardment Squadron attacked the enemy airfield at Sidi Ahmed near the city of Bizerte.

For the next six months, the 97th Bombardment Group conducted missions against

ABOVE: This B-17 Flying Fortress nicknamed *Silver Sheen* of the 341st Bombardment Squadron was shot down over Germany in March 1945. Public Domain US Air Force via Wikimedia Commons

LEFT: Flying Fortresses of the 340th Bombardment Squadron, 97th Bombardment Group fly a mission to Linz, Austria, in 1944. Along with their P-38 Lightning fighter escorts, they leave broad contrails across the sky. Public Domain US Army Air Forces via Wikimedia Commons

LEFT: The emblem of the 97th Bombardment Group, one of the most famous of World War Two, was widely recognised in the Eighth Air Force. Public Domain United States Army Institute of Heraldry JoeCool59 via Wikimedia Commons

LEFT: B-17s of the 340th Bombardment Squadron fly a mission northward into Austria. The bomber in the foreground was later lost in a mid-air collision. Public Domain US Army Air Forces via Wikimedia Commons

enemy troop concentrations, supply depots and convoys, communications centres, shipping in the Mediterranean Sea, and other high value targets. While many of these raids were in direct support of Allied troops battling the Axis forces in North Africa, others were against military and industrial targets in Sicily, Sardinia, Italy, and southern France in anticipation of further offensive action by Allied land forces once North Africa had been secured with the defeat of Panzerarmee Afrika.

After the capitulation of Axis forces in North Africa in May 1943, more concerted efforts were made to soften up enemy defences in other Mediterranean areas, particularly in preparation for Operation Husky, the invasion of Sicily, in July 1943, and Operations Avalanche, Baytown, and Slapstick, the three-pronged Allied invasion of the Italian mainland in September.

In May-June 1943, the 97th Bombardment Group participated in Operation Corkscrew, a heavy bombing campaign against Italian and German forces occupying the Mediterranean island of Pantelleria. During a five-week period, Allied planes flew 5,285 sorties and dropped 6,313 tons of bombs on the island. More than 14,000 individual bombs were dropped on enemy bunkers, pillboxes, and fortified artillery batteries in preparation for the Sicily landings at Syracuse and Gela. During 10 days of continual aerial assault, the Italian and German gun batteries on Pantelleria were reduced to an estimated 47% effectiveness, and on the morning of the June 11, 1943, as the Allied landings commenced, the Italian commander received permission from Rome to surrender the garrison.

Through the summer and autumn of 1943, the 97th Bombardment Group was active in raids supporting the Allied advances in Sicily and then Italy. Concentrated attacks centred at first on the major ports of Messina at the northeastern tip of Sicily and Naples in southwestern Italy. The interdiction of Axis shipping was a priority, particularly as German forces attempted to evacuate from Sicily to the Italian mainland across the narrow expanse of the Strait of Messina. On June 25, 1943, more than 100 Flying Fortresses joined the RAF in pounding Messina while ground troops advanced against difficult German and Italian resistance on the island. The raid lasted only 18 minutes over the target, and it was the largest concentration of Flying Fortresses yet to fly against a European target from bases in North Africa.

After the Allied landings in Italy, the 97th Bombardment Group was engaged in direct support of American and British forces at the embattled Anzio beachhead and in the fighting around Cassino along with the advance through the Po Valley in early 1945.

Once the Allies were well established in Italy and airfields on the plain of Foggia became operational, the 97th Bombardment Group continued tactical operations and resumed its strategic bombing campaign against enemy industrial and military targets across southern Europe. In the summer of 1944, the 97th was involved in the shuttle bombing campaign dubbed Operation Frantic, hitting targets, and then landing at airfields in the Soviet Union, and became the first American bombardment group to land its bombers in Soviet territory.

The 97th participated in four straight days of heavy raids against the Romanian oil production facilities at Ploesti in August 1944, and earned two Distinguished Unit Citations, the first for a raid on an aircraft assembly plant at Steyr, Austria, during Big Week on February 24, 1944, and the second for its aircrews' courage during the August 18, 1944, attack on Ploesti. Strategic raids were conducted against targets in eastern Europe, the Balkans, Czechoslovakia, Austria, and Germany.

ABOVE: Dozens of exploding bombs wreath the Mediterranean island of Pantelleria in a pall of smoke as Allied bombers pound its Axis defenders in June 1943. Public Domain collections of the Imperial War Museums via Wikimedia Commons

Before its deactivation in Italy in 1945, the 97th Bombardment Group occupied a dozen different locations in Britain, North Africa, and Italy. Its aircrews flew 467 combat missions and lost 110 Flying Fortresses. In addition to other firsts, its tour of duty included the first air raid on Germany from Africa and the first air raid on the Italian capital of Rome.

One interesting footnote to the wartime career of the 97th Bombardment Group is its inclusion in a 22-minute film produced in 1942 and titled *Bombers Over North Africa*. The film captures vivid black and white images of early US bomber operations in World War Two. Along with the North American B-25 Mitchell bombers of the 321st Bombardment Group, the B-17s of the 97th are depicted as assisting ground forces in the final defeat of the Axis in North Africa, interdicting supply lines and destroying port facilities.

The film begins with an introduction by Allied Mediterranean theatre commander General Dwight D. Eisenhower and ends with an afterword from General James H. 'Jimmy' Doolittle, commander of the US Twelfth Air Force and later the combined British and American North West African Strategic Air Force. The missions captured on a particular day of filming include strikes on the Sidi Ahmed airfield near Bizerte and the bombing of a road junction at Manouba near Tunis, the capital city of Tunisia.

The film is further notable for its personal perspectives on the airmen and ground crewmen who served. It is among the first to describe their activities in any detail and to present a somewhat poignant and human aspect of men at war. Among other experiences, the men describe the ditching of a damaged B-25 and the shooting down of a German Focke Wulf Fw-190 fighter by a gunner aboard a B-17.

LEFT: B-17s of the 342nd Bombardment Squadron, 97th Bombardment Group attack the Anzio beachhead in early 1944. Public Domain US Army Air Forces via Wikimedia Commons

91st BOMBARDMENT GROUP

RIGHT: The crew of the B-17 Flying Fortress nicknamed *Liberty Bell* poses for a photo prior to a mission with the 91st Bombardment Group. Public Domain US Government via Wikimedia Commons

"I observed 42-31333 receive a direct flak hit approximately between the bomb bay and the number two engine," reported Staff Sergeant George Little, a gunner flying aboard a nearby B-17 bomber during a raid against the rail marshalling yards at Stendal, Germany. "The aircraft immediately started a vertical dive. The aircraft fuselage was on fire and when it had dropped approximately 5,000 feet the left wing fell off.

"It continued down and when the fuselage was about 3,000 feet from the ground it exploded, and then exploded again when it hit the ground. I saw no crew members leave the aircraft or parachutes," Little concluded.

Little had witnessed the demise of the B-17 bomber *Wee Willie*, at the time the oldest B-17 in service with the 91st Bombardment Group and flying its 129th combat mission over Nazi-occupied Europe. While the loss of B-17s was an all too common occurrence in the embattled skies over the continent, that of *Wee Willie* was remarkable for the sequence of stark and gut wrenching images that were captured during its fatal plunge by the automatic camera aboard another B-17 that was ordinarily triggered with 'bombs away' to record images that assisted with post-raid damage assessment. The most shocking photograph shows the fractured left wing twisting away from the aircraft during the free fall.

RIGHT: The B-17 *Wee Willie* plummets earthward as its left wing detaches in this stark photo. *Wee Willie* was assigned to the 322nd Bombardment Squadron, 91st Bombardment Group. Public Domain US Army Air Forces via Wikimedia Commons

Assigned to the 322nd Bombardment Squadron, *Wee Willie* was shot down on the next to last mission of the 91st Bombardment Group on April 8, 1945, and another B-17, *Times A-Wastin'*, was also lost on the mission. Though Sergeant Little saw no chutes, the pilot of *Wee Willie*, 1st Lieutenant Robert Fuller, did survive the crash to be taken prisoner. The eight other crewmen were killed in action.

Wee Willie's end was dramatic, and when the photos were later released, they gave a graphic indication of the harrowing lives that airmen of the Eighth Air Force endured – along with other Allied air personnel – during the bombing campaign against the Nazis in World War Two. And the 91st Bombardment Group was one of the most active in the European theatre. The group was not only famous for one of its 324th Bombardment Squadron B-17s, *Memphis Belle*, that completed 25 missions to great fanfare and publicity, but also due to the fact that it lost more aircraft than any other heavy group in World War Two while its bombers completed 340 missions. The B-17G *Nine-O-Nine*, named for the last three digits of its serial number, 42-31909, flew an incredible 140 missions with the 323rd Bombardment Squadron, between February 25, 1944, and April 1945, believed to be the wartime record for most Flying Fortress missions. Eighteen of these missions were against Berlin.

While the distinction of being the first B-17 to complete 25 missions over hostile territory is widely credited to the bomber *Hell's Angels* of the 303rd Bombardment Group, *Delta Rebel No. 2* of the 323rd Bombardment Squadron, 91st Bombardment Group was, according to recent research, actually the first to achieve this milestone after completing a mission to St. Nazaire, France, on May 1, 1943. *Delta Rebel No. 2* was shot down over Germany three months later.

The group lost 84 B-17s in 1943 and 100 in 1944, while flying missions roughly every other day. Its greatest single mission losses occurred on November 2, 1944, during a raid on a synthetic oil plant near Merseburg, Germany. Thirty-six bombers of the 91st went into the air, and 13 were shot down while a dozen others

BELOW: This B-17, nicknamed *The Liberty Run*, of the 410st Bombardment Squadron, 91st Bombardment Group, was shot down by German flak over the city of Leipzig on July 20, 1944. Public Domain US Army Air Forces via Wikimedia Commons

sustained heavy damage. Forty-nine crewmen were killed and 68 taken prisoner.

Activated on April 14, 1942, at Harding Airfield, Louisiana, the 91st Bombardment Group soon relocated to MacDill Field, Florida, under the command of Lieutenant Colonel Stanley Wray. The group's nickname "Wray's Ragged Irregulars" was popularised with respect to the officer who led its squadrons, the 322nd, 323rd, 324th, and 401st, to war, arriving at Prestwick, Scotland in October 1942 after one B-17 of the 401st crashed in Northern Ireland due to heavy fog, killing the entire crew of eight and a flight surgeon who was also aboard. Initially assigned to RAF Kimbolton, Cambridgeshire, the group reached its permanent base at RAF Bassingbourn near Royston, Cambridgeshire, a few weeks later.

The 91st was to begin its combat career on November 4, 1942, with orders to attack U-boat pens at the harbour of Brest, France. Those orders, however, were changed due to bad weather, and a secondary target, the Luftwaffe airfield at Abbeville, was chosen instead. Just a half hour prior to commencement, the mission was scrubbed. Three days later, the 91st did complete its first combat bombing mission, hitting the port facilities at Brest in the first of 28 missions flown against the high priority U-boat related target in the next eight months. Eight missions were flown in November, seven of them against the port of Brest and the last completed on the 23rd.

That final mission proved costly, shaking the remainder of the group with the loss of three of five B-17s taking part in the raid with two squadron commanders, Major Victor Zienowicz of the 322nd Squadron and Major Harold Smelser of the 324th, being killed in action along with the group navigator and group bombardier.

Early in its combat history, the 91st was engaged in developing tactics, training airmen, and charting the future course of the Eighth Air Force as American air power was increased in Britain. Within weeks of its combat debut, the group was designated for reassignment to the Mediterranean theatre in support of the Operation Torch landings on the coast of North Africa, which took place on November 8, 1942. Four groups were transferred, diminishing the strength of the Eighth Air Force significantly, but the orders sending the 91st to the Mediterranean were suspended in December due to a lack of available facilities in Algeria.

On January 27, 1943, the 91st Bombardment Group flew its first mission into the airspace of the Third Reich, and on March 4 the group earned the first of two Distinguished Unit Citations, pressing its attack against rail marshalling yards at Hamm, Germany, after other groups had aborted and turned for home due to inclement weather. The 401st Bombardment Squadron experienced a difficult day on April 17, 1943, during the 91st Bombardment Group's first attack on the Nazi aircraft industry. Six B-17s of the 401st were shot down during an attack on aircraft assembly installations at Bremen, Germany.

In the spring of 1943, Lieutenant Colonel Wray was promoted to command of the 103rd Provisional Combat Bomb Wing, and Lieutenant Colonel William Reid took command of the 91st, but another shakeup brought Lieutenant Colonel Clemens Wurzbach to command of the 91st in late June as Reid returned to his former group, the 92nd, as commander. Meanwhile, the crew of the Memphis Belle completed its 25 mission tour and was slated to return to the United States. In December, Colonel Claude Putnam succeeded to command of the 91st.

The most famous raid involving the 91st Bombardment Group occurred during the dual attacks against the Messerschmitt Me-109 fighter assembly plant at Regensburg, Germany, and the ball bearing factories at Schweinfurt, Germany, on August 17, 1942. The 91st led the mission to Schweinfurt and lost 10 bombers on that terrible day. During the period from the first Schweinfurt raid to the second on October 14, 1943, remembered as Black Thursday, the 91st Bombardment Group lost 28 Flying Fortresses.

With the resumption of the Eighth Air Force precision daylight bombing offensive in early 1944, the 91st Bombardment Group received its second Distinguished Unit Citation after completing a mission against the Focke Wulf aircraft assembly plant at Oschersleben, Germany, on January 11. The day's missions involved six bombardment groups and three separate targets. Thirty-four Flying Fortresses were shot down over Oschersleben, and a total of 60 were lost over the multiple targets. During Big Week that followed in late February, the 91st lost 10 B-17s, and while leading a raid on Berlin on March 6, six more of its Flying Fortresses were shot down. For the balance of the war, the 91st Bombardment Group struck both strategic and tactical targets, including synthetic oil production centres and transportation infrastructure.

The 91st completed its last combat mission on April 17, 1945, and later flew more than 2,000 former POWs to freedom after the war ended. Among the more than 5,000 airmen who flew with the group, 887 were killed in action and 123 were declared missing, nearly 20% of those engaged. The 91st Bombardment Group lost a total of 197 Flying Fortresses in air combat, while 37 more were so damaged that they never flew again.

LEFT: ***Delta Rebel No. 2*****, a B-17 of the 323rd Bombardment Squadron believed to have been first to complete 25 missions over Nazi-occupied Europe, was shot down by Luftwaffe fighters on August 12, 1943.** Public Domain US Army Air Forces via Wikimedia Commons

ABOVE: The emblem of the 91st Bombardment Group depicts a diving eagle. Public Domain US Government via Wikimedia Commons

LEFT: A B-17 of the 91st Bombardment Group sits on the field at RAF Bassingbourn. Public Domain collections of the Imperial War Museums via Wikimedia Commons

305th BOMBARDMENT GROUP

Among the most active and decorated of bombardment groups within the Eighth Air Force, the 305th was activated on March 1, 1942, at Salt Lake City Army Air Base, Utah, prior to relocating to Geiger Field, Washington, and then Muroc Army Air Field in the summer of that year.

Then-Colonel Curtis LeMay, who was destined for high command and a significant contribution to the bomber offensives both in the European and Pacific theatres, organised and trained the group, which arrived in England in September 1942, and took up residence at RAF Grafton Underwood with the 40th Bombardment Wing. Its three organic squadrons, the 364th, 365th, and 366th, became collectively known as the 'Can Do' group, and each contributed extensive service throughout the war.

The 305th Bombardment Group (Heavy) flew its first combat mission on November 17, just days after settling in. The raid was conducted against St. Nazaire, a port city on the coast of Nazi-occupied France. Attacks on submarine pens, rail yards, shipyards, and other industrial and military targets, took place as the group relocated to RAF Chelveston in December.

The 305th made history on January 27, 1943, participating in the first US Army Air Forces daylight raid into Germany, bombing the harbour infrastructure at the port city of Wilhelmshaven. Fifty-eight B-17 Flying Fortresses and B-24 Liberators dropped 137½ tons of bombs and successfully destroyed numerous warehouses and maintenance facilities while only three bombers were lost, and seven German fighter planes were officially recorded as shot down.

The group received the first of two Distinguished Unit Citations for a mission against a military target in April near Paris, and Major Allen Martini wrote an article titled *Fifteen Minutes Over Paris*, which appeared in the November 20, 1943, edition of the *Saturday Evening Post*, a popular magazine of the period. The major piloted the B-17 nicknamed *Dry Martini III* of the 422nd Bombardment Squadron, and its crew was nicknamed the Cocktail Kids.

Dry Martini III was the lead bomber in the bottom squadron of the formation and the first to drop its bombs on the Renault automobile factory in the vicinity of the French capital city. The Flying Fortresses climbed into spring morning skies that were generally free of clouds, and en route to the target enemy anti-aircraft fire was light. The ordnance was dropped accurately, and Martini wrote that his crewmen burst into song with *The Last Time I Saw Paris* as *Dry Martini III* began the homeward leg of its mission.

Moments later, the situation changed abruptly when at least a dozen Luftwaffe fighter planes were spotted preparing to attack the formation where *Dry Martini III* was in the most vulnerable position. "Having alerted the crew, telling them the enemy was massing ahead and to the left, there was nothing I could do but stay in formation and watch the hostile queue," Major Martini wrote. "… Focke Wulf 190s swarmed in, peeling off and turning upside down, their 20mm cannon making a red line of fire along their wings as they got us in their sights. Gardner and Moberly down in the nose had to bear their brunt. Their .50-caliber machine guns replied furiously as the F-Ws came into range at about 800 yards.

"The tracers were crisscrossing, the ship shuddering with the chain of recoil, as it always did during action, and fighters began to fall. Two F-Ws went down in the first brush, one bursting into flame and twisting away, a red comet, the second disintegrating as a wing collapsed," he continued.

In turn, *Dry Martini III* was hit hard. "Four cannon shells smashed through my windshield, shattering its plastic glass into small fragments; a piece of one shell striking Boyle in the jaw and knocking him out," the major wrote. "I was blinded and so profusely powdered that I picked tiny granules out of my face for days afterward. Otherwise, I was unhurt."

The injured pilot lost consciousness momentarily and recovered, but *Dry Martini III* became a straggler, falling behind formation and becoming more susceptible to attack without the safety of the formation's concentrated .50-calibre machine-gun fire. For another quarter hour, as many as 60 German fighters slashed through the returning B-17s. *Dry Martini III*'s gunners were nearly out of ammunition after clearing the city of Rouen, northwest of Paris. At long last, a squadron of Supermarine Spitfire fighters appeared in the distance, closing rapidly, and chasing off the marauding Luftwaffe planes. When *Dry Martini III* touched down, it had sustained incredible damage, holed by no fewer than 160 German cannon shells and bullets. Five crewmen were wounded, but all survived.

The 305th participated in the difficult raid against the ball bearing

TOP: This photo of a B-17 of the 366th Bombardment Squadron was taken during a mission to Frankfurt, Germany, in October 1943. Public Domain US Army Air Forces via Wikimedia Commons

ABOVE: The insignia of the 305th Bombardment Group (Heavy) is emblazoned with the motto 'Can Do.' Public Domain United States Army Institute of Heraldry via Wikimedia Commons

LEFT: This B-17 Flying Fortress of the 366th Squadron, 305th Bombardment Group, was photographed during a September 6, 1943, mission against Stuttgart, Germany. Public Domain US Air Force via Wikimedia Commons

ABOVE: This B-17 of the 364th Bombardment Squadron, nicknamed *Lady Liberty*, was shot down in August 1943 with the loss of eight crewmen killed and two taken prisoner. Public Domain United States Army Air Forces via Wikimedia Commons

RIGHT: The crew of a 305th Bombardment Group (Heavy) B-17 stands beneath their bomber's wing at RAF Chelveston. Public Domain United States Army Air Forces via Wikimedia Commons

factories at Schweinfurt on August 17, 1943, and miraculously sustained no casualties during the three-hour mission that led to the loss of 60 American bombers. The experience, however, left a lasting impression on those who lived through the enemy aerial onslaught.

And a difficult trial by fire occurred when the Flying Fortresses of the 305th Bombardment Group lifted off for the second Schweinfurt raid on October 14, 1943.

Plagued by circumstances from the beginning, the 305th's mission was harrowing. The bombers climbed through thick fog and cloud cover that shrouded RAF Chelveston and failed to locate the 40th Bombardment Wing, its parent formation, as every navigational point and rendezvous location with the 40th was missed over England. Amid the confusion, the 305th formed up on the 1st Bombardment Wing, and its 15 bombers became an unconventional fourth group in a formation that normally consisted of only three.

A veritable slaughter ensued. Thirteen Flying Fortresses of the 305th were shot down on the day that has lived grimly in the history of the Eighth Air Force as 'Black Thursday'. Sixty of the nearly 300 attacking American bombers were lost, and the 305th sustained 40 killed in action, 20 wounded, and 79 captured on the ground by the Germans after exiting their stricken B-17s. The 305th Bombardment Group loss rate of 87% shocked the Eighth Air Force command establishment, and after the horror of Black Thursday, daylight bombing raids over Nazi Germany were suspended for five months. The bombers had flown much of the mission without fighter escort, and until the long-range P-51 Mustang arrived to provide protection anticipated losses would have proven unsustainable.

After the USAAF bombing offensive resumed, the 305th earned its second Distinguished Unit Citation in a raid on aircraft factories in the heart of Germany in early 1944. Two of its members earned the Medal of Honor for conspicuous gallantry in combat.

Through the heavy raids of Big Week and the remainder of 1944, 305th bombers flew missions against targets in support of the upcoming D-Day landings in Normandy on June 6 and then in suppression of German efforts to repel the invasion. The launch sites for Nazi V-1 buzz bombs were attacked regularly as well. For the balance of World War Two in Europe, missions were flown during Operation Market-Garden, the airborne assault in the Netherlands in the autumn of 1944, and in the Allied response to the German Ardennes Offensive, which resulted in the famed Battle of the Bulge.

All the while, these tactical missions were interspersed with continued bombing of strategic targets in Germany and across Nazi-occupied Europe, including oil facilities at Merseburg, Germany, heavy industrial sites near Berlin, an aircraft assembly plant at Anklam, Germany, and harbour installations at Gdynia in Poland. The group's final combat mission was completed on April 25, 1945.

During the course of World War Two, approximately 800 airmen were killed in action on missions undertaken from RAF Chelveston, and among them were the members of the 305th Bombardment Group who were lost in the embattled skies over Europe. A memorial was erected to their memory some decades ago.

RIGHT: This B-17 of the 365th Bombardment Squadron, nicknamed *Hell Cat*, was damaged in a crash in England in September 1943 and scrapped. Public Domain United States Army Air Forces via Wikimedia Commons

FLYING FORTRESS IN FILM

RIGHT: US Army Air Forces officer and author Beirne Lay is shown climbing into a cockpit. Public Domain US Army via Wikimedia Commons

With the outbreak of World War Two, Beirne Lay was already a veteran of the US Army Air Corps. He was also an accomplished writer for periodicals and had sold a book to Harper Brothers titled *I Wanted Wings*, published in 1937.

Shortly after Lay was recalled to duty, he became a staff officer with then-

colonel Ira Eaker and the Air Corps Information Division. Lay went to England to supervise some film documentary efforts and continued to produce articles for publication. One of these, titled *I Saw Regensburg Destroyed*, was published in the November 6, 1943, edition of the *Saturday Evening Post*. The article was the product of real combat experience.

In August 1943, Lay had flown five combat missions with the 100th Bombardment Group based at RAF Thorpe Abbotts and nicknamed the 'Bloody Hundredth' due to its casualty rate. Lay wrote an in-depth report of an August 17 raid on Regensburg.

"...I had the lonesome foreboding that might come to the last man to run a gauntlet lined with spiked clubs," he reflected. "The premonition was well-founded. At 1017 hours, near Woensdrecht, I saw the flak blossom out in our vicinity, light and inaccurate. A few minutes later, approximately 1025 hours, two Fw-190s appeared at 1 o'clock level and whizzed through the formation ahead of us in frontal attack, nicking two B-17s of the 95th Group in the wings and breaking away beneath us in half-rolls. Smoke immediately trailed from both B-17s, but they held their stations. As the fighters passed us at a high rate of closure, the guns of the group went into action. The pungent smell of burnt powder filled our cockpit, and the B-17 trembled to the recoil of nose and ball-turret guns...."

Promoted lieutenant colonel, Lay was reassigned to command the 487th Bombardment Group, a B-24 outfit, and returned to England in April 1944. His B-24 was shot down during a raid the following month and Lay managed to avoid capture with the help of the French resistance. His second book, *I've Had It: The Survival of a Bomb Group Commander*, was a product of the experience.

BELOW: *Twelve O'Clock High*, starring Gregory Peck, won two Academy Awards in 1949 for its depiction of a B-17 Bombardment Group in combat. Public Domain Twentieth Century-Fox Film Corp. via Wikimedia Commons

Eighth Air Force veteran Sy Bartlett contacted Lay in 1948, asking if he would collaborate on a book and screenplay that would become iconic in the growing fame of the B-17. The two laboured to produce the book *Twelve O'Clock High*, published that year, and the accompanying film of the same name, starring Gregory Peck as Brigadier General Frank Savage, which premiered in 1949. Lay used portions of his firsthand combat reports in a chapter of the book.

The character 'Savage' was a composite of several officers of the Eighth Air Force, but primarily Colonel Frank Armstrong of the 306th Bombardment Group. The film was nominated for three Academy Awards, winning two. Dean Jagger won Best Supporting Actor as Major Stovall, and the film was top in Best Sound Recording. Peck received an Oscar nomination for Best Actor. In 1998, the movie was placed on the US National Film Registry by the Library of Congress as 'culturally, historically, or aesthetically significant'.

While Lay was serving, film director and producer William Wyler led a group of cinematographers who flew combat missions with several B-17 crews, including the 91st Bombardment Group. The result was the landmark documentary *Memphis Belle: A Story of a Flying Fortress*, which premiered in 1944 and includes riveting colour film footage of actual air combat. First Lieutenant Harold J. Tannenbaum, one of the cinematographers, was killed during a bombing mission over France on April 16, 1943. Actor Clark Gable flew at least five missions aboard B-17s and produced numerous bomber training films for the US Army Air Forces along with a 1945 documentary titled *Combat America*. Gable also provided the narration for this 62-minute film.

The story of the B-17 Flying Fortress and the brave men who flew it has been a topic of Hollywood cinema for more than 70 years. In the 1954 film *The High and Mighty*, starring John Wayne, Claire Trevor, and Robert Stack, a US

RIGHT: Famed Hollywood filmmaker William Wyler led the cinematographers that produced compelling colour footage of B-17s at war for the documentary *Memphis Belle: A Story of a Flying Fortress*. Public Domain National Archives and Records Administration via Wikimedia Commons

FAR RIGHT: Actor Matthew Modine stars in the 1990 motion picture *Memphis Belle*. Creative Commons John Garvin via Wikimedia Commons

RIGHT: Gregory Peck appears as Brigadier General Frank Savage in *Twelve O'Clock High*, 1949. Public Domain Twentieth Century-Fox Film Corporation via Wikimedia Commons

BELOW: Tom Hanks and Steven Spielberg served as executive producers for the Apple TV+ miniseries *Masters of the Air*. Public Domain US Department of Defense via Wikimedia Commons

Coast Guard PB-1G air-sea rescue variant of the B-17 is dispatched from San Francisco to rendezvous with a stricken passenger aircraft over the Pacific.

The 1990 motion picture *Memphis Belle* stars Matthew Modine, Eric Stoltz, Harry Connick, Jr., Billy Zane, John Lithgow, and others, in the romanticised story of the crew and B-17 that completed 25 combat missions in the European theatre. The film is a composite of characters in fictionalised situations that are representative of the Eighth Air Force combat experience. Although it was criticised for its liberal inclusion of cliché, *Memphis Belle* debuted at box office number one in Britain and remained there for two weeks.

Among other notable film appearances, the B-17s involved in the Japanese attack on Pearl Harbor are featured in the 1970 production *Tora! Tora! Tora!*, while the big bomber nicknamed *Sentimental Journey* is also seen in Steven Spielberg's 1979 comedy *1941*.

The footage that Wyler's crew compiled in 1943 remained largely forgotten, shunted off in rolls and film cans at the US National Archives for 75 years. All that changed when philanthropist, filmmaker, and explorer Paul Allen backed a research effort through his Vulcan Productions a few years ago. Director Erik Nelson located the long forgotten footage and began a painstaking editing and restoration effort that resulted in the 2018 world premiere of the acclaimed documentary *The Cold Blue* by the National Archives and AFI DOCS, the American Film Institute's annual documentary festival. The film was released through HBO Documentaries the following year to excellent reviews.

"We had to rush to get *The Cold Blue* out because we wanted the [veterans] who were in the movie to see the film while they were around to see it," Nelson told the *Military Times* in 2019. "I'm happy to say that every one of the nine gentlemen we interviewed, the nine heroes, every single one of them is still with us today."

In 2022, Grindstone Entertainment Group acquired the distribution rights for *Wolf Hound*, the story of a B-17 captured by the Germans and put into service by the mysterious Luftwaffe Kampfgeschwader 200. The fictional film stars James Maslow as Captain David Holden, an American fighter pilot intent on rescuing a downed air crew, and Trevor Donovan as Major Eric Roth, a German fighter ace. The Yankee Air Museum in Belleville, Michigan, allowed the filmmakers to feature their B-17G *Yankee Lady* during filming.

Filming for the much anticipated *Masters of the Air* for Apple TV+ began in 2021 and executive producers Tom Hanks and Steven Spielberg presented yet another wartime epic. This particular production features the 100th Bombardment Group and is based on the 2007 book *Masters of the Air: America's Bomber Boys Who Fought The Air War Against Nazi Germany* by Donald L. Miller. Since its release early in 2024, *Masters of the Air* has been favourably compared with the 2001 *Band of Brothers* and 2010 *The Pacific* mini-series from the same team.

FLYING FORTRESS IN CAPTIVITY

ABOVE: This B17D formerly of the 61st Bombardment Squadron, 11th Bombardment Group was captured by the Japanese at Clark Field in the Philippines. Public Domain US Air Force via Wikimedia Commons

RIGHT: A captured B-17E with Japanese markings is shown at an airfield with other Allied aircraft taken during World War Two. Public Domain kumaryu.com/souvenir-from-java via Wikimedia Commons

Inevitably during the course of World War Two, the B-17 would fall into the hands of the enemy. In action early in the Pacific theatre, B-17s were shot down, damaged, and abandoned in various locales, including the Philippines and the Dutch East Indies. The Japanese are known to have recovered at least three Flying Fortresses. At the same time, the Eighth Air Force and other US air forces in the European theatre flew thousands of sorties. Bombers that were lost in action but sustained repairable damage were evaluated and sometimes placed into service by the Luftwaffe, as were damaged aircraft that were forced to land in German-controlled territory.

Further, neutral countries sometimes came into possession of damaged or downed B-17s. Switzerland recorded many violations of its airspace during World War Two, and its fighter planes would often intercept aircraft of the belligerent nations and attempt to force them to land at Swiss airfields. A number of damaged American aircraft did land in Switzerland, and their crews were interned. The Swiss are known to have repaired at least one B-17 with parts taken from other downed bombers and placed it in service with their own air force.

The B-17 was not offered to the Soviet Union through Lend Lease; however, an estimated 73 Flying Fortresses actually came into the possession of the Red Air Force. Some were retained after being damaged and abandoned at bases used during the shuttle bombing raids of Operation Frantic. Others were forced to land in the Soviet Union due to battle damage or mechanical issues. The Soviets managed to place 23 B-17s into service with the 895th Bomber Regiment, but none saw action during the war.

Approximately 40 B-17s are believed to have served with the Luftwaffe after they were repaired and made airworthy, probably with scavenged parts from other downed Flying Fortresses. Generally, the Germans painted these captured bombers with Luftwaffe markings, prominently displaying the black cross on the wings and fuselage along with the swastika on the vertical stabiliser and given the cover designation of the Dornier D-200.

Captured B-17s were used as long-range transports during clandestine operations under the auspices of the shadowy Kampfgeschwader 200. Reports indicate that in the spring of 1944, KG 200 employed captured B-17s in an attempt to set up secret airstrips in North Africa months after the German and Italian ground forces there had surrendered to the Allies. They are also thought to have participated in the insertion of German agents into the Middle East in the autumn of 1944. Other B-17s are believed to have retained American markings and been used in attempts to infiltrate US bomber formations. However, American aircrews became wary of such attempts and were known to have fired on B-17s attempting to join their combat boxes that could not be positively identified.

On at least one occasion, a B-17 with a German crew posed as a crippled straggler, attempting to draw another Flying Fortress toward it to protect against fighter attack. Once the American bomber was lured into range, the supposed cripple was to open fire or call in Luftwaffe fighters to ambush the startled US bomber crew.

The most documented and perhaps the first B-17 to fall into German

BELOW: This B-17 formerly of the 7th Bombardment Group was captured by the Japanese in the Dutch East Indies. Public Domain US Air Force Historical Research Agency via Wikimedia Commons

hands was the B-17G serial no. 41-24585 of the 360th Bombardment Squadron, 303rd Bombardment Group. On December 12, 1942, 1st Lieutenant Paul Flickinger piloted the bomber on a mission against the rail marshalling yards at Rouen, France. It was the bomber's third mission, and the plane sustained damage both en route to the target and during its return flight. Flickinger made a belly landing in a field near the French town of Melun, 60 miles southeast of Paris.

Within hours, the Germans were at work, transporting the plane to Leeuwarden airfield in the Netherlands. The B-17 was repaired and given the code DL+XC, which was painted on its fuselage. After further inspection at the Luftwaffe testing centre in Rechlin, Germany, the B-17, nicknamed *Wulf Hound*, is believed to have toured Luftwaffe fighter bases in Germany and France, allowing pilots to assess thoroughly the strengths and weaknesses of the big bomber, which the Germans had flown for the first time on March 17, 1943. Three months later, *Wulf Hound* was displayed at Lars Airfield near Rechlin during an exhibition of numerous captured Allied aircraft types.

From there the bomber was transferred to KG 200 on September 11, 1943, at Rangesdorf, Germany, for use in secret operations in North Africa. Flying from a covert base in Libya code named Traviata, *Wulf Hound*'s mission was to observe British troop movements. However, on April 16, 1944, the aircraft was dangerously low on fuel, and its pilot, Oberleutnant Dumke, was compelled to ditch off the coast of Greece at Kalamata Bay. All crew members survived.

Other B-17s that fell into German hands and were put to use include *Flak Dancer* of the 544th Bombardment Squadron, 384th Bombardment Group, which landed at an airfield in Laon, France, after sustaining battle damage and was turned over to KG 200 in the spring of 1944, and B-17G serial no. 42-38017, nicknamed *One Mission Lulu* of the 349th Bombardment Squadron, 100th Bombardment Group. *One Mission Lulu* lost an engine when struck by debris from the collision of two other 100th Bombardment Group B-17s during a mission over northern Germany on March 3, 1944. The pilot attempted to reach neutral Sweden, but due to a navigational error the plane landed at Schleswig-Jagel airfield in Germany. The plane was repaired and seconded to KG 200, while its 10 crewmen became prisoners of war.

During a bombing run against an Arado aircraft assembly plant at Anklam in East Prussia on October 9, 1943, the B-17 *Miss Nonalee II* of the 548th Bombardment Squadron, 385th Bombardment Group was damaged, and the pilot again attempted to reach Sweden. The crew, however, was forced to bale out over Nazi-occupied Denmark and rounded up by Danish collaborationist police officers who handed them over to the Germans. Pilot Lieutenant Glyndon Bell stayed with the Flying Fortress and made a forced landing near the town of Varde. He attempted to set fire to the plane but was interrupted by Danish police. After evading capture, he was assisted by the Danish resistance in reaching Sweden. The plane was soon made airworthy and flown to Rechlin. At that point, all traces of it disappeared.

A number of other B-17s were repaired and flown by the Germans, and at least one of these was forced to land at an airfield at Valencia in neutral Spain, on June 27, 1944, while in service with KG 200. The plane and crew were interned for the duration of the war.

The three B-17s that fell into Japanese hands during their 1941 conquest of the Philippines and the Dutch East Indies were repaired and flown to the Imperial Air Force's air technical research laboratory at Tachikawa, near the capital of Tokyo for evaluation. One of these, a B-17D, was judged as an obsolete type, while the other two, both B-17E aircraft, were used to train Japanese fighter pilots in attacking the heavily armed bombers. One of the B-17Es was nicknamed *Tachikawa 105*, and the three bombers also appeared in propaganda films and were exhibited along with other captured Allied aircraft.

The Japanese newspaper *Asahi Shimbun* published a series of photos of the captured Flying Fortresses bearing the rising sun markings of their own armed forces in its monthly magazine titled *Koku Asahi*, which circulated widely throughout wartime Japan. No trace of these aircraft was found after the war, and it has been assumed that they were scrapped by the Japanese, who needed resources for their armaments industry.

ABOVE: A B-17D captured by the Japanese flies with its national insignia of the Imperial Air Force prominently visible. Public Domain ja:画像:B17jp.jpg via Wikimedia Commons

LEFT: Colonel Werner Baumbach of the Luftwaffe headed the clandestine Kampfgeschwader 200. Public Domain audiovis.nac.gov.pl via Wikimedia Commons

LEFT: The Aviation Technical Museum is now located at the former Nazi research site at Rechlin, Germany. Creative Commons Niteshift via Wikimedia Commons

THE B-17 MYSTIQUE

The B-17 Flying Fortress heavy bomber was not the fastest aircraft of its genre. It did not carry the biggest bombload. It was not the most technically advanced. But of all the great bombers that flew during World War Two, it remains by far the most famous.

The reason is simple. The men who crewed it into harm's way praised the Flying Fortress for bringing them home, even when the aircraft itself was grievously wounded. Stories abound of its rugged ability to stay in the air despite severe damage. The pilots who sat at the controls for long hours during hazardous combat missions also lauded the B-17 for its ease of flying and the platform's stability, not to mention its remarkable capacity to absorb tremendous punishment.

No doubt, those airmen who flew aboard the Consolidated B-24 Liberator, the B-17's brother in arms during the daylight precision raids that helped bring the Axis to its knees in World War Two, also adored their airplane. The Liberator was more advanced technically, offered better performance and a heavier bombload, and it was produced in greater numbers than the B-17. Historians acknowledge that the B-24 was initially intended to replace the B-17, although the exigencies of war and preferences of high-ranking air officers brought the two into service as contemporaries.

Still, there is no greater ardour expressed among air veterans than that which has been published exhaustively on behalf of the B-17. Perhaps it was the wide surface of the wing and the broad, towering vertical stabiliser that characterised later variants of the Flying Fortress which took enemy shot and shell more readily than the narrower surfaces of other bombers, that attracted more battle damage. Then again, it might well have been the simple sturdiness of the B-17 airframe that made the difference between life and death or imprisonment for so many. Regardless, the plane gets credit for coming home, and its crews loved their Forts.

Colonel Robert Morgan, pilot of the famed B-17F Memphis Belle, said simply: "She was a Stradivarius of an airplane." Another Eighth Air Force pilot offered: "The plane can be cut and slashed almost to pieces by enemy fire and bring its crew home."

And so, when those airmen who came back to their bases in damaged B-17s actually reached their homes in the United States after World War Two ended, there is no doubt that some of them sat their children and grandchildren down by the fireside and told stories of the great plane. They penned memoirs, made diary entries, and wrote letters. Some of these are still being rediscovered to this day.

In his book *Black Thursday*, author Martin Caidin described a harrowing mission and a remarkable tale of survival aboard a Flying Fortress. "This B-17 met a head-on attack by three Focke Wulf Fw-190 fighters. The gunners exploded two of them, and the top turret poured a stream of shells into the cockpit of the third. With a dead man at the controls, the fighter screamed in, and at a closing speed of 550 miles per hour smashed head-on into the number three engine…The tremendous impact tore off the propeller. It knocked the heavy bomber completely out of formation as though a giant hand had swatted a fly…The fighter cartwheeled crazily over the B-17. It cut halfway through the wing and then sliced a third of the way through the horizontal stabilizer…Pieces of metal from the exploding, disintegrating Focke Wulf tore through the fuselage, and a German gun barrel buried itself in the wall between the radio room

ABOVE: The restored B-17 *Thunderbird* flies during an air show in Houston, Texas, in 2011. Creative Commons Mike Fisher via Wikimedia Commons

LEFT: The B-17G *Aluminum Overcast* rests at an airfield in Madison, Wisconsin. Creative Commons Cory W. Watts via Wikimedia Commons

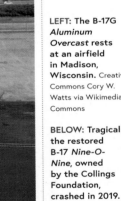

BELOW: Tragically, the restored B-17 *Nine-O-Nine*, owned by the Collings Foundation, crashed in 2019. Public Domain JGHowes via Wikimedia Commons

ABOVE: The B-17D dubbed *The Swoose* due to its hybrid construction is shown in flight. Public Domain US Air Force via Wikimedia Commons

and the bomb bay…Crews of nearby bombers watched the collision. They saw a tremendous explosion, and the bomber hurtling helplessly out of control, tumbling as she fell. They reported when they returned to base that the Flying Fortress had blown up, and that the crew must be considered dead…."

The author went on to report, however, that the bomber was in fact still in the air. Pilot and co-pilot wrestled with all their strength and somehow regained control. "And they brought her all the way back to England and scraped her down for a belly landing on the runway," he concluded. "Postscript: not a man was injured."

RIGHT: The B-17G *Texas Raiders* wings its way above the crowd at an air show in Houston in 2019. This plane was lost in a tragic mid-air collision with a Bell P-63 King Cobra fighter during a 2022 flight. Creative Commons Alan Wilson via Wikimedia Commons

Such stuff might easily be passed off as fiction. But in the case of the B-17 it was reality. Time after time, a cripple came back to base, on many occasions with wounded or dead men aboard…but still it came back.

Through thousands of sorties, even its enemies grew to grudgingly respect the tenacity of the Flying Fortresses and their aircrews. Japanese fighter pilots shied away from them, calling them the 'four-engine fighters'. German pilots said attacking a formation of B-17s was akin to fighting a 'flying porcupine'.

Though the remaining number of Flying Fortresses has dwindled since the end of World War Two, dozens remain as static memorials to the wartime epic they forged in flight. Among them is the *Memphis Belle* on permanent display at the National Museum of the Air Force at Wright-Patterson Air Force Base in Dayton, Ohio. The *Piccadilly Lily II* is maintained by Planes of Fame in Chino, California, a tribute to the original *Piccadilly Lily* of the 351st Bombardment Squadron lost over Bremerhaven, Germany. *Piccadilly Lily II* is believed to have been the last B-17 in US Air Force service, retired in 1959.

In February 1942, Captain Fred Eaton piloted his B-17E on a raid against the Japanese base at Rabaul on the island of New Britain. During his bomb run, the bomb bay doors of the plane became stuck, so the pilot went around again, braving swarms of enemy fighters to deliver his ordnance. With his B-17 damaged and fuel tanks near empty, Eaton knew he could not make the base at Port Moresby in southeastern New Guinea. So, he elected to set the big bomber down in an area that looked like a flat field. It turned out to be a swamp, and the B-17 settled into five feet of water and the cover of jungle foliage. It lay there undisturbed for decades, but pilots who flew over the resting place began to call the old bomber *Swamp Ghost*.

In 2006, the recovery of *Swamp Ghost* was undertaken by entrepreneur and aviation enthusiast Alfred Hagen. The plane was removed piece by piece, and after four years on the dock at Lae, New Guinea, awaiting that government's permission to remove the large artifact, *Swamp Ghost* was shipped to Long Beach, California, in 2010 and then to the Pacific Aviation Museum at Pearl Harbor, Hawaii, in 2013. *Swamp Ghost* is on display there, and restoration is ongoing.

The oldest surviving B-17 is *The Swoose*, which was salvaged and rebuilt in Australia in the early days of US involvement in the war in the Pacific. *The Swoose* took to the air after the tail of one B-17D had been grafted onto the fuselage of another that was originally named *Ole Betsy*. When work on the hybrid was completed, Captain Weldon Smith gave the plane its nickname in reference to a popular tune about a bird that was half swan and half goose.

The Swoose went on to serve as the personal plane of Lieutenant General George Brett, commander of Allied Air Forces in the Southwest Pacific Area, with Captain Frank Kurtz at the controls. After the war, Kurtz saved *The Swoose* from being scrapped, convincing officials of the city of Los Angeles, California, to preserve it as a memorial. The plane was later transferred to the Smithsonian Institution, where it sat in storage until the National Museum of the Air Force took possession in 2008. Restoration work is underway on *The Swoose*, the only surviving example of a B-17D Flying Fortress, the oldest surviving B-17, and the only aircraft of its type that served from the beginning of World War Two to the end.

RIGHT: The recovered B-17 *Swamp Ghost* undergoes restoration in a hangar at the Pacific Aviation Museum. Creative Commons Pacific Aviation Museum via Wikimedia Commons

THE FLYING FORTRESS TODAY

RIGHT: B-17G *Sentimental Journey* sits at an airfield in the spring of 2000. Creative Commons Bill Larkins B-17eaaMay2000 via Wikimedia Commons

RIGHT: B-17G *Sally B* flies in company with a Republic P-47 Thunderbolt fighter plane at the North Weald Fighter Meet in 1986. Creative Commons Dick Gilbert via Wikimedia Commons

BELOW: The B-17G *Yankee Lady*, photographed coming in to land in September 2007, is exemplary of the terrible beauty of the big bomber. Creative Commons Kogo via Wikimedia Commons

At peak inventory, B-17 Flying Fortresses in service with the US Army Air Forces numbered nearly 4,700. As of November 2022, only 45 are known to exist, and fewer than 10 are believed to be airworthy among those registered with the US Federal Aviation Administration. Several of these are not thought to have been operated in more than five years, but there are others undergoing renovation that will possibly fly again one day.

After World War Two, the B-17 remained in service until its last operational US Air Force mission was flown on August 6, 1959, as a target for a test of the AIM-4 Falcon air-to-air missile. In October of that year, the last B-17 in service with the US Coast Guard as an iceberg patrol and air-sea rescue plane conducted its final mission. A few CIA-sponsored covert operations were conducted with the aircraft in the early 1960s, but well before that time thousands of war surplus Flying Fortresses had been sold for scrap.

During its long career, the B-17 served with the armed forces of more than 20 countries. And in the decades that followed World War Two it has remained one of the most remembered and romanticised aircraft of the conflict. It has appeared in many feature films, the subject of thousands of books from technical reviews to memoirs of the 'flyboys' who lived the great trial of air combat from within its unpressurized cabin.

Among the airworthy Flying Fortresses, serial no. 448543 resides with the Erickson Aircraft Collection at Madras, Oregon, and has been restored with the markings of the B-17F *Ye Olde Pub*, famous for the 'Higher Call' incident between an American bomber crew under Lieutenant Charlie Brown and German Me-109 fighter pilot Franz Stigler. The Commemorative Air Force maintains a B-17G nicknamed *Sentimental Journey* that was restored to its wartime configuration in the 1980s after being used in the comedy film *1941*. The Lockheed Vega-built B-17G *Sallie B* flew until 1975 and was used as a survey plane. Extensive restoration led to its appearance in the 1990 film *Memphis Belle*. The Yankee Air Museum in Belleville, Michigan, near the famed Willow Run aircraft factory, maintains the airworthy B-17G *Yankee Lady*.

The Flying Fortress remains popular at air shows, and at times there are opportunities not only to tour these historic bombers, but also to take a ride. Any such experience serves to enrich the appreciation of the B-17's history and heritage. Viewing a single Flying Fortress, whether restored to static display or rumbling across the sky, is a spectacular sight, evoking a glimpse of the awesome might projected by formations of hundreds of the big bombers en route to a life-and-death struggle over the Pacific or above Nazi Germany.

The B-17 remains one of the world's most famous aircraft. It is remembered for several reasons: romance and nostalgia, air power in action, and most of all the courage of the crews who flew it into history and made it a legend.